THE LAW OF SUCCESSION

THE LAW OF SUCCESSION

Richard Hedlund

SECOND EDITION

Hall and Stott Publishing Ltd
27 Witney Close
Saltford
BS31 3DX

British Library Cataloguing in Publication Data

ISBN 978 1 9162431 9 4

Typeset by Style Photosetting Ltd, Mayfield, East Sussex

PREFACE

I'm very grateful for the positive reception given to the first edition of *The Law of Succession* when it was published in 2019, and it has been a great pleasure to update the book for this second edition. This edition includes a variety of new sections as well as updates to the law throughout. Amongst the many developments in succession law that have happened in the past few years are the responses to Covid-19 (Chapter 3) and the reforms to probate procedures introduced in November 2020 (Chapter 11).

Again, I want to thank Martyn Heathcote for his continued support and assistance in updating the textbook. Any errors, of course, are mine.

The law is correct as of 15 March 2021. However, Chapter 10 (Taxation) has been written based on the 2021/22 tax code, as announced in the Budget in March 2021.

Richard Hedlund
Lincoln

CONTENTS

TABLE OF CASES

C

T

TABLE OF LEGISLATION

ABBREVIATIONS

AEA 1925	Administration of Estates Act 1925
AJA 1982	Administration of Justice Act 1982
APR	agricultural property relief
BPR	business property relief
DMC	*donatio mortis causa*
Inheritance Act	Inheritance (Provision for Family and Dependants) Act 1975
MCA 2005	Mental Capacity Act 2005
NCPR 1987	Non-Contentious Probate Rules 1987
NRB	nil-rate band
PR	personal representative
RNRB	residence nil-rate band

Introduction

The law of succession is a vibrant and captivating topic. Historically, it has not received a lot of academic attention, but that has begun to change in the past few decades. Increasingly, more people are developing an interest in this topic, and it is easy to see why. It covers a wide spectrum of human emotion: welcoming new members to the family, dealing with the security (financial and otherwise) of those we love, and ultimately coping with the loss of loved ones. Admittedly, succession and financial planning is not at the forefront of everyone's mind during these momentous occasions, but it does need to feature. 'Be prepared' is always a winning motto. In one way or another, succession law will affect all of us.

This chapter introduces you to the law of succession and the textbook. It covers the following issues:

- What is meant by the law of succession?
- How is succession law structured?
- What are some of the key terms used in succession law?
- What are some of the key sources used in succession law?
- How has English succession law developed over time?

1.1 What is succession law?

Succession law is fundamentally about property and what happens to a person's property when they die. Where does your property go? Can you decide who gets your property? What happens if you die without having made such a decision? Who actually deals with your property? What happens if your wishes are not carried out? What happens to your debts? Succession law also concerns the disposal of the body and how that is carried out.

This can clearly be an emotional subject, and sadly it is a subject that touches all of us. In the recent Singapore case of *Lim Choo Hin (as the sole executrix of the estate of Lim Guan Heong, deceased) v Lim Sai Ing Peggy* [2021] SGHC 52, Chan Seng Onn J noted:

> 'Say not you know another entirely, till you have divided an inheritance with him'. The words of the late Johann Kaspar Lavater, uttered more than two centuries ago, were as sombre as they were prescient. This court has witnessed, on occasions aplenty, the unfortunate legal wars waged between the living over the property of the dead.

Lavater, a controversial Swiss writer and philosopher, was at least right in expressing these sentiments. Regrettably, emotions can run high when a family comes to terms with a bereavement and these emotions can spur legal claims. Some of these claims may be warranted but others will be fuelled by a plethora of (often negative) emotions. That will be evident in many of the cases we will look at, and unfortunately many of these cases show how previously close families completely disintegrate over arguments about the inheritance.

Given the importance that we attach to private property in English (and Western) culture, the question of what happens to your property when you die is really important. Undoubtedly, most people would instinctively say that they want to have some control over what happens to their assets. People who have worked hard to earn money, who have purchased property (maybe even a house), will want to be able to choose who eventually benefits from it. Most will perhaps want to benefit their close family members, but equally they might want to benefit friends or organisations they have been involved with. At the same time, there will be situations where a person feels strongly that a family member should not inherit anything, perhaps because of some family feud. It is important that the law allows for these choices to be made.

Succession law explains how a person can make such choices in their lifetime by writing a will (which is defined below). However, the right to write a will brings with it its own challenges. How do we know that you have made the choice yourself? How do we know that no one else has pressured or forced you into making it? How do we know that your choice has not been brought about by a lack of mental capacity? The law therefore needs clear rules on what amounts to a valid and enforceable will.

Some people die without having a valid will. This is known as dying intestate (again, the definition is explained further below). The law therefore needs clear rules on what happens to a person's property when they die intestate. In English law, the property goes to your 'next of kin', as defined by the Administration of Estates Act 1925. This would be your surviving spouse, children, or other relatives. Where a person leaves no family or relatives, their property goes to the Crown, through a doctrine called *bona vacantia*. There are many reasons why a person might die intestate. They may have a will, but it transpires that it is invalid and thus unenforceable. They may have died unexpectedly, before giving any consideration to writing a will. They may feel that the intestacy rules suit them, meaning there is no need to write a will. They may be put off by the legalese surrounding wills. Finally, some people don't write wills simply because they don't want to contemplate their own death.

So, the first part of succession law applies where a person is still alive and may be deciding what should happen to their property. The second part of succession law begins once the person has died. What happens next? Who becomes responsible for arranging the funeral and who actually takes control of the deceased's property? If you write a will, you generally choose who is to be responsible. Otherwise, the law decides. The person appointed is known as the personal representative (PR). Even choosing the PR is fraught with potential difficulty. What happens if your chosen PR dies before you? What if your family or relatives object to your chosen PR, perhaps because they don't like or trust the PR? So there are rules to deal with these kinds of problems.

Once a PR is legally appointed, their work begins in earnest. The law spells out what the PR has to do. They have to carry out a so-called estate inventory, which in essence means listing and valuing all property owned by the deceased, as well as identifying any debts, such as a mortgage or credit card debts. The PR has to submit the inventory to the tax authority, HMRC, and if the deceased's estate is worth more than £325,000, they have to calculate and pay inheritance tax. This is a particular tax levied on large estates. It is not without controversy, and critics sometimes refer to it as a 'death tax'.

After the PR has dealt with the tax, they have to collect in the estate assets and pay off all of the deceased's debts. Most people have debts and a lot die still indebted. There might be a mortgage on the family home, there might be credit card debts, and goods might have been purchased on credit. Some people might owe other taxes to HMRC, or they might owe wages to their employees, if they ran a business or simply employed a cleaner or gardener. Every person will be different. Understandably, there are a lot of rules on how debts are to be paid, and problems will arise if debts are not properly paid off, or even if they are paid off in the wrong order. The more debts the deceased had, the more complicated it becomes for the PR.

Once all of the debts have been paid off, the PR can finally hand out the remaining property to the beneficiaries. If the deceased left a will, the beneficiaries are those included in the will. If the deceased died intestate, the beneficiaries are, as mentioned above, determined by the Administration of Estates Act 1925. Once the distribution has been completed, the PR is finished in their role.

However, in many instances, the will or intestacy rules state that property is to be held on trust. Here, the PR becomes a trustee, and they may spend a long time (potentially many years) looking after the property as a trustee. For example, a grandparent may leave property on trust for their grandchild, and the PR (who now becomes a trustee) is asked to hold it on trust until the grandchild turns 18. This is where the law of succession most clearly interplays with equity and trusts, which you are likely already to have studied or to be studying alongside succession. This textbook will not go through the rules on trusteeship, as this is beyond the scope of the succession module. It is common for the PR to become a trustee, though it is certainly possible to appoint an alternative trustee. In that situation, the PR's final duty would be transferring the relevant property to the trustee.

It should be clear from the above that the PR has a difficult job. The larger the estate, the more work is needed. If the estate is small and worth less than £5,000, certain simplified rules apply, and a small estate could probably be administered in a few months. Larger estates will take longer. There is a general expectation that the PR's main duties (collecting in all the assets and valuing them, dealing with HMRC, paying off debts, and distributing any gifts (other than those held on trust)) should be completed within a year, though in reality it can take a lot longer than that. For this reason, some choose to appoint a professional PR, such as a solicitor, rather than asking family or friends to take on the role. The only downside to this, of course, is that the professional is going to charge for their services, which will have to be paid out of the estate. So there will be less money available to distribute to the beneficiaries. Ultimately, it is a balance between convenience and cost.

The textbook is, broadly speaking, structured based on the above summary of succession law. **Chapters 2** to **7** look at wills: the rules for making a valid will, how wills are interpreted, how wills can be changed and revoked, and finally the doctrine of mutual wills. **Chapter 8** considers the intestacy rules, to see who inherits when a person dies intestate. **Chapter 9** looks at PRs and how PRs can be appointed. **Chapters 10** to **15** consider the duties of a PR, starting with the tax issues. **Chapter 16** then looks at what remedies are available against a PR if they have not properly undertaken their duties.

By the end of the textbook you will have a solid grounding in succession law, understand the key legal rules, and also have come across various problems with the law and proposals for reform. A brief history of succession law is included later in this chapter, and it will become clear that most of English succession law stems from the 19th century. As we relentlessly make our way through the 21st century, serious questions are being asked about whether the law might be outdated. With Law Commission reforms in the pipeline, this makes studying succession law today even more interesting and relevant.

1.2 Key terms in succession law

This section outlines some of the key terms used in succession law. It is important that you become familiar with them. You will encounter more technical terms in each of the following chapters, and the most important will be defined in 'key terminology' boxes. It is always a useful study and revision exercise to start compiling your own legal dictionary. As you encounter key terms, write them down and also provide your own definition of them.

Will	The first key term to define is a will. A will is a formal legal document in which a person declares what will happen to their property after their death. They can also, amongst other things, declare who they want as their PR or to act as guardian to any children under the age of 18. To be valid, the will has to comply with the formality requirements in ss 7 and 9 of the Wills Act 1837, as well as a host of other legal requirements set out in case law.
Execution	Execution, or to execute a will, refers to the moment when the will is given legal effect by the testator and the witnesses signing the will. It is from the moment of execution that the will becomes a legally enforceable document, albeit one that the testator is free to revoke at any time until their death.
Testator	A testator is the person who creates a valid will. Historically, a female testator was referred to as a testatrix. This gender-specific terminology is less common nowadays, but you need to know the term as it appears in older judgments.
Testate succession	This is a general term for the rules governing succession where a person has died with a valid will.
Intestate succession	This is a general term for the rules governing succession where a person has died without leaving a valid will. It is also referred to as **intestacy**.
Estate	The estate is a term which broadly means all of the property, rights and debts that the deceased had when they died. How the estate is administered and distributed to the beneficiaries will depend on whether the deceased died testate or intestate.
Personal representative	This is the person who administers the estate. Their duties are wide-ranging, but include valuing the estate, collecting in the estate, dealing with inheritance tax, paying off debts and distributing the estate assets to the beneficiaries. There are two types of PRs, as explained below.
Executor	An executor is a PR who is appointed through a will to administer a testate estate. Historically, a female executor was referred to as an executrix.
Administrator	An administrator is a PR who is appointed by the court to administer either (a) a testate estate where there is no executor, or (b) an intestate estate. Historically, a female administrator was referred to as an administratrix.

Administration	This is the legal term for the process by which the PR administers the estate. Where an executor administers a testate estate, this is referred to as **probate**. For various reasons, the administration process is often colloquially referred to as probate, regardless of whether it is a testate estate or an intestate estate being administered.
Non-contentious probate	This term denotes all routine probate matters in court, such as proving a will or appointing a PR.
Contentious probate	This term denotes any probate matter where there is a legal dispute between various parties. For example, the validity of a will might be challenged or there might be a dispute about how the PR has administered the estate.
Beneficiary	A beneficiary is a person who is entitled to the estate (whether the whole estate or a part of it), either through the intestacy rules or through a will. Intestate estates are always held on trust for the beneficiary. In a will, some property might be held on trust for the beneficiary, but some property might not be. Even if the property is not held on trust, the recipient is still called a beneficiary. The definition of a beneficiary in succession law is therefore slightly wider than the definition in trust law.
Testamentary freedom	This is a crucial doctrine in English succession law. It states that a testator has absolute freedom in whom they chose as beneficiaries in their will. Unlike in some other countries, English testators are not required to leave anything to their spouses or children. However, since 1938, certain family members, who are not beneficiaries, have the right to petition the court for financial support from the estate; such financial support is granted at the court's discretion.
Jurisdiction	Finally, a word should be said about jurisdiction. The succession law covered in this textbook applies to England and Wales. For convenience and out of custom, with no disrespect intended, the textbook will refer to this as English law. Scotland and Northern Ireland have their own succession laws. Scottish succession law, which is more heavily influenced by European civil law, differs in many respects. However, a will executed in England can lawfully deal with property that the testator owned in Scotland or Northern Ireland, and vice versa.

1.3 Key sources in English succession law

This section outlines some of the key sources that you need to be familiar with when studying succession law. Ensure that you look at these sources in some detail.

Wills Act 1837	This statute governs the current law on wills. This includes who is entitled to make a will, how a valid will is actually produced, and various rules on how the will is to be interpreted.
Administration of Estates Act 1925	This is a key statute. It governs, first of all, the duties and powers of PRs, and how they go about administering the estate. Secondly, it sets out the intestacy rules, and thus governs who inherits when a person dies intestate.
Senior Courts Act 1981	This statute is really about the procedure in the High Court. Various sections deal with probate matters, including the right of the court to appoint PRs.
Administration of Justice Act 1982	Two sections in this statute are very important, as they govern how wills are to be interpreted and how mistakes in a will can be corrected.
Non-Contentious Probate Rules 1987	This is an important piece of secondary legislation, which outlines the substantive and procedural rules for probate. It must be read together with the Senior Courts Act 1981.

1.4 The historical development of English succession law

As with most aspects of English property law, succession law becomes easier to understand once you have a brief understanding of its history. Prior to the 1850s, there was a divide between how the law treated succession of real property (freehold land and interests in land) and personal property (chattels and intangible property, other than interests in land). Because of this divide, succession law was historically developed in different courts. In the Middle Ages, real succession was a common law matter, dealt with in common law courts, such as the Court of Queen's/King's Bench. Personal succession was originally an ecclesiastical matter, and was dealt with in the Church courts. This means that a lot of succession law has its origin in ecclesiastical law, which in turn was based on the old Roman law. Until 1858, all wills were proven in the Church courts, regardless of whether they concerned real or personal property. For various reasons, including that some property was left on trust, certain succession disputes were also heard in the Court of Chancery, which was the court responsible for equity. It may, in many ways, be considered a remarkable feat that all of this was successfully harmonised in the mid-19th century.

1.4.1 Succession of real property prior to the Wills Act 1837

In the Middle Ages, ownership and control of land was heavily regulated. Following the Norman Conquest in 1066, control of land was seized by the Crown. From this we get the notion that the Crown owns all land. This is strictly speaking not true; it is simply a matter of political reality that the Crown has ultimate control of the land. The Norman Kings created a feudal structure of land control, whereby freehold estates in land were granted to various people, generally the nobility and the Church. They in turn, as feudal lords, could grant lesser estates to other people further down the social hierarchy.

Various restrictions were in place which limited the right of an estate owner to transfer the freehold to another person. In general, the rule of primogeniture applied, which stated that the estate had to pass on intestacy to the eldest legitimate son or male heir, though in the absence of male heirs it could be possible for the land to pass to the owner's daughters. In the absence of any lawful heir, the estate would go back to whoever held a higher estate in the land, which was either a feudal lord, the Church or, ultimately, the Crown. Whoever held the higher estate was also entitled to an inheritance tax.

Herein lies the origin of English trust law. If the estate was held on trust, there would be no succession, and therefore no tax to be paid. Alternatively, in the absence of a legal heir, the estate could be passed on to someone else. The development of trust law through the Middle Ages and into the 16th century is complex and unnecessary to discuss here. Suffice it to say, the use of trusts to avoid inheritance tax was a cause of concern for the King, as it greatly limited tax revenue. Therefore, the original version of the trust (called a use) was banned in the Statute of Uses 1535. The second version, called the trust, which is what we still have today, developed through the cracks in that Statute. Nonetheless, in 1540, the Statute of Wills was passed, which allowed freehold owners to freely pass on their estate to whomever they chose. This was the start of testamentary freedom for real property. A number of feudal restrictions survived until the Tenures (Abolition) Act 1660. The Statute of Wills 1540 was ultimately replaced by the Wills Act 1837, even though the formality requirements for a will devising land were later set out in the Statute of Frauds 1677. The wills were proven in the Church courts until 1858.

1.4.2 Succession of personal property prior to the Wills Act 1837

From Anglo-Saxon times (before the Norman Invasion) and up to the Court of Probate Act 1857, succession of personal property was the purview of the Church. Unlike real property, a medieval testator was allowed to write a will and dispose of his personal property.

However, at least in some parts of England and Wales, the medieval testator did not have absolute testamentary freedom. Rather, the law applied what can aptly be called a rule of threes. The testator had to leave one third of his estate to his widow, one third to his children, and the final third could be freely disposed of. However, the social expectation was that the final third was to go to the Church. That might sound a bit cynical, and the Protestant Reformation did show that the medieval Church spent a lot of its money on itself, but it must also be remembered that, prior to the 16th century, the Church was almost solely responsible for many social matters, such as education and healthcare. The final third, which the Church expected, was in many ways a charitable donation, and undoubtedly a lot of the money would benefit the local community. Whilst women had few legal rights in the Middle Ages, the widow was protected by a special writ she could use to compel the executor to transfer her third to her, known as *de rationabili parte bonorum*.

Following the Protestant Reformation in the 16th century, the rule of threes fell into disuse and was eventually abolished altogether by a series of statutes that repealed the rule in three specific dioceses (York, London, and the Province of Wales). This suggests that the restrictions and the writ only applied in those parts of the country rather than the whole of England.

Either way, from the early 17th century, a testator, in general, had testamentary freedom for both real and personal property. Of course, there were still practical restrictions in place, such as trusts, entailed property, marriage settlements, and dowager rights. Some of those restrictions on ownership remained until the Law of Property Act 1925.

1.4.3 Development of succession law from 1837

The Wills Act 1837, which remains in force today, codified the law on wills. The old distinction between real and personal property was abolished. The Wills Act 1837 did not concern intestacy, which was finally codified in the Administration of Estates Act 1925. However, in 1837, succession disputes could still be heard in different courts. This was obviously a great inconvenience for everyone involved. As stated above, disputes could be heard by the common law courts, ecclesiastical courts, and the Court of Chancery. This problem was finally resolved by the creation of a dedicated court dealing with all succession disputes. Known as the Probate Court, it was created by the Court of Probate Act 1857 and came into existence in 1858.

The separate Probate Court did not last for very long. In 1875, the entire English court system was comprehensively reorganised. A new court was created, then called the Supreme Court. It consists, at trial level, of the High Court and, at the appellate level, the Court of Appeal. In 1875, the High Court was divided into three Divisions. The Queen's Bench Division took over most common law disputes (previously heard in the Court of Queen's Bench). The Chancery Division took over most equitable disputes (previously heard in the Court of Chancery). Finally, there was the Probate, Divorce and Admiralty Division, which took over from a variety of old courts, including the Probate Court. In the legal community this

Division was informally known as the 'Court of Wills, Wives and Wrecks'. All succession disputes were heard in the Probate Division of the High Court. With the creation of the new Supreme Court in 2009, the former was renamed the Senior Court.

This system lasted for about 100 years. In the 1970s, there was a further reorganisation of the High Court. The Probate, Divorce and Admiralty Division was replaced with the Family Division, which remains today (the new Admiralty Court became a subdivision in the Queen's Bench Division). Following this reorganisation, all succession matters begin in the Family Division. Non-contentious probate, namely the routine, day-to-day probate matters, such as appointing PRs and validating wills, is handled by local Probate Registries, which are subsets of the Family Division and are located in many cities and towns around the country. Contentious probate, such as where there is a legal dispute over the validity of a will, is transferred over to the Chancery Division. The Chancery Division will also hear administration claims. One might question why the 1970s reorganisation took place, as it might make sense to have all succession claims heard in a single probate court, in front of specialist probate judges.

It is important to bear in mind this historical development and the current divide between the Family Division and the Chancery Division. In studying succession law, you will encounter judgments from all of these different courts. Therefore, don't be surprised that some pre-1857 judgments come from the ecclesiastical court and that more recent judgments come from either the Family or the Chancery Division.

1.4.4 Future reform of succession law

Whilst there have been more recent changes to succession law, it is true that the bulk of it stems from the 19th century. The Wills Act 1837 still governs the creation of valid wills, and the Act is rapidly approaching its 200th anniversary. The intestacy rules are from 1925, though they have been polished more recently. The rules on PRs and their duties derive primarily from the 19th century. The process for obtaining probate was reformed in 2020, to better take into account new developments in online platforms for managing legal business. Even so, the prevalence of old rules raises the question of whether succession law remains fit for purpose.

To that end, the Law Commission has begun a project on reform of the laws on wills. The Law Commission published a consultation paper in 2017, entitled 'Making a Will' (Law Commission Consultation Paper 231), which suggested a variety of reforms and invited responses from the public. A final report is expected in the coming years, which might lead to a new Bill being put before Parliament to replace the Wills Act 1837. The subsequent chapters will often refer to this consultation paper and the reforms proposed therein. Other chapters will highlight problems that the Law Commission has not looked at this time around, but which will probably need looking at in the near future. This includes the intestacy rules and whether they remain fit for purpose given the social reality of today.

In reading this textbook, you are therefore also encouraged to think critically about the law and to contemplate whether it is in need of reform. Undoubtedly, most of it works perfectly well. It is also beyond doubt that some of it needs to be modernised.

1.5 International aspects of succession law

This textbook only considers succession law as it applies in England and Wales. The other countries in the United Kingdom as well as the Overseas Territories have their own succession laws that may differ from the rules found in English law. Of course, each jurisdiction around the world has its own succession laws as well. Note here the reference to jurisdiction rather than country – in a federal country such as the United States or Australia, each state has its own succession law.

In the modern world, which is increasingly interconnected and subject to people moving for work, studies, relationships, retirement, just for fun, or out of necessity, more and more people own property in multiple jurisdictions. It can be as simple as a person in England owning a holiday home in Spain, or it can be more complex with a person in England owning businesses and having bank accounts and investment portfolios in several different countries around the world. Brexit will obviously have an impact here, but neither Brexit nor Covid-19 will change the fundamental fact that the world is increasingly interconnected. It raises the question of how the property of people who own assets in different jurisdictions is dealt with after they have died.

Unfortunately, in a textbook focusing on English succession law, it is not possible to go through the rules on international succession in any detail. That falls under an area of law known as private international law. However, a few key points can be mentioned. If a person writes a will in England, that will can dispose of property (both real and personal) in any jurisdiction within the United Kingdom. So, for example, owning a holiday home in Scotland does not present a major problem for an English testator. The English will is going to be accepted by the Scottish court. The reverse is, of course, also the case; an English court will accept a Scottish will, disposing of property in England owned by a Scottish testator.

More generally, the English court will accept a will executed in a foreign jurisdiction provided that it was executed in accordance with the rules in that jurisdiction (Wills Act 1963, s 1). However, any question as to the validity of an English will, disposing of property in England, cannot be determined in a foreign court (*Boyse v Colclough* (1854) 1 K & J 124, 69 ER 396; *Clark v Word Wildlife Fund* (Ch D, 2010, unreported)). Only an English court can make a final determination on that point.

English law generally holds that a will as to movable property (personalty) is governed by the law where the testator was domiciled and that a will as to immovable property (realty) is governed by the law where the property is located (*Re Kelly (Deceased)* [2020] EWHC 245 (Ch)). Domicile is a technical legal concept referring, broadly, to the place where a person is intending to make their permanent home. Every person has a domicile of birth but can acquire a domicile of choice by moving to a different jurisdiction, provided they intend to make that jurisdiction their home.

The case of *Rokkan v Rokkan* [2021] EWHC 481 (Ch) can be used as an example of these kinds of interjurisdictional disputes. In short, a Welsh lady called Elizabeth married a Norwegian man called Stein Rokkan. They lived in Norway, where they had two children. After Stein died, Norwegian law provided that his estate should pass to his children, but that Elizabeth could defer that distribution until after her death. That meant that Elizabeth could use Stein's assets during her life. When Elizabeth died, the joint estates should pass to their respective heirs (which, in the case of children, may be the same persons – however, it takes into account that either spouse may have additional children from other relationships). However, after Stein died, Elizabeth returned to Wales, and transferred all her movable assets there (including those from Stein's estate). In Wales, she wrote a will in accordance with English law, that varied from the Norwegian position that the two estates should pass equally to the children. One of the children, Per Rokkan, made a claim arguing that Elizabeth's estate was held on trust in accordance with the Norwegian law, as opposed to passing in accordance with the will. Since Elizabeth died domiciled in Wales, the court held that the succession of her estate was subject to English law. Per's claim was thus dismissed, and Elizabeth's estate (realty in England and all movable property) passed according to the terms of her will. However, Elizabeth also still owned some land in Norway, which passed equally to the two children in accordance with Norwegian law.

To avoid complications and legal disputes, the general recommendation for testators with property in multiple jurisdictions is to execute separate wills in each jurisdiction, complying with the local rules. In general, courts may accept a foreign will that disposes of personal property, but are unlikely to accept a foreign will that disposes of real property. Thus, for example, if an English person owns a holiday home in Spain, the recommendation is to write a separate Spanish will. An English will trying to dispose of that holiday home may not be accepted by the Spanish court, and, if not, the property will pass according to the Spanish rules on intestacy. Similarly, if a foreign national owns personal property in England (such as shares and investments), the English court may accept a foreign will disposing of that property, but the English court may not accept a foreign will disposing of real property in England. If a foreign will is not accepted, the property passes according to the English rules on intestacy. It is to avoid the risk of intestacy that a person should write separate wills in each jurisdiction in which they own property.

summary

The purpose of this chapter has been broadly to outline what succession law is about. It concerns both a person's right to choose what happens to their property when they die, and also what happens after they have died. The chapter has also looked at the historical development of English succession law, to place some of the key concepts and sources in their proper context. The chapter has also listed some key terms and key sources, with which you need to become familiar. They will be looked at in much more detail in each of the following chapters. By the end of the textbook you will have a grounding in English succession law, as well as a critical understanding of how the law might be reformed in the years to come.

chapter 2

Testamentary Intention and Capacity

The previous chapter provided an outline of what succession law covers. Fundamentally, succession law concerns your right to freely choose what should happen to your property once you have died. This right goes to the very heart of private ownership and testamentary freedom, which are principles cherished in English (and Western) philosophy. The choice of what will happen to your property after your death is made in a will.

The will is therefore a very important document. It reflects your final wishes and is your opportunity to provide for family, friends and any other organisations that you want to benefit with your property. Unsurprisingly, therefore, the law prescribes a whole raft of requirements that a will must meet before it is legally valid and enforceable. This chapter, and also the next, look at those legal requirements.

This chapter focuses on mental capacity and testamentary intention. In short, a will is only valid and enforceable if the testator truly intended it to be valid and had the mental capacity to write it. There are four key issues to address:

- *Age:* only an adult can write a will.
- *Mental capacity:* the testator needs to have the required mental capacity to write a will.
- *Knowing and approving:* the testator must know about and approve the contents of the will.
- *Genuine intent:* the testator must not be pressured into writing the will, for example by fraud or undue influence.

This chapter considers each of these requirements in turn. The Law Commission, in its 2017 Consultation Paper 'Making a Will', addressed these issues and made various proposals for reform (Law Commission Consultation Paper 231). The chapter discusses some of these proposals. Thus, by the end of the chapter, you will understand the legal rules for testamentary intention and capacity, recognise some of the problems with the current rules and identify the Law Commission's reform proposals.

2.1 Age

The first legal requirement is that you need to be of a certain age in order to write a valid will. Section 7 of the Wills Act 1837 states that only adults can write a will. This means that you have to be 18 years of age before you have testamentary capacity. Any will written by someone under the age of 18 will not be enforceable in court. The only exception to this rule is the so-called 'privileged will', written by members of the armed forces or those working on ships at sea, which can be created by a minor. Privileged wills are discussed at **3.4.1**.

The Law Commission, however, has proposed that the age limit should be lowered to 16 (Law Com 231, [8.28]). To determine whether that is appropriate, it is necessary to look at the age of consent more generally, both in England as well as in other jurisdictions. In England, 18 is today seen as the age where a child becomes an adult, and, as such, 18 is the age requirement for several important legal acts. Voting in a political election and drinking alcohol are notable examples. Further, property law holds that only adults can own legal estates in land (Law of Property Act 1925, s 1(6)). This means that the age of 18 might also be suitable for testamentary capacity.

However, the age requirement for a number of other legal acts is 16. This includes being able to consent to medical treatment. Indeed, a person under 16 can consent to medical treatment if they are sufficiently mature and are able to understand what is going on (*Gillick v West Yorkshire and Wisbech AHA* [1986] AC 112). Subject to parental consent, a person over 16 can marry or join the armed forces. In Scotland, a person over 16 can vote in local elections, and there have been repeated calls for the voting age to be lowered to 16 in elections in England and Wales as well. These developments come as part of a broader move to recognise and respect the personal autonomy of young people. This might suggest that it is appropriate to lower the age of testamentary capacity to 16, as proposed.

Lowering the age of testamentary capacity to 16 is also supported by developments in some other jurisdictions. There is no universal consensus on the age of testamentary capacity, though in many jurisdictions the age requirement is 18. However, there are exceptions. The age of testamentary capacity in Singapore is 21. In British Columbia, Canada, the age of testamentary capacity is 16. In the United States, most states have 18 as the age of testamentary capacity, but the state of Georgia has it at 14. However, Scotland has the lowest age, where a person over 12 is deemed to have testamentary capacity.

Other jurisdictions have 18 as the general age of testamentary capacity, but allow for exceptions. In Ontario, Canada, for instance, a person under 18 may write a will if they are married or are about to marry. In the Australian states, the right of married minors to write wills is recognised, and beyond that the courts have the right to authorise any minor to write a will if the court is satisfied that the minor 'understands the nature and effect of the proposed will' and that it is 'reasonable' to do so (see, for example, the Succession Act 2006 (New South Wales, Australia), s 16). Similarly, in New Zealand, an unmarried minor can write a will if they can satisfy the Family Court that they understand the 'effect' of a will (Wills Act 2007 (New Zealand), s 9).

It is clear that there is no general trend on the age of testamentary capacity. However, there are many jurisdictions that have either lowered the age of testamentary capacity from 18 or give the courts discretion to allow minors to write wills. Given that the age requirement for a number of legal acts in England and Wales is 16, the Law Commission is surely right to propose lowering the age of testamentary capacity to 16.

However, as the Law Commission rightly notes, this will still not solve disputes arising with children under the age of 16. A tragic example is the case of *Re JS (Disposal of Body)* [2016] EWHC 2859 (Fam), [2017] 4 WLR 1, where a 14-year-old girl dying of cancer wanted her body to be cryogenically frozen, in the hope that a cure might be found in the future. However, as a minor, she could not write a will and therein appoint an executor, who would be responsible for the disposal of the body. The court had to intervene because there was a disagreement between the two parents, with the mother accepting the girl's wish for cryogenic freezing and the father opposing it. The court made the mother the sole administrator and prevented the father from interfering with the mother's decision. Thankfully, however, these sorts of disputes are rare, and can be resolved by the courts.

key terminology

Executor: the person appointed by the will to arrange the disposal of the body and administer the deceased's estate, such as paying off debts and distributing the property to the intended recipients (called beneficiaries). See **Chapter 9**.

Administrator: the person appointed by the court to administer the deceased's estate, in situations where there is no executor.

example

Disposal of the body

A person may, in their will, include directions as to how they want their body to be disposed. This could include burial or cremation. However, the law says that such directions are only 'wishes' and have no legal effect. It is for the personal representative (PR) (whether an executor or administrator) to dispose of the body, and whilst the PR may want to give effect to the testator's wishes, the PR is not legally bound to do so: *Williams v Williams* (1881-82) LR 20 Ch D 659.

2.2 Testamentary capacity

So, as it stands, you can write a valid will once you have become an adult. The next requirement imposed by the law is the need for what is called testamentary capacity. This means that you must have the requisite mental capacity to write a will. In other words, when writing a will, you cannot be subject to any mental illness or disorder that would prevent you from fully understanding the legal effect of the will. This section of the chapter explores the legal test for testamentary capacity.

To fully understand the test for testamentary capacity, it is necessary to turn back the clock more than 150 years. This takes us to the dawn of the Victorian Age. This era was a time of great innovation, and society was fascinated by all manner of new inventions and developments. A greater interest in psychology and mental health was no exception.

Psychology became an independent school of study in the latter half of the 19th century, and influential psychologists such as Sigmund Freud and Carl Gustav Jung started publishing their works in the early 20th century. Nonetheless, 19th century English case law demonstrates a deep-rooted interest and fascination with mental health. It was in this era, decades before Freud, that English law developed its test for whether a testator had mental capacity. This means that the test predates any modern understanding of mental disorders or illnesses. It is for this reason that the Law Commission has proposed replacing the existing test with the more modern test found in the Mental Capacity Act (MCA) 2005, which is more in tune with 21st century developments in mental health.

The first section below looks at the early cases which led up to the existing test. The second section considers the existing test in detail. The third section focuses on issues around time, namely when does the testator need to have mental capacity? The fourth section looks at how mental capacity is proved in court. The final section examines the modern test in the MCA 2005 and considers the Law Commission's arguments as to why it thinks succession law should adopt that test.

2.2.1   Delusions: the original test for testamentary capacity

The current test for testamentary capacity is set out in a case called *Banks v Goodfellow* (1869-70) LR 5 QB 549. However, it is useful to put this case into context by looking at the cases that came before it. What did they say and how was the law changed in *Banks v Goodfellow*?

The cases that predate *Banks v Goodfellow* talked about delusions. They asked whether the testator had been suffering from any delusions that had affected their ability to make rational decisions. For instance, a testator might have become convinced that his daughter was possessed by the devil, and therefore he excluded her from his will. This is what happened in the case of *Dew v Clark* (1826) 3 Add 79, 162 ER 410, and unsurprisingly the will was found to be invalid. The judge, Sir John Nicholl, presented a test for when a testator is under a delusion:

> Wherever the patient once conceives something extravagant to exist, which has still no existence whatever but in his own heated imagination; and wherever, at the same time, having once so conceived, he is incapable of being, or at least of being permanently, reasoned out of that conception; such a patient is said to be under a delusion.

In this test, the law asked whether the testator had a delusion – namely believing in something extravagant and unreal – and whether or not the testator could, either permanently or temporarily, be reasoned out of it.

On paper, it should be fairly straightforward to figure out if someone has a delusion. As in *Dew v Clark*, if the testator believed that their child was possessed by the devil, then, yes, they might be suffering from a delusion. (It is, however, important to note that such beliefs are socially accepted in some parts of the world as a result of religious teachings, and it cannot be said that all those who hold those beliefs are truly delusional; it is always a question of fact for the court.) If the testator believed that the Prime Minister (two Prime Ministers in fact!) was coming to their house at night to have what the judge called 'improper connections' with them, then, yes, they might be suffering from a delusion, as was the case in *Waring v Waring* (1848) 6 Moo PC 341, 13 ER 715. If the testator believed that there was an international conspiracy working against them, implicating their family, then again, yes, they might be suffering from a delusion, as was the case in *Kostic v Chaplin* [2007] EWHC 2298 (Ch). If the testator believed that aliens had landed on their farm, and that the former Iraqi dictator Saddam Hussein had been trying to break in, then, yes, they might be suffering from delusions, as was the case in *Lloyd v Jones* [2016] EWHC 1308 (Ch). All of these are 'extravagant' ideas which only exist in the testators' minds.

However, the test set out in *Dew v Clark* comes with some problems. Sir JP Wilde, in the case of *Smith v Tebbitt* (1867) LR 1 P&D 398, criticised it with some dramatic flair:

> But surely, sane people often imagine things to exist which have no existence in reality, both in the physical and moral world. What else gives rise to unfounded fears, unjust suspicions, baseless hopes, or romantic dreams?

There will undoubtedly be a lot of people who have deep-seated beliefs that others might find strange or odd, but which in no way affect that person's mental capacity. A belief in something 'extravagant' which cannot be objectively proven undoubtedly encompasses a wide range of religious, philosophical and political ideas. However, it cannot be said that just because a person subscribes to a particular religion or philosophy, they suddenly lack mental capacity.

A second, more practical, problem with just referring to delusions is that the delusion might not actually impact on the testator's decision-making process. If so, there is no need for the delusion to invalidate the will. This has led to a clarification in later case law. The delusions have to actually affect the testamentary decision-making process and must cause the will to contain or not contain a particular beneficiary or gift. For instance, in *Lloyd v Jones*, cited above, the testator believed that aliens were landing on her farm and that Saddam Hussein was trying to break in. This is clearly a delusion, by any definition, but it had no bearing on how the testator wrote her will. On the facts, the will was upheld.

The courts came to recognise the limitation of simply talking about delusions. This led to the test in *Banks v Goodfellow*, which remains in use today. It added three new requirements, but the fourth requirement retains the essence of the old law, ensuring that the testator does not suffer from a delusion or disorder of the mind. As such, *Banks v Goodfellow* builds on the older test, but it was not a complete replacement.

2.2.2 *Banks v Goodfellow:* the current test for testamentary capacity

key case

Banks v Goodfellow (1869-70) LR 5 QB 549

The testator in this case was a man called John Banks. Unfortunately, he suffered from some form of mental illness (which was not explained and perhaps not fully understood at the time). Due to this, he had spent time in a mental hospital (which at the time was called a 'lunatic asylum'). He continued to suffer from delusions for the rest of his life. These delusions were very tragic. He believed that a man called Featherstone Alexander was molesting him, notwithstanding the fact that Featherstone Alexander had died many years earlier. Mr Banks also believed that he was being molested by devils or evil spirits.

Mr Banks nonetheless managed his own affairs. In December 1863, Mr Banks executed a will in favour of his niece, Margaret Goodfellow. Mr Banks died in 1865. The question for the court was whether the will was valid or whether the estate should pass on intestacy to the children of Mr Banks' half-brother. After a trial, the county court found in favour of the will. An appeal was lodged, but the Queen's Bench also found in favour of the will.

The court drew a clear distinction between what it called complete and partial insanity. Mr Banks was partially insane, in that he had certain delusions, which did not affect his ability to conduct his daily affairs. The court looks suspiciously at a will executed by a person with delusions, but in this case held that there was no reason to invalidate a will if the delusions were not present at the time of execution or if they had no impact on the testamentary decisions.

key terminology

Execution of a will: this is the legal act done to create a valid will. In short, it requires that the will is in writing, and the testator must sign the will in the presence of two witnesses, who then also sign it. See **Chapter 3**.

The Court in *Banks v Goodfellow* laid down the current test for testamentary capacity.

> It is essential to the exercise of such a power that a testator shall understand the nature of the act and its effects; shall understand the extent of the property of which he is disposing; shall be able to comprehend and appreciate the claims to which he ought to give effect; and, with a view to the latter object, that no disorder of the mind shall poison his affections, pervert his sense of right, or prevent the exercise of his natural faculties – that no insane delusion

shall influence his will in disposing of his property and bring about a disposal of it which, if the mind had been sound, would not have been made.

It is commonly accepted that this is a four-part test. In more modern parlance, the four-part test can be presented as follows:

(1) The testator must understand the nature and act of writing a will.

(2) The testator must have an understanding of what property he or she owns.

(3) The testator must understand who should be considered as potential beneficiaries.

(4) The testator's decision-making must not be affected by any mental illness or disorder.

However, in *Banks v Goodfellow*, Cockburn CJ states 'with a view to the latter object', which seems to link the third and fourth requirements. This has led to some confusion as to whether this is a four-part test or whether the third and fourth parts are joined together. In *Burgess v Hawes* [2013] EWCA Civ 94, the Court of Appeal suggested that it was a three-part test. However, in *Sharp v Adam* [2006] EWCA Civ 449, the Court of Appeal said that it was a four-part test. The Law Commission argued that it would be 'illogical' to limit the fourth requirement, on the impact of the mental illness or disorder, to the third requirement (Law Com 231, [2.40]). This chapter will proceed on the basis that there are four separate parts to the test.

2.2.2.1 The first requirement: the testator must understand the nature and act of writing a will

Under the first requirement, when you are writing a will, you have to understand what a will is and what it does. In short, the law requires that the testator understands that they are setting out what will happen to their property when they die. The testator should also understand that wills are what we call ambulatory, namely that they only take effect on death and can be changed or revoked at any time until then.

The testator only needs to understand the immediate consequences of their decision, namely that they are deciding how their property will be distributed when they die. The testator does not need to understand any collateral consequences of that decision. So, for example, in the case of *Simon v Byford* [2014] EWCA Civ 280, the testator left her shares in the family company equally to her children. This had the effect of creating a voting deadlock, since her children would now have an equal amount of shares. A voting deadlock amongst the shareholders might make it more difficult to run the company. However, the deadlock was a collateral consequence; the will was upheld since the testator understood the immediate consequence of her action, namely that she was disposing of her property in equal shares to her children once she died.

2.2.2.2 The second requirement: the testator must have an understanding of what property he or she owns

Secondly, the law requires that you have an understanding of what property you own. In the case of *Waters v Waters* (1848) 2 De G & Sm 591, 64 ER 263, the court said that the testator is only required to have a general understanding of their assets, but they do not have to know 'every atom of [their] property'. For many people, no doubt, that would be an unrealistic expectation. The courts have therefore emphasised that this is not a memory test. Capacity is not lost simply because the testator has forgotten that they own this or that property. If the testator has forgotten about some property that they own, they can be reminded of that fact. As Lewison LJ lamented in *Simon v Byford*:

> Once I knew the dates of all the Kings and Queens of England, and the formula for Hooke's law; and was 'capable' of remembering them. Now I would have to look them up.

The real question is whether the testator has the capacity to actually understand what property they have. So, for example, in the case of *Wood v Smith* [1993] Ch 90, the testator was adamant that he had investments valued at around £17,000, and he was trying to dispose of them in his will. In reality, his investments were valued at around £105,000. The testator was repeatedly told of the real value, but he could not comprehend that information. The will was thus invalid.

2.2.2.3 The third requirement: the testator must understand who should be considered as potential beneficiaries

Thirdly, the law requires you to have an understanding of whom you should consider as beneficiaries in the will. This usually includes family and friends. It is still not a memory test. The question is whether you have the capacity to understand who may expect to inherit, such as your family and friends, even if you have to be reminded of particular individuals.

It is important not to misunderstand this requirement. English law recognises testamentary freedom, meaning that you are free to leave your property to whomever you want, and consequently, subject to the family provision rule, you can exclude family and friends (see **Chapter 15**). The mental capacity test simply requires you to understand who the likely beneficiaries are.

The case of *Couwenbergh v Valkova* [2008] EWHC 2451 (Ch) is illustrative. It is a sad case, demonstrating the negative consequences of dementia. The testator, Mrs Adams, was suffering from dementia (by all accounts caused by old age) and had not only forgotten about her family members but could not recognise them in person. Even if they introduced themselves to her in person, she would not know who they were. The judge summarised her state thus: 'Mrs Adam was having difficulty in recognising persons who should have been wholly familiar to her and she would repeat herself in the course of the same conversation.' On the facts, the court decided that her will was invalid.

There is a clear difference between being able to recognise a potential beneficiary (such as a child) and then consciously excluding them from your will (as the law permits) and not being able to recognise family or friends at all due to some mental illness or disorder. The court in *Boughton v Knight* (1872-1875) LR 3 P&D 64 emphasised testamentary freedom, stating that a potential beneficiary, such as a child, can be consciously excluded from the will for any reason, however frivolous or mean-spirited that reason might be. For example, the playwright William Shakespeare famously gave to his wife his 'second-best' bed. Capricious decisions on their own do not point to a lack of mental capacity.

2.2.2.4 The fourth requirement: the testator's decision-making must not be affected by any mental illness or disorder

The fourth part of the test states that if any mental illness or disorder means that any of the three above requirements cannot be met, the testator lacks capacity and the will is therefore invalid. There is no fixed legal list of mental illnesses or disorders. The law develops alongside medical science. The court in *Re Key* [2010] EWHC 408 (Ch), [2010] 1 WLR 2020 emphasised this point:

> Psychiatric medicine has come a long way since 1870 in recognising an ever widening range of circumstances now regarded as sufficient at least to give rise to a risk of mental disorder, sufficient to deprive a patient of the power of rational decision-making, quite distinctly from old age and infirmity.

As seen above, the Victorian judgments focused on delusions, and this is how the early tests were formulated. *Banks v Goodfellow* itself was a case about delusions, and the test in fact still refers to that. It is true that delusions continue to arise in modern cases as well. Two such cases, *Kostic v Chaplin* [2007] EWHC 2298 (Ch) and *Lloyd v Jones* [2016] EWHC 1308 (Ch), were mentioned above. However, our understanding of mental health has come a long way since 1870, and the courts are using the fourth part of the test to keep the law up to date.

For example, in the case of *Sharp v Adam* [2006] EWCA Civ 449, the testator had multiple sclerosis, which, possibly due to MS's impact on cognitive function, had poisoned his mind against his daughters. He therefore disinherited his daughters. They challenged the will and the court declared that the will was invalid. In *Re Key*, the testator wrote a new will one week after his wife of 65 years had died, and the court held that bereavement had the potential to undermine capacity. Dementia, as seen in *Couwenbergh v Valkova*, is another example, and it is a mental condition that is on the rise as the population gets older and lives longer. There is also a wider recognition of the impact of depression, which the Office for National Statistics suggests affects almost one in five people. These developments in psychology are included within the fourth part of the test, as they can impact on the testator's decision-making process.

It is very important to emphasise that testamentary capacity is only lacking if the mental illness or disorder actually affects the decision-making process when the testator prepares and executes the will. For example, in *Vegetarian Society v Scott* [2013] EWHC 4097 (Ch), a testator with schizophrenia had his will upheld in court, as his mental disorder had not affected his decision-making process. The will was challenged as he had disinherited family members and, despite not being vegetarian himself, left around 80% of his estate to the Vegetarian Society. Even though that decision may appear unusual, it was done consciously by a testator who knew what he was doing, and thus was a decision that, as the judge put it, 'the law respects and upholds'.

In light of how psychology has developed over time, it is very important that any discussion of the *Banks v Goodfellow* test does not become focused on delusions. The test is more versatile than that, and the courts have been able to keep the test up to date. Nonetheless, because of its age and reference to delusions, the Law Commission has proposed replacing the *Banks v Goodfellow* test. This will be further discussed later on in the chapter.

2.2.3 Time: when does the testator need to have testamentary capacity?

The testator needs to satisfy the testamentary capacity requirements at the time when the will is executed, that is to say, when the will is signed and witnessed (see **3.1**).

What happens if the testator does have a mental illness or disorder and regularly moves in and out of capacity? The law states that the will is valid as long as it was executed at a time when the testator did have capacity. In the case of *Chambers and Yatman v Queen's Proctor* (1840) 2 Curt 415, 163 ER 457, the testator was suffering from various delusions over the course of three days. On the fourth day he executed a will, with three witnesses. On the fifth day, he sadly committed suicide. On the facts, there was nothing to suggest that the testator was suffering from any delusions on the fourth day when the will was executed. Therefore, the will was upheld. Ultimately, as discussed in the section below, it becomes a question of fact whether the testator had capacity at the time the will was executed, and this must be proven by the propounder of the will.

key terminology

Propounder: the person (generally the named executor) who applies to court, after the testator's death, in order to get a grant of probate.

Probate: the legal process through which an executor (sometimes an administrator) administers the estate (see **Chapter 11**).

There is one exception to the general rule, which derives from the case of *Parker v Felgate* (1883) 8 PD 171. If a testator gives instructions to their solicitor for a will to be drafted, and they have mental capacity when giving those instructions, the will is still valid even if the testator did not have full capacity when actually executing the will. The only requirement is that the testator understands that they are signing their will based on the instructions already given.

2.2.4 Burden of proof: proving testamentary capacity

The burden of proving that the testator had testamentary capacity when executing the will, or when giving instructions for the will if the *Parker v Felgate* exception is used, lies with the propounder of the will. The propounder is the person who takes the will to court to prove it, and normally this will be the executor named in the will (see **Chapters 9** and **11**). Parke B explained in the case of *Barry v Butlin* (1838) 2 Moo PC 480, 12 ER 1089 that 'the *onus probandi* lies in every case upon the party propounding a Will; and he must satisfy the conscience of the Court that the instrument so propounded is the last Will of a free and capable Testator'. However, the process is normally much more straightforward. The process was explained more recently in the case of *Re Key* [2010] EWHC 408 (Ch), [2010] 1 WLR 2020:

> (i) While the burden starts with the propounder of a will to establish capacity, where the will is duly executed and appears rational on its face, then the court will presume capacity. (ii) In such a case the evidential burden then shifts to the objector to raise a real doubt about capacity. (iii) If a real doubt is raised, the evidential burden shifts back to the propounder to establish capacity none the less.

This passage shows that there is a three-stage process. The majority of wills remain in the first stage and do not proceed beyond that. If the will is (a) duly executed and (b) appears rational, then testamentary capacity is presumed, and there will be no need for the propounder to provide any evidence. Rather, it is for a challenger to the will to 'raise a real doubt' as to the testator's mental capacity. The challenger's burden of proof is not to actually prove a lack of capacity, but merely to show that there are real doubts as to capacity. So, how can this be done? The challenger might, for instance, show that the testator was often forgetful or confused about common tasks or people, and thus might not satisfy the second or third *Banks v Goodfellow* requirement. The challenger might, perhaps, provide some medical evidence as to a mental illness or disorder. Each case will, of course, turn on its own facts. If there is real doubt, the propounder will need to provide evidence to prove that the testator did satisfy the *Banks v Goodfellow* test. It is only in this situation that a full trial might take place.

As noted, most wills do not move beyond the first stage, because they are duly executed and appear to be rational or because the will is not challenged by anyone. A challenge is most likely to come from a person who either would benefit from an earlier will (if the testator had made an earlier will) or from the intestacy rules (if the testator had not made an earlier will).

key terminology

Intestacy: a person dies intestate where they do not have a valid will. The Law Commission suggests that 40% of the adult population do not have wills (Law Com 231, [1.1]) (see **Chapter 8**).

Let us look more closely at when a testator is presumed to have testamentary capacity. There were two requirements identified in *Re Key*:

(a) A duly executed will: this will be discussed at **3.1**. In short, the will has to be in writing, signed by the testator, and also signed by at least two witnesses (Wills Act 1837, s 9).

(b) The will appears rational on its face: a will is rational where it relates to the testator's life. Most wills satisfy this requirement where the testator leaves their assets to family, friends or organisations that they have been associated with. As noted above, English law recognises testamentary freedom, and there is nothing immediately irrational about cutting family or friends out of a will.

If necessary, the propounder will need to prove that the will does relate to the testator's life. A good example is the case of *Austen v Graham* (1854) 8 Moo PC 493, 14 ER 188. The testator was a man called James Graham. He had spent many years living in India and, perhaps unusually in colonial times, had absorbed and adopted the local cultures and traditions. He held himself out at various points as a follower of both Hinduism and Islam. On his return to England, some doubts were raised as to his mental health, as he was said to have engaged in wild and extravagant behaviours (though it seems very possible that these 'doubts' were just xenophobia on the part of his social circle). James Graham wrote a will in which he left almost his entire estate to the Turkish Ambassador in London, to be used for (a) the poor of Constantinople (modern-day Istanbul) and (b) the creation of a monument in Constantinople with a burning flame and his name engraved upon it.

The validity of this will was challenged, but the court decided that the will was rational. The court explained how it went about determining whether a will is rational on its face, and the guidance remains useful today:

> With reference to this allegation, and the evidence adduced in support of it, we must examine into the life, habits, and opinions of this gentleman previously to the time when his insanity is alleged to have commenced; for the same behaviour, language, and testamentary dispositions which would be absurd and irrational in a native of England, living according to English habits, and entertaining or professing a belief in Christianity, might not necessarily bear the same character when proceeding from a native of India, or from one who, from an early period, had adopted its manners and modes of life, and who entertained or professed a belief in [Islam].

If there are any doubts as to whether the will is rational, the court will have to investigate the life of the particular testator. It will look at what kind of life they lived, what values they believed in, and, if necessary, what religious beliefs they professed. This will be used to determine whether the terms of the will are rational. Each testator is different, so the test of whether the terms of the will are rational is a subjective test.

If the terms of the will are irrational, then testamentary capacity cannot be presumed. It then falls on the propounder to prove that the testator did have testamentary capacity and that the irrational terms of the will were the free choice of the testator.

The process is demonstrated below.

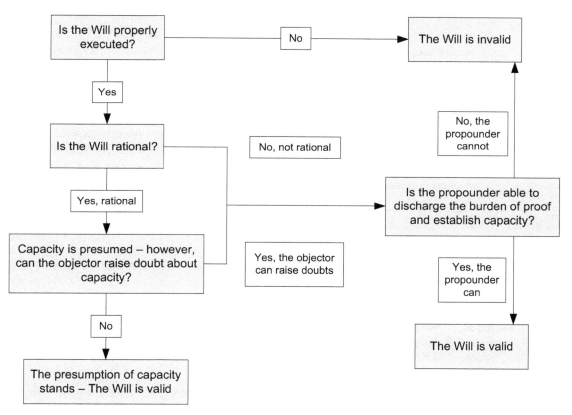

2.2.4.1 Evidence used to prove testamentary capacity

Each case turns on its own facts, so there are no firm rules on what evidence will be most effective in proving that the testator had testamentary capacity. To begin with, it must be emphasised that the question of whether or not the testator had testamentary capacity is a legal question, not a medical question. It is for the judge, not a doctor, to make a decision based on all available evidence.

The starting point will likely be the witnesses to the will, who were present when the will was executed. This is one of the reasons why witnesses are required. They can hopefully speak to the testator's state of mind when the will was executed. Beyond that, the court will likely consider witness statements from family and friends, who can also speak to the testator's mental state around the time when the will was executed. Family and friends are the people who most likely knew the testator the best, and they are therefore in a good position to explain the testator's mental state. However, the court must be wary of any bias in the statements provided by family and friends, especially if the challenged will benefits one of them or has excluded another. The risk is that the family and friends are, whether consciously or subconsciously, trying to paint a picture which benefits them.

The court will likely also hear from professional witnesses. This may be the solicitor who advised the testator and drafted the will. This may be any medical professional who has been treating the testator, such as their GP or a specialist consultant. The court can also hear from expert witnesses. This may be an expert medical professional, for example a professor in psychiatry, who will be able to explain the medical issues in more depth. The professional witness is unlikely to ever have met the testator, so their expert insight has to be considered in that light. In the case of *Edkins v Hopkins* [2016] EWHC 2542 (Ch), the judge said that the court should be 'cautious about putting too much weight on experts who did not see [the testator] as opposed to the witnesses who did'. Ultimately, of course, it is for the trial judge to determine the reliability of each witness and how much weight is given to their testimony.

key case

Re Key [2010] EWHC 408 (Ch), [2010] 1 WLR 2020

A man called George Key died in 2008. His wife, Sybil, to whom he had been married for 65 years, had died in 2006. At the time when Sybil died, George had an existing will, executed in 2001, which gave almost all of his estate to his two sons, at the expense of his two daughters. When Sybil died, the daughters learnt of the 2001 will and its contents. Immediately, they pressured George to write a new will. He did so, within a week of his wife's death, and the new will gave almost all of his estate to his daughters, at the expense of his sons. When George died, the sons challenged the new will, saying that George had not had testamentary capacity because he had executed the new will whilst distraught over the death of his wife.

The court considered evidence from the children, who unsurprisingly gave different accounts: the sons argued that their father lacked capacity and that the 2006 will was invalid; the daughters argued that he had capacity and that the 2006 will was therefore valid. Certain of George's friends and neighbours also gave conflicting evidence, ranging from that George was distraught due to the bereavement, to that George was upset but was the 'same George' he always was. The solicitor who had prepared the 2006 will gave evidence, but he was not entirely trustworthy, because he had failed to prepare a proper attendance note, which all lawyers should do after meeting a client. There were also two expert witnesses. The sons called a psychiatrist, who had examined George before George's death. The daughters called a distinguished Professor in Old Age Psychology, with considerable experience in giving expert evidence, but who had never met George. Nonetheless, the

Professor's specialism was more relevant to testamentary capacity than that of the psychiatrist. On balance, the court found that the psychiatrist's evidence was to be given more weight, on the basis that he had actually met George. This mishmash of witnesses, with their conflicting stories, shows the difficulties there can be in determining whether someone had testamentary capacity.

The court decided, based on the evidence, that George did not have mental capacity when executing the 2006 will. Instead, the court admitted the 2001 will into probate.

2.2.4.2   The Golden Rule

The courts have laid down a so-called Golden Rule, which solicitors and other will-drafters are recommended to follow where they advise an elderly or infirm client. Solicitors should satisfy themselves that the testator does in fact have mental capacity. This is something that can be done by asking for a medical opinion, perhaps from the testator's GP, before the will is executed. As explained in *Re Key*:

> The substance of the golden rule is that when a solicitor is instructed to prepare a will for an aged testator, or for one who has been seriously ill, he should arrange for a medical practitioner first to satisfy himself as to the capacity and understanding of the testator, and to make a contemporaneous record of his examination and findings.

The presence of a medical opinion will not be determinative of testamentary capacity, which can still be challenged in court after the testator has died. However, a medical report is strong evidence that the will's propounder can rely on to satisfy the court that the testator did in fact have capacity.

In the alternative to obtaining a medical opinion prior to the execution of the will, in *Re Simpson (Deceased)* (1977) 121 SJ 224, Templeman J recommended that the execution of a will of an elderly or infirm testator should be made in the presence of a medical professional. The medical professional should make a formal note of the event, which could be used as evidence in court, if needed. Ironically, Lord Templeman himself did not execute his final will in front of a medical professional, nor was a medical report obtained, despite Lord Templeman possibly suffering from dementia; a point used, after his death, to argue that his own will was invalid on the grounds of lack of testamentary capacity. That challenge was unsuccessful and his will was admitted to probate; *Re Baron Templeman of White Lackington (deceased)* [2020] EWHC 632 (Ch).

The Golden Rule is a (strongly) recommended guideline, but it is not a firm rule and there are no professional consequences for the solicitor if no medical report is sought. For example, in the case of *Kunicki v Hayward* [2016] EWHC 3199 (Ch), [2017] 4 WLR 32, the solicitor who drafted the disputed will could not properly explain the Golden Rule to the judge, suggesting a lack of understanding of what it entailed; nonetheless, on the evidence as a whole, the judge held that the testator had testamentary capacity. The reason for following the Golden Rule is simply to try to avoid unnecessary litigation about testamentary capacity, which is always challenging given that the testator has died and can no longer give their own evidence.

2.3 The Mental Capacity Act 2005

There are many areas of the law where the question of whether a person has mental capacity is relevant. For making wills, the test in *Banks v Goodfellow* is used. For other areas of the law, a new statutory test has been introduced by the Mental Capacity Act (MCA) 2005. The MCA 2005 is used to determine whether an adult person has mental capacity for a wide range of juridical acts. This includes whether a person has capacity to live independently, capacity to manage their personal finances, such as paying a mortgage, rent or bills, or capacity to consent to medical treatment.

The relevant sections of the MCA 2005 are ss 2 and 3, which are set out below:

2 People who lack capacity

(1) For the purposes of this Act, a person lacks capacity in relation to a matter if at the material time he is unable to make a decision for himself in relation to the matter because of an impairment of, or a disturbance in the functioning of, the mind or brain.

(2) It does not matter whether the impairment or disturbance is permanent or temporary.

(3) A lack of capacity cannot be established merely by reference to—

(a) a person's age or appearance, or

(b) a condition of his, or an aspect of his behaviour, which might lead others to make unjustified assumptions about his capacity.

...

3 Inability to make decisions

(1) For the purposes of section 2, a person is unable to make a decision for himself if he is unable—

(a) to understand the information relevant to the decision,

(b) to retain that information,

(c) to use or weigh that information as part of the process of making the decision, or

(d) to communicate his decision (whether by talking, using sign language or any other means).

(2) A person is not to be regarded as unable to understand the information relevant to a decision if he is able to understand an explanation of it given to him in a way that is appropriate to his circumstances (using simple language, visual aids or any other means).

(3) The fact that a person is able to retain the information relevant to a decision for a short period only does not prevent him from being regarded as able to make the decision.

(4) The information relevant to a decision includes information about the reasonably foreseeable consequences of—

(a) deciding one way or another, or

(b) failing to make the decision.

In practice, the s 3 test is not too different from the requirements in *Banks v Goodfellow*, although s 3 is set out in more general terms since it is designed to apply to a wide range of situations.

The question that has arisen following the introduction of the MCA 2005 is whether it replaces the test in *Banks v Goodfellow*. Unfortunately, the courts have not been able to give a definitive answer. In the case of *Scammell v Farmer* [2008] EWHC 1100 (Ch), the judge suggested that the MCA 2005 did not apply to testamentary capacity, and, at any rate, the testator had died before the Act came into force. In the case of *Re Key* [2010] EWHC 408 (Ch), [2010] 1 WLR 2020, the judge said that the MCA 2005 had not replaced *Banks v Goodfellow*, at least not in that case since the will was executed before the Act came into force. The same point was made by the Court of Appeal in the case of *Simon v Byford* [2014] EWCA Civ 280, namely that the MCA 2005 did not apply because the will predated the Act coming into force. These cases seem to suggest that the MCA 2005 does apply to wills executed after the Act came into force on 1 April 2007. However, these statements are all obiter, since the wills in question predated the MCA 2005.

In the case of *Re Walker* [2014] EWHC 71 (Ch), on the other hand, the court firmly stated that the MCA 2005 has not replaced *Banks v Goodfellow*. Strauss QC pointed out three important, though subtle, differences between the two tests.

The first relates to proving capacity. As discussed above, under *Banks v Goodfellow*, once a challenger has raised doubt, it is for the propounder of the will to prove capacity. Under the MCA 2005, it is for the challenger to prove a lack of capacity (MCA 2005, s 1(2)). This, in effect, reverses the burden.

The second difference relates to relevant knowledge. The phrasing in the MCA 2005 is much broader than in *Banks v Goodfellow*, which requires only an understanding of what a will is, what property the testator owns, and who the potential beneficiaries are. As noted above, the *Banks v Goodfellow* test is not one of memory. The testator does not need to remember every item that they own or remember every family member that they have; the question is only whether they have the capacity to understand the information, if necessary once they have been reminded of it.

The third difference relates to s 3(4), which refers to 'reasonably foreseeable consequences'. As mentioned in *Simon v Byford* above, the *Banks v Goodfellow* test only asks that the testator understands the immediate consequences of their act, namely that they are creating a will that takes effect when they die. It does not ask them to understand collateral consequences. In *Simon v Byford*, leaving the company shares to her children in equal shares would create a voting deadlock, but that was a collateral consequence and there was no need for the testator to appreciate this. Arguably, s 3(4) goes further and encompasses collateral consequences. Using the MCA 2005, the will in *Simon v Byford* might have been invalidated, although under *Banks v Goodfellow* it was upheld.

The view in *Re Walker* was approved in the case of *James v James* [2018] EWHC 43 (Ch). The judge agreed that there were differences between the two tests, meaning that the courts should continue to apply *Banks v Goodfellow*. Further, there is nothing in the MCA 2005 that suggested it had anything to do with testamentary capacity. The judge remarked that it is 'a principle of statutory interpretation that Parliament is assumed not to intend to overrule well-established rules of the common law without clear words'. If the MCA 2005 had been intended to replace *Banks v Goodfellow*, Parliament would have said so.

It is very unsatisfactory that the law is in this state of uncertainty. The *Banks v Goodfellow* test continues to be applied by default today. The decisions in *Re Walker* and *James v James* are undoubtedly correct, but they are only High Court decisions. In the absence of Parliamentary intervention, a decisive decision of the Court of Appeal or Supreme Court would be welcomed.

The Law Commission, appropriately, decided to address this issue in its 2017 consultation report. There, it recommended adopting the MCA 2005 test (Law Com 231, [2.66]). This is for a number of reasons. First, it would provide consistency in the law, meaning that all questions of capacity are decided using a single test. Secondly, it would ensure internal consistency within succession law. Where a person loses capacity within the meaning of the MCA 2005, the Court of Protection (a specialist court dealing with mental capacity matters) can create a statutory will; the court writes a will on behalf of the incapacitated person. It means that, today, a solicitor needs to use *Banks v Goodfellow* for their general clients and the MCA 2005 test for those clients whom the Court of Protection has said have already lost capacity. Thirdly, the MCA 2005 is more in tune with modern advances in mental health and psychiatry. In particular, there is no mention of delusions, which is an unfortunate remnant from the 19th century. The Law Commission further proposes that the *Banks v Goodfellow* criteria, namely understanding one's property and one's family and friends, should be adopted in a formal Code of Practice, which would clarify what is meant by relevant information in s 3 (Law Com 231, [2.73]). In this way, the *Banks v Goodfellow* test would not disappear altogether, but would continue to be used as guidance when the s 3 test is applied. Adopting the MCA 2005 would, however, impact on the issues identified in *Re Walker*, so there would necessarily be some changes needed to the operation of testamentary capacity.

2.4   Knowing and approving

So far, the chapter has shown that to write a valid will, the testator needs to be an adult and have testamentary capacity. There are, however, many more requirements. The next requirement to be considered is called 'knowing and approving'. It must be proven that the testator knew and approved of the contents of the will. As the court said in the case of *Strum v Fuller* [2001] EWCA Civ 1879, [2002] 1 WLR 1097, the will has to 'truly represent the testator's testamentary intentions'. Those who challenge a will often raise a lack of knowledge and approval alongside their claim that the testator lacked testamentary capacity, so most cases consider both issues.

The process for proving knowledge and approval of the terms is closely linked to the process for proving testamentary capacity. Where the will is duly executed (see **3.1**), namely it has been signed by the testator and at least two witnesses, the court will presume that the testator knew and approved of the will (*Re Burns (Deceased)* [2016] EWCA Civ 37). Further, the court will presume knowledge and approval if certain conditions are met. The strongest presumption that the testator knew and approved of the will is where the testator either personally wrote the will, actually read through the will, or had the will read out loud to them (*Barry v Butlin* (1838) 2 Moo PC 480, 12 ER 1089). It is therefore good practice for a solicitor to ensure that the testator reads the will, or has it read to them, before the will is executed. This is, however, solely a presumption and can be challenged.

The burden of proof for knowing and approving traditionally comes in two stages: first, the challenger has to raise some doubts as to whether the testator truly knew and approved of the will, referred to as 'exciting the court's suspicion', and, secondly, if that has been done, the propounder has to prove knowledge and approval. This mirrors the burden of proof required for testamentary capacity. In more recent cases, however, the courts have doubted the utility of the two-stage approach. In the case of *Gill v Woodall* [2010] EWCA Civ 1430, [2011] Ch 380, the court argued that, ultimately, it is a question for the judge to determine, following a trial, whether there was knowledge and approval. This decision has to be based on all the evidence available. Whilst this is true, knowing who has the burden of proof is also important. It would be unnecessary and disproportionate if propounders had to prove knowledge and approval for every single will. Therefore, disputes have to start with a challenger raising real doubt.

A challenger can excite the court's suspicion in different ways. The court will look at the circumstances in which the will was executed. In *Gill v Woodall*, the disputed will gave the residue of the estate to the RSPCA, despite the testator having previously referred to the charity as, amongst other things, 'a waste of time'; this excited the court's suspicion. Further, the testator had attended the solicitor's office to execute the will. However, she suffered from agoraphobia (a fear of leaving one's home), meaning that she was in discomfort and could not take in what the solicitor was saying during their meeting; as such she could not be said to actually have known what was in the will (a different outcome might have been reached if the solicitor had attended the testator's home, where she might have been more comfortable).

The court will be extra vigilant where the person who prepared the will (for instance, the solicitor who drafted the will) is also a beneficiary under the will. The same applies where the will was signed by someone else on the testator's behalf, which the law permits (see **3.1.2.2**). The court will also be vigilant where the testator is blind or illiterate, where, unfortunately, it is easier for an unscrupulous party to write a will that the testator does not in fact approve of.

The propounder has to satisfy the court that the testator knew and approved of the will. Reading the will to the testator is a good start but will not always be sufficient. In the case of *Poole v Everall* [2016] EWHC 2126 (Ch), the will was prepared by the testator's carer, and it left 95% of the estate to the carer. The testator was allowed to read through the will before signing it. On the facts, that was not sufficient, because the testator did not consult with anyone else, nor did the carer point out how large a share he was to receive. Ideally, there will be further evidence from people who are not beneficiaries, and thus have no personal agenda when giving evidence to the court, to the effect that the testator knew and approved of the will's contents. What evidence can be used for proving knowledge and approval varies from case to case. For example, in the case of *In the Goods of Geale* (1864) 3 Sw & Tr 431, 164 ER 1342, a deaf and illiterate testator's will was upheld because he had communicated acceptance through a personal sign-system used by the family. Ultimately, it is a question of fact whether each particular testator knew and approved of the will's contents.

2.5 Testamentary intention

In addition to being an adult, having testamentary capacity, and knowing and approving the contents of the will, the testator must finally intend to create a valid will. This is known as having testamentary intention. There are a number of things that the testator must intend in order for the will to be valid.

First, the testator must intend for the provisions in the will to take effect on his or her death. If the intention is for the provisions to have immediate effect, there is no will but at best an outright gift. Secondly, the will must also be intended to be revocable, also referred to as ambulatory, at any point until the testator's death. This means that the testator knows that they can change their mind at any time. Finally, the testator's intention must be their own, and they must not be unlawfully influenced by someone else when deciding to write the will.

Whether the testator has testamentary intention is a question of fact. For example, in the case of *Lister v Smith* (1863) 3 Sw & Tr 282, 164 ER 1282, the testator was trying to evict a tenant, who was the mother-in-law of the testator's daughter. As such, the testator wrote a codicil, which removed his daughter from his will. This action was intended solely as a threat to evict the tenant. On the testator's death, the court decided that the codicil was invalid, because the testator had never intended for it to take effect.

key terminology

Codicil: this is a document that amends the original will. For example, the codicil might add or remove a particular beneficiary. The codicil must be formally created in the same way as a will, namely in writing, signed by the testator, and signed by two witnesses. If the amendment is minor, executing a codicil might be easier than having to write an entirely new will.

The testator's intention must be to create a will, taking effect on their death, and revocable until that point; however, there is no requirement of an intention to create an English will. For example, in the case of *Re Berger (Deceased)* [1990] Ch 118, a Jewish man prepared a Jewish will (known as a zavah), which he intended to take effect in a Rabbinical Court. The zavah complied with all of the formality requirements in English law and the testator clearly had testamentary intention. On that basis, the English court granted probate to the zavah (once translated from Hebrew into English).

Other than demonstrating that the purported will was just a joke or for show, as in *Lister v Smith*, there are two main grounds on which a will can be invalidated based on an absence of testamentary intention. They are testamentary undue influence and testamentary fraud. Furthermore, the will itself may be a forgery and not prepared by the testator.

2.5.1 Undue influence

Undue influence is a general equitable doctrine that allows a gift or contract to be set aside where one party has been unlawfully pressured into giving the gift or signing the contract. Students might have encountered this doctrine when studying Contract Law, Land Law or Equity & Trusts. Testamentary undue influence is related, but it works slightly differently.

To prove testamentary undue influence, it has to be shown that the testator was coerced into executing the will (*Re Edwards* [2007] EWHC 1119 (Ch)). The burden of proof lies on the person who alleges the undue influence and there is a high hurdle. There will rarely be direct evidence of the coercion taking place, as such things will take place in private, but it may be proven by surrounding circumstances. So, what are some of the factors that might point towards undue influence? The court will have to look at the testator's emotional or mental condition, and the court will consider the testator's age, their general health, and whether they are relying on another party to manage their daily lives. At the same time, the court will also look at the alleged coercer's emotional or mental condition, considering, for example, whether they have a forceful or manipulative personality.

The coercion has to overpower the testator, so that the will does not reflect the testator's true intentions. This means that a clear distinction has to be drawn between undue influence and, for instance, family members making emotional pleas to get this or that property in the will. The latter is surely quite common, and there is nothing untoward about asking to be included in a will. The same can be said for charity appeals, such as those often shown on TV, which very openly draw on a person's emotions. Undue influence requires something more than that. So, for example, in the case of *Schrader v Schrader* [2013] EWHC 466 (Ch), a will was set aside for undue influence where the son, who was described as having a forceful personality, manipulated his mother, described as frail and vulnerable (she was in her 90s and was reliant on her son after a bad fall in her home), into writing a will with certain terms that benefitted him.

2.5.2 Testamentary fraud

Testamentary fraud, also referred to as fraudulent calumny, is a related claim. It occurs where the testator has been lied to and writes a will based on those lies. The person telling the lies has to do so deliberately, or without caring whether the statement is true or false. There is no fraud if the person genuinely believed the lie to be true. So, for example, in the case of *Wilkinson v Joughin* (1866) LR 2 Eq 319, the testator married a woman who claimed to be a widow, and then included her in his will. It transpired that the woman was not actually a widow (she was still married to her first husband who was very much alive), meaning that her marriage to the testator was void. The gift to her in the testator's will was struck out based on her fraud. In the case of *Re Edwards* [2007] EWHC 1119 (Ch), the testator had two sons, Terry and John. Terry did not like John and made baseless accusations against him. This resulted in the testator, the mother, leaving her whole estate to Terry. After being challenged, the court decided that the will was invalid. However, the judge based his decision on undue influence (namely that Terry had coerced his mother into writing the will), but the facts more closely resemble testamentary fraud.

The case of *Re Edwards* shows that there is an overlap between undue influence and fraud (and that coercion can follow from the lies, or vice versa). In both situations, the will as written does not reflect the testator's true intentions and it must therefore be invalidated. These claims also overlap greatly with the requirement that the testator knew and approved the contents of the will. Clearly, if the will was produced as a result of undue influence or fraud, the testator did not approve of its contents. Someone objecting to the validity of such a will therefore has several avenues available when going to court. The burden of proof is on the person alleging the fraud. The court noted in *Clitheroe v Bond* [2020] EWHC 1185 (Ch) that 'the court can draw inferences from all the circumstances but as with any allegation of fraud the strength of the evidence has to rise in proportion to the seriousness of the allegation'. Strong evidence may therefore be needed to prove that testamentary fraud took place.

2.5.3 Forgery

The will may also turn out to be a forgery, written by someone other than the purported testator. The court would refuse to put the forged will into probate, meaning the deceased either died intestate (without a valid will) or died testate leaving an earlier valid will.

For example, in the case of *Face v Cunningham* [2020] EWHC 3119 (Ch), one sister (Rebeca Face) tried to probate a will she claimed was executed by her father. The validity of the will was doubted by her two siblings. The court found that the will was indeed a forgery and could not, of course, be put into probate. The document had actually been written by Rebeca, who had asked two other people to put their names on the document as purported witnesses. Importantly, the court directed that a copy of the judgment should be forwarded to the Crown Prosecution Service, for a possible fraud prosecution. It is worth noting that, as a result, the father died intestate, and Rebeca and her two siblings took one third each of his estate (see **Chapter 8**). Her entitlement to inherit on intestacy was not affected by the fraud, as they are distinct legal issues. Similarly, in *Re Patel (Deceased)* [2017] EWHC 133 (Ch), the court refused to probate a will it found had been forged by the deceased's son. A crucial issue here was that the homemade will was written in English despite evidence that the deceased did not know or understand English.

Forging a will could also amount to a criminal offence of fraud. Section 1 of the Fraud Act 2006 identifies three specific types of fraud: first, in s 2, fraud by false representation, which is to say, the defendant knowingly makes a misleading or untrue statement about fact or law, with the intention of making a benefit for themselves or causing another to suffer a loss; secondly, in s 3, fraud by failing to disclose information that the defendant is under a duty to disclose, again with the aim of making a benefit for themselves or causing a loss to another; and thirdly, in s 4, fraud by abuse of position, which arises where the defendant is in a position of authority where they are expected to protect the financial interests of another person, and instead dishonestly abuse that position to make a gain for themselves or to cause a loss to another.

In the case of *R v Phillips (Karen)* [2012] EWCA Crim 588, the Court of Appeal imposed a sentence of six months' imprisonment, suspended for two years, on a defendant who had forged her partner's will. The Court of Appeal took into account time already served after the Crown Court had handed down a sentence of eight months' imprisonment. Whilst not formally reported, newspaper articles also give details of various people who have been sentenced in the Crown Court for fraud, having forged a will. For example, in 2015 a woman was sentenced to 21 months' imprisonment by Teesside Crown Court for forging her husband's will, to make herself the sole beneficiary. In 2016, a couple were jailed for six months for forging a will and committing theft from the estate by Nottingham Crown Court. In 2019, a man was sentenced to 12 months' imprisonment for forging his mother-in-law's will. Remember that sentencing for a criminal offence is done by the judge using the sentencing guidelines, taking into account all the relevant circumstances of the case, and a range of aggravating and mitigating factors. That explains the variations in the sentences handed down in these cases.

2.6 Further reading

Law Commission, *Making a Will* (Consultation Paper 231, July 2017), Chs 2 (Testamentary capacity), 7 (Knowledge and approval and undue influence) and 8 (Children making wills).

Rich, Barbara, 'What does "want of knowledge and approval" mean in the 21st century' [2008] Private Client Business 303–10.

Kerridge, Roger, 'Undue Influence and Testamentary Dispositions: A Response' [2010] Conv 129–44.

Kerridge, Roger, 'Wills made in Suspicious Circumstances: The Problem of the Vulnerable Testator' (2000) 59 CLJ 310–34.

Frost, Martyn, *A Victorian tragedy: the extraordinary case of Banks v Goodfellow* (Wildy, Simmonds & Hill Publishing, 2018).

Sloan, Brian, 'Burdens, presumptions and confusion in the law on want of knowledge and approval' [2017] Conv 440–62.

This chapter has begun to look at the legal requirements for writing a valid will. As we have seen, there are quite a few such requirements (and more are discussed in the next chapter):

- A testator has to be an adult before they can write a valid will.
- A testator must have mental capacity, as determined by the test in *Banks v Goodfellow*. The Law Commission has proposed replacing *Banks v Goodfellow* with the Mental Capacity Act 2005 test, since the 2005 Act is more in tune with modern developments in mental health and psychiatry.
- The testator must know and approve of the contents of the will.
- The testator must have testamentary intention, namely intending that the will disposes of his or her property on death and remains revocable until that time.
- Testamentary intention can be set aside on the basis of testamentary undue influence or testamentary fraud or that the will itself was a forgery.

It should be clear from this how seriously the law treats wills. They are very important documents and it is essential that the will truly reflects what the testator wanted. If the will was written under the influence of a mental illness, or if the testator did not know what the will included, or if the testator was coerced or misled into writing the will, the law cannot allow the will to be enforced.

The next chapter will look at the formality requirements for writing a valid will, contained in s 9 of the Wills Act 1837. The formality requirements have been alluded to several times in this chapter, and now it is time to look at them in detail.

Formality Requirements for a Valid Will

In the previous chapter, we began looking at the legal requirements for writing a valid will. It was said that a will is a very important document, and therefore the law insists on these requirements to ensure that the will truly reflects the testator's wishes. The previous chapter looked at the age requirement, the need for testamentary capacity, the requirement that the testator knows and approves the contents of the will, and the requirement that the testator has genuine testamentary intention.

This chapter continues to look at the remaining legal requirements for writing a valid will, namely the formality requirements set out in s 9 of the Wills Act 1837. There are five issues to address:

- *Writing*: the will has to be in writing.
- *Signature*: the will has to be signed by the testator.
- *Intention*: the signature must indicate the testator's intention to create the will.
- *Witnesses*: the testator's signature has to be witnessed and the witnesses must themselves sign the will. The chapter will look at the temporary changes to the witnessing rules introduced during the Covid-19 pandemic.
- *Exceptions*: there are exceptions to the formality requirements, including the doctrine of privileged wills under s 11 of the Wills Act 1837 and the doctrine of *donatio mortis causa*. The chapter will also look at the doctrine of secret trusts, as well as implied trusts and proprietary estoppel.

The chapter examines each of these issues. The Law Commission, in its 2017 Consultation Paper 'Making a Will', also addressed these points and made proposals for reform (Law Commission Consultation Paper 231). These proposals are also discussed. By the end of the chapter, you will understand the formality requirements for a valid will and the key exceptions to those requirements, recognise some of the problems with the current rules and identify the Law Commission's reform proposals.

3.1 Wills Act 1837, s 9

The formality requirements for writing a valid will are set out in s 9 of the Wills Act 1837. They are detailed below, but first it is important to say a few words on why the formality requirements are there. The Law Commission argues that the formality requirements serve four functions (Law Com 231, [5.6]). These functions are complementary to each other:

(1) 'Evidentiary function': complying with the formality requirements (such as having the will signed by the testator) provides evidence that the will is genuine and was made by the testator, rather than someone else. The will also serves as durable proof of what the testator's intentions are; the written document is more reliable than witnesses claiming that the testator promised them certain property. Oral promises might be genuine but they are difficult to prove.

(2) 'Cautionary function': having to follow the formality requirements highlights the importance of the will and hopefully ensures that the testator carefully considers what to put into the will. It reflects the fact that ownership of property, especially valuable property such as a house, is a serious thing, and it should not be too easy to lose it.

(3) 'Channelling function': the formality requirements provide for a well-defined procedure to move, or channel, property from the testator to the intended beneficiaries.

(4) 'Protective function': as discussed in the previous chapter, the testator must intend to create a will, and they must not be influenced by fraud or undue influence. The formality requirements help protect against such abuse.

However, the formality requirements unfortunately also have an inadvertent fifth, prohibitive, function. On the one hand, the formality requirements might be a barrier to people making wills in the first place. On the other hand, there is the unfortunate reality that otherwise genuinely intended wills might be invalidated because they fail to comply with all of the formality requirements. In the end, the four key functions identified by the Law Commission have to be balanced against the risk of the formalities being a barrier – it is not always easy to find the correct balance.

Having identified why the formality requirements are there, it is now time to look at s 9. The version set out here, and discussed in this part of the chapter, was in place from when s 9 was amended by the Administration of Justice Act 1982 until 31 January 2020. Section 9 has been temporarily amended during the Covid-19 pandemic (see **3.1.6** below) to take into account social distancing requirements. The law will revert back to the version set out here after 31 January 2022 (unless the Covid-19 amendment is extended – indeed, the Covid-19 amendment may also be repealed earlier than 31 January 2022 – make sure to check what rule applies).

9   Signing and attestation of wills

No will shall be valid unless—

(a) it is in writing, and signed by the testator, or by some other person in his presence and by his direction; and

(b) it appears that the testator intended by his signature to give effect to the will; and

(c) the signature is made or acknowledged by the testator in the presence of two or more witnesses present at the same time; and

(d) each witness either—

(i) attests and signs the will; or

(ii) acknowledges his signature, in the presence of the testator (but not necessarily in the presence of any other witness),

but no form of attestation shall be necessary.

In simple terms, the will has to be in writing, signed by the testator in front of two witnesses, who then sign the will themselves. This is the mantra for remembering s 9: writing, signed and witnessed. However, in reality, there is a bit more to it than that. Unfortunately, a lot of complications have arisen, not least because many wills are home-made without the benefit of professional advice. This has led to the court having to make countless decisions on whether individual wills satisfy s 9. The chapter now looks at each of these requirements in turn.

3.1.1 The will has to be in writing (s 9(a))

The first requirement is that the will has to be in writing. Unlike some other jurisdictions, English law does not recognise oral (also known as nuncupative) wills. However, as noted later in this chapter (at **3.4.4**), an oral promise of an inheritance may form the grounds of a claim under a constructive trust or proprietary estoppel.

Thus, a valid will must be written down. Because it also has to be signed, the writing requirement is taken to mean that the will must be written down on a piece of paper, or some other surface material. In the case of *Hodson v Barnes* (1926) 43 TLR 71, a sailor had written his will on a large eggshell, which the court decided was acceptable (however, the will failed due to a lack of genuine testamentary intention, and it might be difficult to prove that the testator was serious about making a will if it was written on something as novel as an eggshell).

Today, most wills are written on a computer, before being printed out to be signed. It is also possible to purchase 'will packs', which are pre-written templates where the testator can simply add names and other details (such as a monetary value) in the blank spaces provided. Fully handwritten wills, which are known as holographic wills, are probably less common today, but these would of course have been the norm in the days before typewriters and computers.

There are no requirements as to what instrument is used to write the will. There is only one important rule to note here: if a will is written in both pen and pencil, the law presumes that the notes in pencil were intended only as a draft and therefore do not form part of the will (*In the Goods of Adams* (1872) LR 2 P&D 367). This presumption can be rebutted by some proof that the testator intended the pencil notes to form part of the will. As said, however, today most wills are typed on a computer, so this rule will have limited practical use.

There is also no requirement as to what language the will is written in. As long as an English or Welsh (in Wales) translation can be provided to the court, the will itself can be written in any language. In the case of *Whiting v Turner* (1903) 89 LT 71, a will written in French was accepted into probate. In the case of *Re Berger (Deceased)* [1990] Ch 118, which was discussed in the previous chapter, a will written in Hebrew was accepted into probate. The case of *Kell v Charmer* (1856) 23 Beav 195, 53 ER 76 is another good example. The testator owned a jewellery business. As part of his bookkeeping, he used a range of homemade symbols to indicate different financial values. The testator then used the same symbols in his will. The court accepted the will into probate after the personal representative had demonstrated, with the help of a codebook from the jewellery business, what those symbols meant.

3.1.2 The testator must sign the will (s 9(a))

The second requirement in s 9(a) is that the will is signed. There are two ways of satisfying this requirement. First, and most commonly, the testator can personally sign the will. Secondly, and advisable only if required on medical grounds, the testator can direct someone else to sign the will on their behalf. The law must allow someone else to sign on the testator's behalf in circumstances where the testator cannot sign personally, perhaps because of a physical disability.

3.1.2.1 The testator signs personally

Ideally, the testator will personally sign the will by adding their signature at the end of the document. In order to protect wills which are genuine (in the sense that they actually reflect the testator's intentions), the courts have taken a rather liberal view on what amounts to a signature. The courts have defined a signature as 'the name or some mark which is intended to represent the name' (*Hindmarsh v Charlton* (1861) 8 HL Cas 160, 11 ER 388). Ordinarily, of course, the testator will sign with their full name. However, different signatures have been used and upheld by the courts. For example, in *In the Estate of Cook* [1960] 1 WLR 353, the will was signed *'Your loving mother'*, which the court decided was perfectly acceptable. Another example is the case of *Re Chalcraft* [1948] P 222, where the testator only managed to sign half her name before slipping into unconsciousness and later dying. The court found that the signature was valid.

Prior to 1983, s 9 of the Wills Act 1837 stated that the signature had to be 'at the foot or end' of the will. This rule was strictly adhered to by the court, but it carried the risk of invalidating perfectly genuine wills simply because the signature was not in the correct place. Section 9 was therefore amended by the Administration of Justice Act 1982. Since 1983, the signature can be placed anywhere on the document. A good example can be found in the case of *Wood v Smith* [1993] Ch 90. Here, the testator made a holographic (handwritten) will. The testator began by writing '*My will by Percy Winterbone …*', but there was no other signature on the document. The court found that the will had been validly signed, since the testator had actually written out his name (however, the will itself was found to be invalid due to a lack of testamentary capacity). In the case of *Weatherhill v Pearce* [1995] 1 WLR 592, the testator had handwritten an attestation clause that read, '*Signed by the said testator Doris Weatherhill in the presence of us …*', which was followed by the signature of two witnesses. The court found that the testator had validly signed the will by writing her own name in pen in the attestation clause.

key terminology

Attestation clause: this is a clause inserted at the end of the will, which specifies that the testator and the witnesses have signed the will. An attestation might read along the following lines:

Signed by the said [testator] as his/her last Will in the presence of us both, present at the same time, who at [testator's] request, and in [testator's] presence and the presence of each other, have signed our names as witnesses.

The testator and the witnesses will sign next to the clause.

3.1.2.2 The testator directs another person to sign on their behalf

If the testator cannot personally sign the will, another person can 'guide' the testator's hand so as to create the signature. Alternatively, the testator can direct the other person to sign it on their behalf. In this case, the signer has to sign the will in front of the testator, and the signer should use their own name, rather than the name of the testator (*Re Clark* (1839) 2 Curt 329, 163 ER 428). The will's attestation clause should also indicate that the will has been signed by the signer on the testator's behalf.

There is no rule on who can sign on the testator's behalf. It can be anyone, including someone who is also a beneficiary under the will. In the case of *Barrett v Bem* [2012] EWCA Civ 52, [2012] Ch 573, the Court of Appeal argued that a beneficiary should ideally not be the signer, but it did not go so far as to make this a rule. The court's suggestion is based on the risk of fraud or undue influence. It can be difficult to prove that the testator intended a gift to take effect, or even knew and approved of the contents of the will, if the will contains a gift to the person who also signed it, purportedly on the testator's behalf. The Law Commission echoed this concern, and it has proposed a rule that if a beneficiary under a will is the signer, the will is valid but the gift to the beneficiary is void (Law Com 231, [5.54]). This would have the same effect as the current rule, discussed below, which says that a gift to a witness is void, even though the will as a whole remains valid.

3.1.3 The testator must intend that their signature gives effect to the will (s 9(b))

The requirement in s 9(b) states that when the testator signs the will, the testator must intend to give the will legal effect. As seen in the previous chapter, for any will to be valid, the testator must have genuine testamentary intention. The case of *Lister v Smith* (1863) 3 Sw & Tr 282, 164 ER 1282 was mentioned at **2.5**, where a codicil (amending an existing will) was invalid because it was written in jest. The testator therefore did not intend, through his signature, to give effect to the codicil.

The testator's intention is generally evidenced through an attestation clause, although s 9 does not formally require the inclusion of an attestation clause. They are always included in professionally drafted wills. Next to the attestation clause, the testator and the witnesses all sign their names. Intention, for the purpose of s 9(b), is presumed where the will has a formal attestation clause, so it is wise to include one.

As said, professionally drafted wills always include an attestation clause. However, they may not appear in homemade wills. If the will does not have an attestation clause, the witnesses may be required by the court to sign an affidavit of due execution or provide a witness statement to explain the circumstances in which the will was executed.

key terminology

Affidavit of due execution: a formal legal document (namely, a sworn statement) signed by the witnesses to a will that lacks an attestation clause. In it, the witnesses swear that the will was properly executed in accordance with s 9 of the Wills Act 1837. The affidavit is presented to the probate court.

key legislation

Non-Contentious Probate Rules (NCPR) 1987: this is an important piece of secondary legislation, which outlines the substantive and procedural rules of probate. The NCPR 1987 will be referred to throughout the textbook.

Under r 12(1) of the NCPR 1987, if the will lacks an attestation clause, the court will ask at least one of the witnesses to sign an affidavit or provide a witness statement to explain the circumstances in which the will was executed. The affidavit must be signed before a commissioner for oaths, which usually means a solicitor. Allowing the witness to sign a witness statement, as opposed to a formal affidavit, was introduced in November 2020, as part of the overall work of streamlining the probate process. A witness statement must be signed by the person making it, but it does not have to be signed before a commissioner for oaths, which makes it an easier legal document to prepare, especially by a lay person who may not have easy access to legal advice. In terms of the probate process, how it works, and how it was changed in November 2020, see **Chapter 11**.

If no witness can be found (perhaps because the witnesses predeceased the testator), any other person present when the will was executed can sign an affidavit or provide a witness statement.

However, if there is no one available to give an affidavit or witness statement proving that the will was properly executed (perhaps because everyone present predeceased the testator), r 12(2) allows the court to instead accept an affidavit or witness statement from any person (such as a family member) who can prove that the signature on the will really is that of the testator. If necessary, this can also include a handwriting expert who can provide evidence that the signature is genuine.

A sample affidavit is produced below, based on the sample will included in the next chapter. As seen, it is actually a fairly straightforward document, based on easily accessible templates. A witness statement would contain the same kind of information but would not be signed in the presence of a commissioner for oaths. Most likely it would be prepared by the witness at home and be submitted directly to the probate court.

Note in clause 1 of the affidavit that the witness states that she has marked the will with the letter 'A'. The original will is shown to the witness when they are preparing the affidavit or witness statement (see NCPR 1987, r 10), and as proof of this the witness should make another mark on the will. Ordinarily, this mark is going to be a letter. The original will, with the new mark on it, and the affidavit or witness statement are then sent to the probate court. If need be, the court will provide a facsimile copy of the will, rather than the original.

LINCOLN

DISTRICT PROBATE REGISTRY

IN THE HIGH COURT OF JUSTICE

FAMILY DIVISION

I, Dot Parker of 12 Bristol Road, Gainsborough, DN21 9TL, make oath that:

1. I am one of the two subscribing witnesses to the Will of Dorothy Smith, of 1 Lincoln Avenue, Lincoln LN30 1AB. The other subscribing witness to the Will is Lucina Xi. The Will is dated the 30th of August 2018. The Will has been produced to me and I have marked it with the letter A.

2. The Testator executed the Will on the 30th of August 2018 by signing her name as that name now appears on the Will in the presence of me and Lucina Xi, with both of us present at the same time. After the Testator had signed the Will, we each attested and signed the Will in the presence of the Testator.

Sworn by the above named deponent

Dot Parker (Solicitor)

at 12 Bristol Road, Gainsborough, DN21 9TL

this 2nd day of January 2019

---

before me:

Zack Bagins

Solicitor/Commissioner for oaths

3.1.4 The testator signs or acknowledges their signature in the presence of two or more witnesses, present at the same time (s 9(c))

The requirement in s 9(c) is that the testator's signature is either (a) made in the presence of at least two witnesses, or (b) that a prior signature is acknowledged to the witnesses. Both of the witnesses must jointly see the testator either sign or acknowledge a prior signature. The will is not valid if the testator signed the will in the presence of only one witness and later acknowledged that signature to a second witness; both witnesses must be present together.

Two examples can be given. In the case of *Brown v Skirrow* [1902] P 3, the testator took her will to a local shop and asked the two shopkeepers to be her witnesses. They agreed. However, before the testator could sign the will, one of the shopkeepers became distracted by another customer. Therefore, only one of them actually witnessed the testator signing. Later, when the other customer had left, the testator acknowledged her signature to the other shopkeeper. However, the court found that the will was invalid. This is an example of where s 9 has invalidated an otherwise genuine will, but, as noted above, the formality requirements, including the witnesses, are there for a reason. More recently, in the case of *Re Singh* [2011] EWHC 2907 (Ch), a will was found to be invalid because the two witnesses claimed in court that they had never met before – clearly they had not been present together when the testator had signed the will.

The law only requires that the witnesses see the testator sign a document or acknowledge a prior signature on the document. The witnesses do not need to know that they are in fact witnesses to a will. Nor do they actually have to see the signature itself; it is sufficient that they see the testator sign a document (*Smith v Smith* (1866) LR 1 P&D 143). Normally, of course, they will see the signature when they sign their own names.

It is worth emphasising that s 9(c) states that there have to be 'two or more' witnesses. Normally, in practice, there will only be two witnesses, but nothing stops a testator from using more than two witnesses.

3.1.4.1 Who can be a witness?

In short, anyone can be a witness. There are, however, some legal and practical considerations to take into account.

First, a witness must be able to physically see what is going on, such as the testator signing the will. This has led the court to suggest that a blind person cannot be a witness (*Re Gibson* [1949] P 434) except in what the judge called 'peculiar' circumstances. Today, a blind person might be able to witness a will written and signed in braille.

There is no mental capacity requirement for witnesses, in the way that testators need to have mental capacity. The only requirement imposed by the law is that they can see and are conscious of the will being signed by the testator (*Hudson v Parker* (1844) 1 Rob Ecc 14, 163 ER 948). This suggests that the witness cannot, for instance, be intoxicated with drink or drugs.

There are no formal age requirements for a witness, which means that children can legally witness a will. In the case of *Wilson v Beddard* (1841) 12 Sim 28, 59 ER 1041, one of the witnesses was a 14-year-old child. However, since the witness has to be conscious of what is going on, it seems unlikely that very young children can be valid witnesses. This, however, has not been adjudicated on; at any rate, this would be fact-specific and would depend on the maturity of the particular witness. The Law Commission stated that whilst this rule might seem 'surprising', there was no reason to change it (Law Com 231, [5.27]).

The Wills Act 1837 also includes a few further rules on who can or cannot be a witness. The most important rule is found in s 15. It says that if a beneficiary is a witness, they will lose their interest under the will, although the will itself remains valid. The same applies if a spouse or civil partner of a beneficiary is a witness; the beneficiary will lose their interest but the will itself remains valid. This rule ensures that witnesses do not act in self-interest, for example by swearing that a will was properly executed (so that they can claim their beneficial interest under it) when in reality the will was not properly executed. The Law Commission proposes that s 15 be extended to also include a witness's cohabitant (Law Com 231, [5.59]). This is on the basis that more and more people today cohabit instead of getting married or entering into a civil partnership. Section 15 therefore serves a very important function, but it should not be misunderstood: beneficiaries or their spouses can be witnesses and the will remains valid; the consequence is simply that the gift to them is void.

What if there is a surplus of witnesses? Remember that s 9 says that there has to be at least two witnesses. What if there are three witnesses, but only one of them is also a beneficiary. Here there are two independent witnesses, so does the third one, who is also a beneficiary, have to lose their interest? Prior to 1968, the answer was yes, the superfluous witness would lose their interest (*In the Estate of Bravda* [1968] 1 WLR 479). This was perhaps unfair to that beneficiary, and the law was quickly changed. Since 1968, a superfluous witness is allowed to take their interest, provided that there are two independent witnesses (Wills Act 1968, s 1(1)).

If a gift is void under s 15, the starting point is that it falls into the residue of the estate and passes to the residuary beneficiaries. If s 15 affects the residue (because the will was witnessed by a residuary beneficiary or their spouse/civil partner), the property instead passes on intestacy (see **Chapter 8**).

Two further sections are important to take note of. Section 16 of the Wills Act 1837 allows the testator's creditors to be witnesses, and s 17 allows the named executor to be a witness.

3.1.5 Each witness must attest and sign the will or acknowledge their signature in the presence of the testator, but not necessarily in each other's presence (s 9(d))

The final requirement under s 9 is that the witnesses attest and sign the will. Whilst the testator must sign or acknowledge their signature in the presence of both witnesses together, the witnesses do not thereafter have to sign their names in each other's presence. When the first witness has signed the will, they can leave the room before the second witness signs. However, the testator must be present for each of the witnesses' signatures. This can be contrasted with *Brown v Skirrow* (above), where the testator signed in front of only one shopkeeper and later acknowledged the signature to a second shopkeeper. The witnesses did not jointly see the testator sign the will. Had they done so, it would not have mattered that one of the witnesses later became distracted by a customer. Ultimately, it is good practice for the testator and all of the witnesses to sign the will together.

Section 9 provides that the witnesses both attest and sign. By attest, the law means that the witnesses must have seen the testator sign and be willing to confirm that in court, if required (*Bryan v White* (1850) 2 Rob Ecc 315; *Sherringford v Sherringford* [2005] EWCA Civ 326). No specific form of attestation is required by law; in general, the witness's signature is proof of having attested the will. As discussed further at **11.4.5**, the witnesses may be called to court to give evidence of how the will was executed, if there are any challenges to its validity.

The testator must have testamentary capacity whilst the witnesses sign the will, or at least be aware of what is happening if the rule in *Parker v Felgate* is applied (see **2.2.3**). In the case of *Re Chalcraft* [1948] P 222, mentioned above at **3.1.2.1**, the testator slipped into unconsciousness halfway through signing her name. The court found that her signature was valid. The Court took a liberal approach on capacity, upholding the testamentary document even though the witnesses signed immediately after the testator slipped into unconsciousness. The judge noted that the courts have a 'degree of latitude' when deciding whether the testator had testamentary capacity at the requisite time.

The courts have also taken a fairly liberal approach to what is meant by 'in the presence of' the testator. The witnesses have to sign in the presence of the testator, and it has been found sufficient that the testator is able to see the signature being made. This liberal approach has led to some strange outcomes. In the case of *Casson v Dade* (1781) 1 Bro CC 99, 28 ER 1010, the testator signed the will in front of the two witnesses. Because she was asthmatic, she then had to step outside for some fresh air. Once outside, she sat down in her horse-drawn carriage. Technically, she could see the witnesses signing the will through the carriage window and the office window. On that basis, the court found that the witnesses had signed the will in the testator's presence. A different outcome was found in the case of *Tribe v Tribe* (1849) 1 Rob Ecc 775, 163 ER 1210. The testator was ill and was lying in her bed. She signed her will in front of the two witnesses. Then, to keep her warm, the curtains around the bed were drawn shut. The witnesses signed the will in the room. The court found that the will was invalid, because the testator (hidden behind the drawn bed curtains) could not see the witnesses sign the will. The witnesses were therefore not in her presence.

3.1.6 Specific amendments to s 9 brought in during the Covid-19 pandemic

The Covid-19 pandemic saw the introduction of strict curbs on people meeting up together, especially outside of households or support bubbles. This, of course, caused a problem when the law simultaneously asked a testator to sign their will in the presence of two independent witnesses.

The law made an allowance for this in the Wills Act (Electronic Communications) (Amendment) (Coronavirus) Order 2020 (SI 2020/952). These regulations temporarily amended s 9 to allow for remote witnessing of wills, such as by making use of video-conferencing platforms. Many practical concerns remain on how to go about proving that the will has been validly witnessed in this manner, which are likely to be litigated in future court cases.

The Ministry of Justice (MoJ) provided guidance on how to remotely witness a will. To begin with, ideally, the attestation clause will be drafted in a way that explains that the will is remotely witnessed in accordance with the regulations. A standard attestation clause is found in the sample will in **Chapter 4**, and this standard clause could be amended to say that the witnesses observed the testator's signature via video-conferencing and that the testator later observed their signatures via video-conferencing.

The actual process of executing the will might go as follows. First, the parties should set up a video-conference, where the two witnesses can clearly see the testator sign the will (ie the document has to be in frame; it is not enough to see the testator's face with the will being signed out of frame). The MoJ guidance says that if the witnesses do not know the testator (for example, if they are employees of the law firm that drafted the will for the testator), the testator should hold up an ID document to the camera (such as a passport or driving licence) to prove their identity.

The will must then be taken to each witness in turn for them to sign it. The MoJ guidance suggests that this should be done within 24 hours, but accepts that it can be longer if the will has to be sent in the post. The risk, of course, is that the testator dies before both witnesses have had a chance to sign the will, which means it would not be valid. A video-conference has to be set up again between the witness and the testator. There are therefore two (if the witnesses are together) or three (if the witnesses are apart) separate video-conference meetings that have to be set up for this to work. Each party should hold the will up to the camera so everyone is in agreement that it is the same document on each occasion (rather than a copy or a forgery). Ideally, the witness will show each page of the will, to ensure that no extra pages have been added as part of a fraud or forgery. The testator must be able to see the witness sign the will (again, the document has to be in frame). If possible, the MoJ guidance says that the sessions should be recorded, which would obviously amount to strong evidence of due execution if any doubts are raised before the court after the testator has died.

When the two witnesses in turn have signed the will, it should be returned to the testator or to a law firm for safe-keeping.

The regulations only applied for wills made between 31 January 2020 and 31 January 2022. Thereafter, unless the rule is extended (or, indeed, shortened if the Covid-19 pandemic is brought under control earlier), the law reverts back to s 9 as it has stood since 1982 (as explained above). To avoid potential disputes, any person who did execute a will by remote witnessing may well choose to execute a new will in the usual manner as soon as that is possible. At this point, it is not known how many testators have made use of remote witnessing.

The benefit of this rule is in allowing wills to be executed in a socially distant manner. However, the risks and downsides are several. First, the testator may die during the process (whilst the document is being sent to each witness), which means that the will is not properly executed and thus has no legal effect. Secondly, the witnesses may tamper with the will, as it is in their sole possession, and they may add or remove text (such as inserting a new page). Thirdly, the testator loses confidentiality, as the witnesses are in sole possession of the will and are able to read it (normally, the witnesses might only see the attestation clause at the end of the will, with no ability to read the whole document). Fourthly, there is a risk that the will is lost in the post, which would mean that (a) the process has to start over, and (b) it poses a confidentiality risk if a third party gains access to the document. It remains to be seen how these regulations work in practice and whether there will be any appetite to retain remote witnessing in s 9 after 31 January 2022.

3.2   The presumption of due execution

Where a will has, on its face, been executed in accordance with the formality requirements, the law presumes that it has been validly executed, even if there are minor irregularities. The presumption of due execution is generally traced back to the judgment of Lord Penzance in *Wright v Rogers* (1865-69) LR 1 P&D 678. Lord Penzance observed:

> The Court ought to have in all cases the strongest evidence before it believes that a will, with a perfect attestation clause, and signed by the testator, was not duly executed, otherwise the greatest uncertainty would prevail in the proving of wills.

This makes the probate process a lot easier as the court can put a will into probate where there is an attestation clause with the testator's signature and the signature of two witnesses. If required, the court may ask for a witness statement from one of the witnesses, to explain the circumstances in which the will was executed, which is discussed further in **Chapter 11**.

A couple of examples can be given to explain the application of the presumption. In the case of *In the Estate of Denning* [1958] 1 WLR 462, a will was signed on the front by the testator, with two witness signatures appearing on the back of the page. This is irregular, as one would expect the witnesses' signatures to be next to the testator's signature. However, the court applied the presumption and put the will into probate. More recently, in the case of *Kentfield v Wright* [2010] EWHC 1607 (Ch), there was some uncertainty as to whether the testator had signed in the presence of both witnesses at the same time, or whether one witness had signed later on. As there was no clear evidence either way (a long time had elapsed and, understandably, the witnesses had forgotten exactly what had happened), the presumption was applied, and the will was put into probate.

The court has said that the 'strongest evidence' is required to rebut the presumption (*Channon v Perkins* [2005] EWCA Civ 1808). What evidence is required will depend on the circumstances, such as what kind of irregularity is being complained about. The stronger the appearance of due execution, the stronger the evidence needed to rebut the presumption. In particular, the presumption is stronger where there is a proper attestation clause (*Gardiner v Tabet* [2021] EWHC 563 (Ch)).

One of the reasons for the presumption is, as seen in *Kentfield*, that memories fade over time, and that the oral evidence a witness gives in court as to the execution, which might have happened years if not decades earlier, might inadvertently be incorrect. Therefore, the written evidence of the will itself carries a lot of weight. If the witnesses are not available (such as having pre-deceased the testator), the court will consider evidence of the surrounding circumstances, which can include witness statements from other parties who may have knowledge of the relevant circumstances when the will was made (*Re Relton (Deceased)* [2019] EWHC 4055 (Ch)). However, the application of the presumption and the evidence needed to rebut it will always be fact-specific.

3.3 Reform of s 9 of the Wills Act 1837

Section 9 was enacted nearly 200 years ago and has met with only minor changes, including that the testator's signature can now be placed anywhere on the will, rather than having to be at the end. However, a lot of things have changed in the past 200 years. In particular, new technologies have emerged which do not fit neatly within the current formality rules. The Law Commission has discussed a whole range of changes to the formalities. Some, such as who can sign on the testator's behalf, and excluding a witness's cohabitee from inheriting under the will, have been mentioned above.

There are two major developments worth looking at in more detail. The first is whether English law should adopt a so-called 'dispensing power', where the courts can accept wills even where the will has not complied with all of the formality requirements. The second is, looking to the future, whether wholly electronic wills (including video wills) should be permitted.

3.3.1 Dispensing power

As it stands, a will has to comply with all of the formality requirements set out in s 9. As mentioned at the start of the chapter, the formalities are there for several good reasons: to provide durable proof of the testamentary wishes and to safeguard against abuse. Nonetheless, where the formalities are strictly adhered to, injustices can also arise.

One concern is that a person instructs their solicitor to draft a will, but the person dies before they are able to actually execute the will. This situation arose in *Davey v Bailey* [2021] EWHC 445 (Ch), where an elderly man died of a heart attack before he was able to execute the will that he had asked his lawyer to draft. This meant that various family members, who had been promised certain inheritances, missed out (those family members unsuccessfully made a claim for *donatio mortis causa*, which is explained at **3.4.2** below).

A further concern is that a testator believes that they have executed a will, but the execution is invalid as they have not fully complied with all of the formality requirements in s 9. In *Brown v Skirrow* [1902] P 3, the will was invalid because when the testator signed the will, one of the witnesses (both shopkeepers) was dealing with a customer. Therefore, the will was not signed in the presence of both witnesses. However, there was nothing to suggest that this was not a genuine will and it was very unfortunate that the testator's wishes could not be carried out. In *Tribe v Tribe* (1849) 1 Rob Ecc 775, 163 ER 1210, the testator was shielded by a curtain drawn around her bed for warmth. Again, it can be seen as rather unfair that her testamentary wishes could not be carried out, simply because her nurses wanted to keep her warm. At the same time, these cases also show why the formalities are important. In *Tribe v Tribe*, for example, how is the testator to know that the witnesses (or anyone else, for that matter) did not tamper with the will after the testator had signed it?

The law is faced with a difficult balancing exercise, between trying to save a testator's genuine wishes and enforcing the formalities to prevent fraud and abuse. English law comes down on the side of the formalities, which are strictly applied. However, other countries, such as Australia and New Zealand, have allowed their courts to save purported wills that do not comply with the formalities but which do represent the testator's true testamentary intentions.

For example, under s 14 of the Wills Act 2007 (New Zealand):

14   High Court may declare will valid

(1)   This section applies to a document that—

    (a)   appears to be a will; and

    (b)   does not comply with section 11 [the formality requirements]; and

    (c)   came into existence in or out of New Zealand.

(2)   The High Court may make an order declaring the document valid, if it is satisfied that the document expresses the deceased person's testamentary intentions.

The statutory provisions in New Zealand and Australia look to the testator's intentions. If the court is satisfied that the document, which 'appears to be a will', genuinely reflects the testator's intentions, the court can allow it into probate. A few examples can be given to illustrate the operation of the dispensing power and to explain why such a rule should be introduced into English law.

First, the courts in Australia and New Zealand have used their dispensing powers to probate unexecuted wills, where the would-be testator died before the execution was possible (consider, as an example, *Mitchell v Mitchell* [2010] WASC 174 from Western Australia). This could avoid disappointing family members who might have been promised inheritances and could also relieve them from having to bring alternative claims, such as *donatio mortis causa*, proprietary estoppel, or seeking a constructive trust (these claims are discussed later on in this chapter).

Secondly, the dispensing power can be used to probate documents that do not meet the formality requirements but do set out the testator's testamentary wishes. A few examples can be given. *Re the Estate of Wai Fun Chan* [2015] NSWSC 1107 is a case from New South Wales, Australia. Here, a mother made a video recording before she died. In it, she gave some moral exhortations to her children, but she also gave instructions for how her property was to be distributed once she had died. These instructions were contrary to what was said in her existing will. The court in New South Wales allowed the video recording into probate, as a codicil which amended the existing will.

key terminology

Codicil: a formal document, executed in accordance with the formality requirements in s 9 of the Wills Act 1837, which makes changes to an existing will. For instance, if the will gives £1,000 to John Smith, the codicil can change the monetary value, for instance, to £2,000. This can be easier than writing a new will from scratch.

Re Nichol [2017] QSC 220 is a case from Queensland, Australia. A man composed a text message in which he explained that he wanted his brother David and nephew Jack to get his property. The message ended with the words 'My will', together with a smiley face and a paperclip symbol. The text was addressed to the brother, David, but was never actually sent. The message was written as a suicide note as the testator then took his own life. The court allowed the text message into probate as an informal will, as the judge was satisfied that it did represent the testator's true wishes.

This decision follows on from the earlier Queensland case of *Re Yu* [2013] QSC 322, in which the testator had composed several documents on his iPhone, including one which began with the words 'This is the last Will and Testament ...' of the testator, Karter Yu. He then committed suicide. The court allowed the iPhone document into probate as an informal will, as the judge was satisfied that it did represent the testator's genuine testamentary wishes.

These cases are good illustrations of how a dispensing power would work. Video recordings and electronic documents, such as texts, cannot today satisfy the formality requirements in s 9 of the Wills Act 1837. It also takes into account the risk of would-be testators dying unexpectedly before they can execute their will. The Law Commission in its consultation paper discusses the potential of introducing a dispensing power into English law (Law Com 231, [5.105]). There are obviously concerns when it comes to dispensing with the formality requirements, since they are there for a good reason. At the same time, it seems only fair for the court to have some discretion to allow documents into probate where they genuinely reflect the testator's wishes. Ultimately, it would be for the court to decide, on the available evidence, whether the document did reflect the testator's wishes.

3.3.2 Electronic wills

Because the will has to be signed by the testator and by the witnesses, an English will currently has to be in writing. However, developments in technology raise the question of whether the law should allow a testator to create a fully electronic will. Gradual developments in other jurisdictions have laid some of the groundwork.

An example can be given from the US state of Tennessee. In the case of *Taylor v Holt*, 134 S.W.3d 830 (2003), the testator wrote his will on a computer and, in front of the two witnesses, added a computer generated version of his signature. The document was then printed and the two witnesses signed the will. The Court of Appeals in Tennessee allowed the will into probate, saying that the stylised electronic signature was a 'mark representing the name' and thus complied with Tennessee's equivalent to s 9. There is a very small possibility that this case would have been decided the same way in England, given the case law on s 9 which allows 'marks' representing the name. However, no such case has arisen in England, and it is difficult to predict what the courts would do. Going back to Tennessee, it is not clear what the outcome would have been if both the witnesses had also added electronic signatures and if the document had never been printed out. In English law, it is unlikely that the courts would accept this. However, given the relentless pace of technological developments, these are questions that the law has to figure out, and probably quite soon. Of course, in the short term, introducing a dispensing power into English law would address the issue.

Several US states have legislated to allow for fully digital wills, including Nevada, Arizona, Indiana and Florida. The US Uniform Law Commissioners have also adopted the Electronic Wills Act 2019, which is a template that individual states are free to adopt, either verbatim or with state-specific amendments. It has so far been adopted by Utah and Colorado. These developments show that digital wills are going to feature in the future, as more and more legal acts and services move online.

During the Covid-19 pandemic, English law introduced temporary changes that allowed for remote witnessing of a will via video-conferencing. However, digital wills go one step further, by having the will exist solely as a digital file. Only time will tell whether English law will permit electronic documents into probate as valid wills. It seems likely, almost inevitable, but there are practical concerns that have to be addressed first. That, however, is a technological rather than legal question.

3.4 Exceptions to the formality requirements

Whilst English law today does not have a dispensing power, the law does recognise some limited exceptions to the formality requirements. The two main exceptions are the doctrines of privileged wills and *donatio mortis causa*. This section will also look at the doctrine of secret trusts, as well as implied trusts and proprietary estoppel. The latter topics will only be looked at briefly, and more detailed discussion of these issues can be found in a textbook on Equity & Trusts.

3.4.1 Privileged wills (Wills Act 1837, s 11)

The doctrine of privileged wills derives from ancient Roman law. Like English law today, Roman law imposed a whole range of formality requirements for a will to be valid. The Romans also realised that it would be impractical for soldiers, whilst on military duty at the far reaches of the Empire, to comply with all of those requirements. Roman law therefore allowed any solider who was *in expeditione* (which translates as anyone on a military tour of duty, or expedition) to validly dispose of their property without having a formal will. When English succession law introduced the formality requirements discussed above in the Statute of Frauds 1677, Parliament decided also to adopt the Roman law doctrine of privileged wills. The doctrine was extended to sailors and mariners who were at sea. This doctrine was then re-enacted in s 11 of the Wills Act 1837:

> **11 Soldiers and mariners wills excepted**
>
> Provided always, that any soldier being in actual military service, or any mariner or seaman being at sea, may dispose of his personal estate as he might have done before the making of this Act.

The phrasing of s 11 is not particular helpful; in essence, it refers back to the old law found in the Statute of Frauds 1677. Note that the language in s 11 refers only to 'personal estate'. The rule was later modified in the Wills (Soldiers and Sailors) Act 1918, which extended the doctrine of privileged wills to also encompass real property.

A privileged will can be created in any format, including as an oral statement. If it is in writing, it does not have to be signed or witnessed. A privileged will can also be created by a minor. The testator must still show testamentary intention and have testamentary capacity, in the same way as for an ordinary will.

3.4.1.1 Soldier being in actual military service

A soldier is defined as anyone who is serving in any of the armed forces, including the reserve forces. The Law Commission has suggested extending the privilege to civilians and civilian contractors who work alongside the armed forces in combat areas (Law Com 231, [5.80]).

The phrase 'in actual military service' has been broadly defined by the courts. In the case of *Re Wingham (deceased)* [1949] P 187, it was explained as 'actually serving with the Armed Forces in connection with military operations which are or have been taking place or are believed to be imminent'. This raises a few key points. The privilege does not apply during peacetime, nor does it apply to anyone who is stationed on routine duty in the UK, since they are not serving in connection with a military operation. The privilege starts to apply once the soldier has been given orders to participate in an operation, even though the soldier might still be residing at home or at a UK base. The courts will generally give the soldier the benefit of the doubt.

In the case of *Re Jones* [1981] Fam 7, the privilege was held to apply to a soldier who was stationed in Northern Ireland during the Troubles. Deployment to Northern Ireland in those circumstances was regarded as a military operation. It is not clear whether the privilege would apply to a soldier placed on non-routine guard duty, for example around strategic locations in London, to assist the police during times of increased terror threats. Considering *Re Jones*, it is possible that the privilege would apply.

The privilege did not apply in the case of *In the Estate of Grey* [1922] P 140. A soldier stationed in barracks in London tried to make a privileged will, but the court held that he was not able to do so, since he had no orders to serve in an actual military operation. It was irrelevant that large parts of the Army were on active duty in Germany, as part of post-World War I operations. In contrast, the privilege did apply in the case of *In the Estate of Colman* [1958] 1 WLR 457. Here, a soldier on leave in England made a privileged will. This was upheld by the court, since the soldier was under orders to serve in Germany as part of post-World War II operations. It did not matter that the will was made whilst the soldier was on leave in England; the relevant consideration was that he was under orders to serve in a military operation.

3.4.1.2 Mariner or seaman being at sea

The term mariner has been broadly construed. In short, it applies to anyone serving on a ship. For example, in the case of *In the Goods of Hale* [1915] 2 IR 362, the privilege was applied to a typist onboard a cruise ship. In the case of *In the Estate of Knibbs* [1962] 1 WLR 852, the privilege was applied to a barman on board another cruise ship.

The term 'being at sea' has been interpreted along the same lines as 'in military service'. The privilege applies to anyone who is under orders to sail, even if they are still residing at home awaiting departure (*Re Servoz-Gavin* [2009] EWHC 3168 (Ch), [2011] Ch 162). It does not apply to a sailor who does not have any orders to sail (*Re Rapley (Deceased)* [1983] 1 WLR 1069). The case of *In the Goods of Admiral Austen* (1853) 2 Rob Ecc 611, 163 ER 1431 is informative as to what is meant by 'being at sea'. Admiral Austen made a privileged will and then made several privileged codicils whilst serving abroad. Some of these codicils were made whilst the Admiral was stationed in Hong Kong; he was under orders to be at sea, even though he was residing ashore. Other codicils were made whilst serving on a riverboat on the Rangoon River, in what is today Myanmar (formerly Burma).

The Law Commission notes that the privilege remains justifiable for members of the armed forces (which, of course, includes the Royal Navy) given the particular circumstances of their work. However, the Law Commission doubts whether today there is any justification for extending the privilege to civilian mariners. Ships are safer and communication technologies are much better today than 100 or more years ago. The Law Commission therefore proposes to remove the privilege for civilian mariners and extend it only to members of the armed forces and, as noted, civilian contractors working alongside the armed forces in combat zones (Law Com 231, [5.78]).

3.4.2 *Donatio mortis causa*

Donatio mortis causa (DMC) is another doctrine adopted from the old Roman law. Colloquially, it is probably best known as a deathbed gift. The law accepts that a person, on their deathbed, cannot reasonably be expected to comply with all of the formality requirements. Therefore the law allows for this narrow exception. Since it is involves an *inter vivos* gift, DMC has more to do with gifts than it has to do with wills and succession, but it is important to understand what DMC is and how it works.

DMC sits awkwardly between a gift and a will. Gifts have their own formality requirements, namely that the donor has to have donative intent and the property has to be transferred. Some transfers, such as land, have to be in writing. Wills, of course, have to comply with s 9 of the Wills Act 1837. DMC disapplies these formalities. The Court of Appeal judgment in *King v Dubrey* [2015] EWCA Civ 581, [2016] Ch 221 has greatly clarified how DMC works.

There are three requirements for property to pass through DMC:

(1) The donor must contemplate their impending death.

(2) The donor makes a gift which will only take effect if and when the contemplated death occurs; until then the donor can revoke the gift.

(3) The donor must deliver dominion over the property to the intended recipient.

These three requirements will be looked at in turn.

3.4.2.1 The donor must contemplate their impending death

This requirement states that the donor must be contemplating their impending death and that this death must come from a specified cause. It is not sufficient to philosophically recognise that everyone dies eventually. In the case of *Wiles v Allington* [1931] 2 Ch 104, the donor was terminally ill with cancer and knew that she had no chance of survival. She was therefore contemplating death from a specific cause. The same was the case in *Sen v Headley* [1991] Ch 425. In the case of *Re Craven's Estate (No 1)* [1937] Ch 323, the donor was awaiting an operation and knew that she might die from it. It suggests that the first requirement for DMC is met by anyone who is about to have surgery under general anaesthesia, given that all such surgeries come with a (relative) risk of death. It also means that the impending death does not have to be certain. Mrs Craven, for instance, might have survived her operation (sadly, she did not). A DMC gift fails if the donor survives the foreseen cause, and the recipient must return the gift to the donor.

3.4.2.2 The donor makes a gift which will only take effect if and when the contemplated death occurs; until then the donor can revoke the gift

The gift in question must only take effect when the donor dies. If it is meant to take effect immediately, it can only be a lifetime gift, and must thus comply with all formality requirements for the transfer of ownership. Certain types of property, such as land, shares, cars, and so on, have specific formality requirements, which generally means that various forms and documents have to be completed. The DMC gift cannot therefore have immediate effect; rather, the recipient will only become the owner once the donor has died. This means that the donor can change their mind at any time before they die and revoke the gift.

3.4.2.3 The donor must deliver dominion over the property to the intended recipient

This third requirement is in complete contradiction to the second requirement. Nonetheless, the donor has to hand over dominion of the property to the recipient (which means that the recipient must physically return the property if the donor changes their mind or survives the foreseen death).

In *King v Dubrey*, the court explained that dominion can have three meanings:

(a) physical possession of the property itself;

(b) physical possession of a key or any other item with which to access the property;

(c) physical possession of any documents that signify ownership of the property.

Dominion can therefore mean getting physical possession of an item, such as a book. It can mean getting keys, such as the keys to a car or to a safety deposit box. It can also mean getting possession of documents that prove ownership, such as issued share certificates.

3.4.2.4   What property can be passed through DMC?

In theory, at least, all kinds of property can be passed through DMC. This includes both real and personal property. When it comes to personal property, handing over dominion is relatively straightforward. The key exception would be shares and other intangible property, where the donor would have to hand over ownership certificates.

Real property, in particular a freehold title, is more complex. In the case of *Sen v Headley* [1991] Ch 425, the court said that unregistered land could pass through DMC, provided that the donor had handed over the title deeds. It is not clear whether DMC can apply to registered land, though it is possible (but very unlikely) that handing over the keys to a house would suffice. In the case of *In the Estate of Exler* [2017] EWHC 1189 (Ch), the judge referred to *Sen v Headley* and noted that since that case, 'land is capable of passing' through DMC, making no distinction between registered and unregistered land. However, *Exler* also concerned unregistered land, so no formal decision has been made on registered land.

The Court of Appeal in *King v Dubrey* warned about future expansion of DMC, given the risk of fraud and abuse when the formality requirements (either for gifts or for a will) are not complied with. Therefore, it is unlikely that the courts would expand DMC to include registered land.

key case

King v Dubrey [2015] EWCA Civ 581, [2016] Ch 221

Margaret Fairbrother made a will in 1998, in which she gave most of her property to various charities and the rest as gifts to various friends. James Dubrey and Joan Dubery were the executors. Kenneth King was Margaret's nephew. He had not had a very successful life. In 2007 he went to live with Margaret, who was becoming old and frail. In return for caring for her, he lived at her home and she gave him an allowance.

Several times, Margaret said that Kenneth would get the house when she died. The house was unregistered, and she handed him the title deeds, repeating her wish that he get the house when she died. Shortly before she died, Margaret wrote a document, purporting to be a will, in which she appointed Kenneth her executor and gave him her entire estate. However, the document was not witnessed, and therefore did not comply with s 9. Thus, when she died, her 1998 will was entered into probate. Kenneth brought a DMC claim in order to get ownership of the house.

The Court of Appeal agreed that the third requirement had been met, since Kenneth had been handed the title deeds to the house. However, neither the first nor second requirement had been met. Whilst Margaret had been old and frail, she had not been contemplating her impending death – she did not know of any particular cause from which she would die, other than that it would eventually happen from natural causes. Nor was the gift of the house conditional on her death – the words used, that Kenneth would get the house when she died, suggested a testamentary intent rather than a gift conditional on death. Therefore, Kenneth's DMC claim failed.

3.4.2.5   What are the problems with DMC?

This chapter has demonstrated that the formality requirements are there for a reason. Having a will in writing provides durable proof of the testator's intentions. Complying with the formality requirements protects against fraud, undue influence and other forms of abuse. Further, all dispositions concerning land have to be in writing, as set out in s 53(1) of the Law of Property Act 1925. This is because land is valuable and no one should risk losing it because of a casual conversation. This raises the question as to why the doctrine of DMC is there in the first place.

The Law Commission noted that DMC 'softens the hard edges of formalities law' (Law Com 231, [13.47]). There is some merit in this assertion. It is difficult to anticipate all possible circumstances, and deathbed gifts might be justified in some cases. People on their deathbed might not have access to a legal adviser who can draft a will for them, and they might anyway have other things on their mind. DMC might be appropriate here. However, the risk of abuse is very real. People on their deathbed may not have their full mental and physical fortitude, and they may be physically or emotionally vulnerable. For example, a child looking after their dying parent might threaten to walk away unless they are given the property. How would someone weakened by illness respond to that? Jackson LJ, in *King v Dubrey*, expressed his 'mystification' as to why DMC had been adopted into English law and noted that 'even Roman jurists found the concept of DMC perplexing'. Indeed, Scotland recently abolished DMC altogether from Scottish succession law (see s 25 of the Succession (Scotland) Act 2016).

The future of DMC is therefore debatable. Since the Law Commission proposes to leave the law as it is, it is unlikely that any future legislation will abolish DMC in England. However, following the statements by Jackson LJ in *King v Dubrey*, the courts will likely keep a close eye on DMC and ensure that the doctrine does not expand any further. Cases like *Exler* show that the courts do take a rather dim view of anyone trying to advance a DMC claim without having foolproof evidence. Time will tell.

3.4.3   Secret trusts

When a testator dies, their will is put into probate (see **Chapter 11**). At this point, the will becomes, essentially, a public document. It is open to family and friends to 'inspect' the will. They may want to do so to see if they are beneficiaries and, if so, what they are going to inherit. They may also want to inspect the will to ensure that there are no irregularities, such as non-compliance with the formality requirements, or that the will is not a forgery. If they have any suspicions about the will, this can be raised with the court. For these reasons, it is important that the will is a public document.

However, this might be a problem for the testator, for instance where they want to keep the identity of their beneficiaries hidden from their family and friends. A classic example is a testator wanting to benefit a mistress or any children that have resulted from an extramarital affair. There may be other reasons, such as wanting to benefit members on both sides of a family feud without the other side finding out, as that could cause more upset. A parent might also want to benefit their children unequally, without them finding that out.

That is where secret trusts come in. They provide a means for a testator to leave a gift without disclosing the identity of the beneficiary on the face of the will. The law recognises two types: a fully secret trust and a half-secret trust.

Let us explore both types in turn on the basis that a testator wants to benefit someone called Alicia without the testator's family finding out about it. The testator instead uses their friend Seun as a go-between, as the testator's family know about Seun and will not be surprised that he is named in the will.

3.4.3.1   Fully secret trust

The testator can use a fully secret trust, which does not appear at all on the face of the will. The will might therefore simply read: 'I leave £10,000 to my friend Seun.' To anyone who inspects the will, Seun is the beneficiary of the £10,000. However, separately, the testator has asked Seun to pass on the £10,000 to Alicia. Seun is thus a secret trustee and Alicia is a secret beneficiary, but this will not be known to anyone who reads the will.

The benefit here is that only Seun (and whoever else the testator has told) knows about the existence of the secret trust. If the testator's family and friends inspect the will after the testator's death, they will not learn that Alicia is the ultimate beneficiary.

The obvious drawback is that the testator has to really trust that Seun will carry out his promise of passing the property on to Alicia. Unless Alicia knows that she is a secret beneficiary (if the testator told her about the gift), there is nothing in practice stopping Seun from keeping the £10,000 for himself. He is, after all, named as the beneficiary in the will. If no one else knows about the secret trust, who will stop Seun from keeping the property himself? For this reason, the testator should ideally inform both the secret trustee and the secret beneficiary about the terms of the secret trust.

3.4.3.2 Half-secret trust

Given that risk, the testator may choose to use a half-secret trust instead. The half-secret trust does appear on the face of the will but without disclosing the identity of the beneficiary. The testator may write, for example, 'I leave £10,000 to my friend Seun to hold on trust on the terms that I have disclosed to him.' Separately, the testator must have informed Seun that he is to hold the £10,000 on trust for Alicia.

The benefit here is, again, that only Seun (and whoever else the testator has told) knows about the identity of the beneficiary. The second benefit is that everyone knows that Seun is a trustee. That means that there is no risk of Seun keeping the £10,000 for himself.

The drawback is that it might only be Seun who knows the terms of the trust. He cannot keep the £10,000 for himself, but the risk is that he will still not give it to Alicia, but perhaps benefit someone else closer to him. Another drawback is that the family might become curious about the identity of the secret beneficiary, which can obviously create suspicion and drama, and could put Seun in an awkward position if the family begin insisting that he reveal the beneficiary's identity.

The testator has to consider the benefits and risks associated with either a fully or half-secret trust and make a choice. Ultimately it comes down to placing considerable trust in the secret trustee (which, perhaps more than ever, really brings home why it is called a 'trust').

3.4.3.3 Requirements for a valid secret trust

There are three main requirements that a testator must meet in order to create a valid secret trust (see *Ottaway v Norman* [1972] Ch 698).

The first requirement is intention, namely an intention to create a valid trust. You will find more information on the certainty of intention to create a trust (as well as the certainty of subject matter and certainty of objects requirements) in an Equity & Trusts textbook (generally, see *Knight v Knight* (1840) 3 Beav 148, 49 ER 58).

The second requirement is communication. This means that the testator must communicate the terms of the secret trust to the secret trustee. For a fully secret trust, the communication can happen at any time before the testator dies, regardless of whether it is before or after the will is executed. For a half-secret trust, the communication must be before or contemporaneous with the execution of the will. It cannot happen after the will is executed.

The third requirement is acceptance by the trustee. The acceptance can be either express or implied. In *Moss v Cooper* (1861) 1 J & H 352, 70 ER 782, the court said that silence amounts to implied acceptance. It follows that if the will-beneficiary does not want to be a secret trustee, they must clearly say no to the testator.

A few other rules are worth mentioning. In a fully secret trust, the trustee can also be one of the beneficiaries (*Re Freud* [2014] EWHC 2577 (Ch)). However, in a half-secret trust, the trustee cannot be one of the beneficiaries (*Re Rees* [1950] Ch 204). The law has not clearly justified the distinction between the two. In a fully secret trust, if the trustee dies before the testator, the gift fails outright and passes to the testator's next of kin on a partial intestacy (*Re Maddock* [1902] 2 Ch 220). No judgment seems to have decided what happens if a half-secret trustee dies before the testator, but the same outcome is likely. If the terms of the half-secret trust are known, the court may save the half-secret trust and appoint a replacement trustee, applying the maxim that 'a trust will not fail for want of a trustee'. If the secret beneficiary dies before the testator, the trust should fail (this is the general rule where beneficiaries die before the testator) and the trustee should hold the property on trust for the testator's next of kin. However, in *Re Gardner (No 2)* [1923] 2 Ch 230, the court said that the trustee should hold the property on trust for the beneficiary's estate. This is a deviation from the general rule, and it is generally argued that *Re Gardner (No 2)* was wrongly decided and would not be followed by a court today.

3.4.3.4 Justifications for enforcing the secret trust

The secret trusts go against s 9 of the Wills Act 1837, which says that the terms of the will must be in writing, and the will itself must be formally executed in the presence of witnesses. For secret trusts, the identity of the beneficiary is not written down in the will. Yet, the courts enforce the secret trust. There is no firm justification as to why, but various theories have been presented.

The main theory is known as the fraud theory. The secret trust is enforced because if the will-beneficiary is allowed to keep the property for themselves, after having promised the testator that they would pass the property on to a third party, that would amount to equitable fraud (*McCormick v Grogan* (1869-70) LR 4 HL 82 and *Blackwell v Blackwell* [1929] AC 318). Whether the secret trust is an express trust enforced to prevent fraud or a constructive trust imposed by the court to prevent fraud is subject to debate.

A second theory is the *dehors the will* theory. It says that secret trusts arise outside of the will, meaning there is no issue that they do not comply with the Wills Act (*Re Snowden* [1979] Ch 528). This is because they are communicated to the trustee separately from the will. The main problem with this theory is that the trust is constituted by legal title passing to the trustee through the will when the testator dies, meaning the will is integral to the existence of the trust. Separately, it has been argued that the theory should actually say *dehors the Wills Act* (see the argument in David Wilde, 'Secret trusts: dehors the Wills Act (not the will)' [2020] Conv 163–76). This is because secret trusts pre-date the Wills Act, and since Parliament choose to ignore secret trusts when passing the Wills Act in 1837, it suggests that the Wills Act has nothing to do with secret trusts. They can therefore be enforced by the courts even though they do not comply with s 9.

Unfortunately, it is still not settled whether secret trusts are express trusts enforced to prevent fraud; constructive trusts imposed by the court to prevent fraud; express trusts enforced as they arise outside of the will and therefore do not need to comply with the Wills Act; or express trusts enforced on their own merit since the Wills Act has nothing to do with them. Despite this uncertainty, the courts continue to enforce secret trusts wherever the requirements set out above have been met.

3.4.4 Implied trusts and proprietary estoppel

A claimant can seek to obtain property from the estate of a deceased person by claiming a beneficial interest through an implied trust or proprietary estoppel. This is a major topic in its own right that will be covered in greater detail in an Equity & Trust textbook; what follows is a quick summary to understand how these claims can override the provisions of a will or the outcome of an intestacy.

3.4.4.1 Resulting trusts

A claimant can claim a resulting trust over property if they have financially contributed to its purchase price (*Dyer v Dyer* (1788) 2 Cox Eq Cas 92, 30 ER 42). The contribution can be to a deposit on the property, the full purchase price, or to mortgage repayments if the mortgage was taken out specifically to fund the purchase (*Burns v Burns* [1984] Ch 317). The claimant can obtain a beneficial interest equal to the portion that they contributed (*Winkworth v Edward Baron Development Co Ltd* [1986] 1 WLR 1512). The law presumes that the resulting trust arises in those situations, and the claimant can obtain a formal declaration of a resulting trust from the court. The legal owner can rebut the presumption by proving that the financial contribution was, in fact, a gift.

However, the law generally presumes that any contribution made by a spouse for their spouse to obtain property, or by a parent for their child to obtain property, is a gift. This is known as the presumption of advancement. The spouse or parent can rebut the presumption of advancement by proving that the contribution was not intended as a gift but as a loan or investment. This is very important as many parents assist their children in purchasing a house. The law presumes this to be a gift and the parents cannot ask for their money back, unless they can show that it was clearly intended to be a loan.

Today, the courts recommend claimants to use the common intention constructive trust (CICT) as the basis for their claim as opposed to the resulting trust, as the CICT can take into account a wider range of factors beyond simply the purchase price contributions.

3.4.4.2 Common intention constructive trust

Where two people buy a house together, they jointly own the property. Using the TR1 form (which is the conveyancing form provided by the Land Registry), they can indicate if they want to hold the beneficial interest on a joint tenancy or a tenancy in common. The courts will generally regard a formal declaration of trust in the TR1 form as binding and conclusive.

However, two people can jointly own a property without making a formal declaration of trust. Here, the law presumes that the beneficial interest is held on a joint tenancy. The parties can use the CICT to argue that the beneficial interest is instead held on a tenancy in common (TiC), meaning the parties have separate shares of the beneficial interest. They can also use the CICT to change how the beneficial interest is divided (rather than having two TiC shares of 50% each, the parties may have TiC shares of unequal value). The process for determining if the parties had a common intention to hold the property on a TiC, and how those shares are to be quantified, is set out in *Stack v Dowden* [2007] UKHL 17, [2007] 2 AC 432 and *Jones v Kernott* [2011] UKSC 53, [2012] 2 WLR 1121.

The common intention to hold the property on a TiC can be either express or implied. An implied common intention is more likely in family home disputes, where family members are less likely to make formal agreements. Rather, their intention is implied based on detriment suffered by the claimant. Detriment can be established based on a range of factors, including their financial contributions to the property as well as non-financial matters, including childcare. The common intention as to how to quantify the TiC shares can be express, implied, or imputed by the courts, as a last resort. The court will be looking at the same factors to make a decision on quantification.

Two people may live in the same house even though the house is owned by only one of them. The claimant, as the non-legal owner, can use the CICT to obtain a beneficial interest as an equitable tenant in common. In *Lloyds Bank plc v Rosset* [1991] 1 AC 107, the House of Lords said that the claimant could really only rely on financial contributions, such as to the purchase price, the mortgage, or renovations to the house. This was a rather strict approach. In *Stack v Dowden*, the House of Lords adopted a more flexible approach, allowing the judges to consider non-financial contributions to the family home, such as providing childcare. However, *Stack v Dowden* and *Jones v Kernott* were both cases concerning joint legal owners. There has been considerable debate thereafter whether the more flexible approach also applies to single owner claims, where the claimant has no legal or beneficial interest at all. The matter is still unresolved.

As noted, the CICT will be explained in more detail in an Equity & Trusts textbook. However, the key point here is that a claimant can claim a beneficial interest in property through the CICT. Many cases have arisen where a relationship has come to an end; however, the claim can also arise where one party has died, and the survivor claims an interest in the property through a CICT, regardless of the terms of any will or what would happen on an intestacy. The CICT is not limited to cohabiting parties in a relationship. It applies wherever someone has helped the legal owner of property in a way that gives rise to a common intention that the claimant is to have a beneficial interest, including between parents and children as well as between business partners.

3.4.4.3 Proprietary estoppel

A claimant can seek a remedy under the claim of proprietary estoppel. The three requirements for the claim were laid down by the House of Lords in *Thorner v Major* [2009] UKHL 18, [2009] 1 WLR 776. The first is that the legal owner makes a promise or assurance to the claimant that the claimant is to obtain the property, or some interest in the property. The second requirement is that the claimant relies on this promise in a reasonable manner. The third requirement is that the claimant suffers a detriment due to this reliance. If the claim is successful, the court will award a remedy, which will be the least necessary to provide justice on the facts. That can include awarding a beneficial interest in the property under a constructive trust, but it can also provide equitable compensation.

In *Thorner v Major*, and in many similar cases thereafter, the claimant had worked free of charge on a family farm, on the expectation of inheriting the farm when the current owner died. In *Thorner v Major*, the legal owner died intestate, necessitating the claimant's claim to obtain the farm through proprietary estoppel.

The claim has also been used to try to obtain a family home. In *Jennings v Rice* [2002] EWCA Civ 159, [2003] 1 P & CR 8, the claimant had done odd jobs in the house belonging to Mrs Royle over a number of years, which included acting as her carer. He had worked free of charge on the promise that he would inherit the house when Mrs Royle died. However, she died intestate, meaning that the house passed to her next of kin. Mr Jennings claimed proprietary estoppel and was successful. However, the court awarded him equitable compensation of £200,000, as opposed to the house itself.

What these claims show (whether the resulting trust, the common intention constructive trust, or proprietary estoppel) is that the next of kin (on intestacy) or the will-beneficiary may not actually obtain the property that they think they are entitled to, as someone else may successfully claim the property through an implied trust. These equitable remedies are quite flexible and fact-specific, so each case is different. Equally, if someone has suffered detriment in relation to a specific property that they were expecting to obtain, they can make a claim to court if they realise that someone else is legally entitled to the property as a next of kin or as a will-beneficiary. It is important that testators understand that they cannot deny someone property simply by leaving it in a will to someone else, if that person has been promised the property and they have suffered detriment in reliance on that promise. The CICT and proprietary estoppel are powerful remedies in those situations.

3.5 Further reading

Law Commission, *Making a Will* (Consultation Paper 231, July 2017), Chs 5 (Formalities), 6 (Electronic Wills), 13 (*Donationes Mortis Causa*).

Borkowski, Andrew, 'Reforming Section 9 of the Wills Act' [2000] Conv 31–42.

Critchley, Patricia, 'Privileged Wills and Testamentary Formalities: A Time to Die?' (1999) CLJ 49–58.

Hedlund, Richard, 'Introducing a Dispensing Power in English Succession Law' (2019) 25(7) Trusts & Trustees 722–29.

Hedlund, Richard, 'Digital Wills as the Future of Anglo-American Succession Law' [2020] Conv 230–45.

summary

This chapter has considered the formality requirements for writing a valid will. The will has to be in writing, signed by the testator or by someone else on the testator's behalf, and that signature has to be witnessed by at least two witnesses who then sign the will themselves.

The chapter then considered potential future reforms, including the introduction of a dispensing power to save documents which do not meet all of the formality requirements, and future developments towards electronic wills.

Lastly, the chapter considered two key exceptions to the formality requirements: the doctrine of privileged wills and the doctrine of *donatio mortis causa*. These are both doctrines adopted from Roman law that English law has developed over the past centuries. They are narrow exceptions to the formality requirements. The chapter also considered the doctrine of secret trusts and the relevance of various types of implied trusts, and how that can impact on testators.

Example of a Will

Studying the rules around wills is difficult without actually looking at a will. Therefore, this chapter contains a sample will, which is considered in detail. This allows a better understanding of the formality rules discussed in the previous chapter and also sets the scene for the following chapters.

The sample will is representative only. It shows one way in which a will can be drafted, but it is certainly not the only way. The will includes a range of common clauses, but that does not mean that all wills need to include these clauses. Additionally, the will includes a few less common clauses, which are there for educational purposes. The way a will is set out and the clauses it contains depend entirely on the nature of the estate and what the testator is seeking to achieve. Having set out the sample will, the chapter then offers an explanation of each of the clauses.

In outline, the chapter addresses three key issues:

- It demonstrates what a typical will looks like.
- It sets out common will clauses.
- It explains the purpose of these clauses.

4.1 Example will

Last Will and Testament

I, Dorothy Smith, of 1 Lincoln Avenue, Lincoln LN30 1AB,

Widow, Being of Sound Mind, **HEREBY REVOKE** all former Wills and testamentary dispositions made by me **AND DECLARE** this to be my last Will and Testament _____

1. I WISH for my organs to be donated for medical purposes, and for my body to be cremated and my ashes scattered in The Wash; _____

2. I DECLARE that I have for a long time been very disappointed in my son, for reasons which he knows, and I knowingly and deliberately exclude my said son from this Will; _____

---

3. I APPOINT my niece Zara Jones, of 20 London Road, Bristol, BS42 1DW, and Dot Parker, Solicitor, of 12 Bristol Road, Gainsborough, DN21 9TL, or failing her the partners at the date of my death in the firm of Parker and Parker, of the same address, or the firm which at that date has succeeded to and carried on its practice (and in so doing I express the wish that only one of such legally qualified partners shall act as executor and act on its trusts) (hereinafter called 'my Trustees') to be Executors and Trustees of this my Will; _____

4. I GIVE to my said niece Zara Jones £20,000 absolutely; _____

5. I GIVE to my said niece Zara Jones my freehold property, known as 1 Lincoln Avenue, Lincoln LN30 1AB, absolutely; _____

6. I MAKE the following gifts absolutely:_____

> (i)To John Anderson: my Grandfather Clock, Mantel Clock, Oak Corner Cupboards, Oak Bookcase, Oak Record Cabinet, Small Oak Round Folding Table and Jacobean Style Carved Oak Desk; _____

> (ii)To Sarah Pike: All Brass and Copper Artefacts in my home; _____

> (iii)To Geoffrey Jones: my Antique Banjo Barometer; _____

7. I GIVE DEVISE AND BEQUEATH the whole of my estate of whatsoever kind and wheresoever situate both real and personal **UNTO** my Executors and Trustees **UPON TRUST** to sell call in collect and convert the same into money with power in their absolute discretion to postpone the sale calling in collection and conversion of such part or parts thereof as they shall think fit without being responsible for loss and **TO HOLD** the net proceeds of such sale calling in collection and conversion and my ready money and such part or parts of my estate as shall for the time being remain unsold and unconverted **UPON TRUST** as follows: _____

> (i)To pay thereout my just debts funeral and testamentary expenses; _

> (ii)As to the residue thereof for my beloved children (which, for the avoidance of doubt, includes my stepdaughter Lisa Smith, of 12 Shadow Lane, Market Rasen, LN8 2AB) and my said niece Zara, as shall survive me, and if more than one in equal shares absolutely; __

8. ANY Trustee being a solicitor or other person engaged in any profession may act and shall be entitled to charge and be paid all professional or other charges for any business or act done by him or his firm in connection with the trusts hereof including acts which a Trustee could have done personally. _____

IN WITNESS whereof I have hereunto set my hand to this my Will this

30th   day of   August   Two thousand and eighteen

SIGNED by the said	*Dorothy Smith*
as and for her last Will in the presence of us both being present at the same time who at her request in her presence and in the presence of each other have hereunto subscribed our names as witnesses:-	*Dot Parker* (solicitor) *Lucina Xi* (trainee solicitor)

4.2 Discussion of the will clauses

This is the will of Dorothy Smith. The attestation clause at the end tells us that the will was executed on 30 August 2018. It was done so in the presence of two witnesses: a solicitor and a trainee solicitor at the law firm of Parker and Parker.

4.2.1 Preamble

The preamble to the will is very important and serves a number of functions. First, it identifies Dorothy Smith as the testator. Secondly, it begins to address the issue of testamentary capacity. Of course, the phrase 'being of sound mind' is not, in and of itself, proof of Dorothy's testamentary capacity, but it might be a prompt for Dorothy and the will-drafter to review Dorothy's mental state before the will is executed.

Thirdly, the preamble also revokes all of Dorothy's previous wills. The need to have a revocation clause will be discussed further in **Chapter 6**, but, in brief, it is not sufficient simply to write a new will or even to declare that this will is your final one. Any previous will would remain valid, as stated in s 19 of the Wills Act 1837. The revocation clause is therefore vital to ensure that this will, and nothing else, determines how your property is going to be disposed of after your death. Even if the will is the first one you ever write, a revocation clause is recommended, so that there is no doubt or confusion after you have died.

4.2.2 Clause 1

In clause 1, Dorothy gives directions as to what she wants to happen to her body once she has died. She wants her organs to be used for medical purposes (which is rather vague) and for her body to be cremated and her ashes scattered across the Wash (an area of land and sea between Norfolk and Lincolnshire).

At first glance, this might seem like a reasonable request to include in a will. However, the law actually says that such instructions are not legally binding (*Williams v Williams* (1882) 20 Ch D 659 – see **13.5.1**). The personal representative (PR) has a duty to lawfully dispose of the body, but this may well happen before the will is located and read. The PR can certainly take the testator's instructions into account, that is only polite, but the PR is not bound to follow them. Therefore, whilst clause 1 may appear in a professionally drafted will, instructions as to the funeral and potential organ donations should be made elsewhere. This includes registering as an organ donor with the NHS and telling family and friends about your funeral wishes. Again, even if you tell your family about your funeral wishes, neither they nor the PR hold any legal obligation to carry out your wishes.

4.2.3 Clause 2

In this clause, Dorothy explains that she has excluded her son from inheriting anything from her estate. To some, this might be a surprising thing for a parent to do. Indeed, in an ideal world, perhaps, everyone would get along with everyone. In reality, however, family disputes can escalate beyond the point of no return. In English law, a testator is entitled to disinherit their family. There is no legal obligation to leave anything at all to your spouse, partner or children. This is in stark contrast to many civil law countries, such as Spain, where (subject to a few rules on disinheritance), as a matter of course, part of a parent's estate has to go to the children.

In English law, a disinherited family member does have a right to petition the court to receive some money from the estate. In short, they will have to establish that they have a genuine financial need for it. However, there is no automatic right to an award. The court will determine whether the petitioner will get a financial award out of the estate by using a list of factors, which are set out in the Inheritance (Provision for Family and Dependants) Act 1975. This process is discussed in detail in **Chapter 15**.

4.2.4 Clause 3

The purpose of clause 3 is to appoint executors. An executor is one type of PR, who is responsible for administering the testator's estate. The appointment of PRs is discussed further in **Chapter 9**, and the various duties and responsibilities of PRs are discussed in **Chapters 10 to 14**.

This appointment clause makes two appointments. The first is a lay appointment, namely the niece Zara. The second is a professional appointment, namely the solicitor Dot Parker. The appointment clause also states that if Dot Parker cannot undertake the duties of executor, perhaps because she has predeceased the testator or simply retired from practice, then another partner from the firm can be appointed as the executor instead. The substitution provision clarifies that it applies to the firm even if it has been renamed, has moved or has been amalgamated or taken over by another firm. If the firm has simply closed down, there will be no appointment. Ideally, in real life, should that occur then Dorothy Smith would be recommended either to write a new will with a new appointment clause or to execute a codicil with a new appointment (codicils are discussed in **Chapter 6**).

It is very important to include an appropriate substitution provision in an appointment clause, so that it is always clear who the executor will be. If it is not clear, it may be necessary to take the will to court, but this may be costly and cause unnecessary delay. The appointment process is discussed further in **Chapters 9** and **11**.

4.2.5 Clause 4

The first actual gift in the will is contained in clause 4. Here, Dorothy gives £20,000 to her niece Zara. This gift can be categorised under three headings. First, because it is personal property, the gift is properly called a legacy (though today the term gift is commonly used). Secondly, it is a general gift, that is to say a gift of financial value, rather than a gift of something specific. Thirdly, it is a pecuniary gift, since it is a gift of money. Clause 4 is therefore a general pecuniary legacy. The different types of gifts and how they are distributed to beneficiaries are discussed in **Chapter 14**. In this case, Zara is entitled to £20,000 in cash from the estate.

4.2.6 Clause 5

Clause 5 is a gift of freehold property. This gift can be categorised under two headings. First, because it is real property, it is properly called a devise (though, again, today the term gift is also commonly used for real property). Secondly, it is a specific gift, since it refers to a particular asset (the freehold title at 1 Lincoln Avenue). Clause 5 is therefore a specific devise.

4.2.7 Clause 6

Clause 6 contains a series of specific legacies, namely a variety of household artefacts. Subject to the need to pay off debts (see **Chapter 13**) and ademption (see **Chapter 6**), the named beneficiaries will receive those specific items.

4.2.8 Clause 7

Clause 7 is the residue clause. The residue refers to everything that is left once any general and specific gifts have been accounted for. The executors are to collect in all other assets, which will now be held on trust (here the executors become testamentary trustees). As trustees, they are given the right to sell all of the residuary property to raise cash (this is commonly done). The clause then specifies how the residue (generally, the cash) is to be distributed.

First, and illustrating the most common way of drafting a residue clause, the residue will be used to pay off all debts. This includes funeral expenses, the cost of administration and any personal debts of the testator (such as credit card debts). The payment of debts is covered in detail in **Chapter 13**.

Secondly, the remainder of the residue will be distributed in equal shares to Dorothy's children and Zara. The law has a broad definition of the term 'child' or 'issue' but, generally, stepchildren are not included in that definition. This is discussed further in **Chapter 5**. Whether or not a stepchild is included in the definition is a matter of interpretation (see *Reading v Reading* [2015] EWHC 946 (Ch)). To avoid any uncertainty or confusion, Dorothy therefore does the right thing to specifically mention that her stepdaughter Lisa is to be included as a beneficiary. As discussed elsewhere, this is one of many examples where the law might now be out of step with social reality and therefore in need of reform.

The residue clause raises an important point of interpretation, namely that the will has to be read as a whole. Clause 7 has to be read together with clause 2, which states that Dorothy has excluded her son from the will. The beneficiaries in clause 7 therefore include all of Dorothy's children, including her stepdaughter, but not her son. To be on the safe side, and to avoid any potential litigation, this should ideally be made clear in clause 7 itself. For example, rather than saying 'my children', Dorothy could have listed the children she wanted to benefit.

4.2.9 Clause 8

Clause 8 is a traditional charging clause. It allows professional executors, such as a solicitor, to charge for their work and to compensate themselves out of the estate. Charging clauses were always included in professionally drafted wills where a professional executor was appointed. However, ss 28 and 35 of the Trustee Act 2000 now provide an automatic right for a professional PR to charge for their work. The will can, on the other hand, exclude their right to charge, though this may cause the professional PR to refuse to act. Therefore, today, charging clauses are strictly speaking not necessary, although there is no harm if one is included.

4.2.10 Attestation clause

The will ends with the attestation clause. Here, complying with s 9 of the Wills Act 1837, Dorothy signs the will in the presence of at least two witnesses, who then themselves sign. Though a date is not formally required under s 9, it is always included in a professionally drafted will. If the will was witnessed remotely, using the Covid-19 amendment to s 9, the attestation clause should be reworded to reflect that that process has been used. The formality requirements behind the attestation clause were discussed in **Chapter 3**.

4.3 Further reading

Seaman, Jennifer, 'Commonplace mistakes in drafting wills and trusts and what can be done to resolve them' (2015) 21 T&T 438–48.

summary

This chapter has looked at a sample will. It included a variety of clauses, some of which are more common than others. The clauses were then discussed one by one. The purpose of that discussion was to flag up key issues in succession law, such as PRs, types of gifts, interpretation of wills, and the idea of testamentary freedom. All of these issues, and many more, will be discussed in more detail in the other chapters in this textbook. As you read through the textbook, you may wish to refer back to this chapter.

chapter 5

Rectification and Construction of a Will

Where a testator has written a will, the hope is that the will clearly and unambiguously explains what the testator wants to happen to their property. However, sometimes that does not happen. The will might not state what the testator intended, or the words used might be ambiguous and difficult to understand. In these situations, the personal representative (PR) can go to court to ask for assistance, either to change the wording of the will or to construct (that is to say, interpret) the words used.

This chapter addresses the following issues:

- *Rectification:* the courts are allowed to make changes to the wording of a will under s 20 of the Administration of Justice Act (AJA) 1982 if the will does not reflect the testator's intentions.
- *Construction (1):* the common law provides the key rules for how a will is to be constructed (interpreted), and case law has, over time, defined key words and phrases commonly used in wills.
- *Construction (2):* furthermore, the courts are allowed to construct (interpret and define) any ambiguous words used in the will under s 21 of the AJA 1982.

There has been a lively debate, involving both judges and academics, as to whether rectification (changing the wording of a will) should come before or after construction (interpreting the words used). The conventional approach is that rectification comes first, to ensure that the will reads the way the testator intended. Only thereafter can the words used be interpreted (Law Reform Committee, Nineteenth Report, *Interpretation of Wills*, Cmnd 5301 (1973)). However, recent cases have started with construction before considering rectification (see, for example, *Reading v Reading* [2015] EWHC 946 (Ch)). Unfortunately, the Supreme Court in *Marley v Rawlings* [2014] UKSC 2, [2015] AC 129 did not fully resolve the issue.

The Law Commission, in its recent consultation, notes that the two doctrines 'overlap', since, before a will can be rectified, the court has first to determine what the testator intended, which means interpreting the will (Law Commission Consultation Paper 231, [9.24]). It is likely that it makes no major practical difference whether rectification or construction comes first, provided that, in the end, the court is satisfied that the will does express the testator's intention.

5.1 Rectification

Regardless of whether rectification or construction should come first, this chapter will follow the conventional approach and start by discussing rectification. The power to rectify wills was introduced by s 20 of the AJA 1982. It allows the court to materially alter a will, by adding, removing or amending particular words or phrases, to ensure that the will reads as the testator truly intended:

20   Rectification

(1)   If a court is satisfied that a will is so expressed that it fails to carry out the testator's intentions, in consequence—

(a)   of a clerical error; or

(b)   of a failure to understand his instructions,

it may order that the will shall be rectified so as to carry out his intentions.

(2)   An application for an order under this section shall not, except with the permission of the court, be made after the end of the period of six months from the date on which representation with respect to the estate of the deceased is first taken out.

(3)   The provisions of this section shall not render the personal representatives of a deceased person liable for having distributed any part of the estate of the deceased, after the end of the period of six months from the date on which representation with respect to the estate of the deceased is first taken out …

…

Section 20 has three important subsections. Subsection (1) is the operative part. It explains that there are two grounds on which a will can be rectified. Rectification can take place if the will does not reflect the testator's intention, either because of a clerical error or because the drafter failed to understand the testator's instructions. These two points will be expanded upon below. Subsection (2) says that an application for rectification must be made within six months after probate is granted. This is to ensure that the PRs are able to complete the administration of the estate and begin distributing the property, without fearing that disappointed beneficiaries might later on bring opportunistic claims. However, the court is given discretion whether to allow a claim that is submitted late. Sometimes this is necessary as the administration process can run for several years. Subsection (3) provides protection to the PRs. If they have distributed the estate after the six-month period, they are not liable to compensate a disappointed beneficiary if the court permits an out-of-time rectification later on.

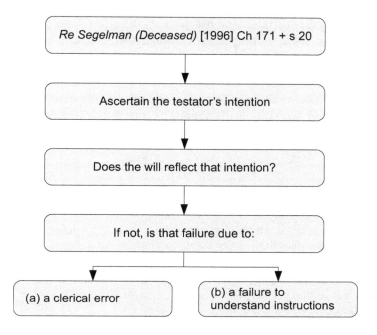

When a rectification claim is made, the court in *Re Segelman (Deceased)* [1996] Ch 171 explained that three questions have to be asked. The first is to ascertain what the testator's true intentions actually were. The second is to determine whether the will reflects those intentions. If not, the third question is to ask whether the will fails to reflect those intentions because of either a clerical error or a failure to understand instructions. It follows that a will might not reflect the testator's intentions, but that this failure was not caused by a clerical error or by the drafter misunderstanding instructions. This could include situations where the solicitor drafting a will simply did not understand what various legal terms meant. Here, the PRs or disappointed beneficiaries could instead bring a professional negligence claim against the solicitor (see **Chapter 16**). The court, however, would not be allowed to rectify the will in such circumstances.

5.1.1 Clerical error

When looking at the judgments, it seems that most rectification claims proceed on the basis that there has been a clerical error. This is true even in cases that, on the facts, seem to be more about a failure to understand instructions. This might suggest that a failure to understand instructions actually counts as a clerical error. However, since s 20(1) clearly separates the two, it is important to understand what is really meant by a clerical error.

The first issue to be determined is who can commit a clerical error. Obviously, the solicitor taking instructions and drafting the will can commit a clerical error. So can anyone employed at the relevant firm, for example a clerk, typist or administrator who has dealings with the document. The courts have also said that a testator, preparing a homemade will, can also commit a clerical error, by accidentally adding or removing words (*Re Williams (Deceased)* [1985] 1 WLR 905).

The second issue concerns what is actually meant by a clerical error. The key case on this point is the Supreme Court decision in *Marley v Rawlings* [2014] UKSC 2, [2015] AC 129, which adopted a wide definition.

key case

Marley v Rawlings [2014] UKSC 2, [2015] AC 129

This case concerned a husband and a wife, who wanted to execute new wills. They decided to draw up so-called mirror wills, which are identical to each other in every respect. In these wills, each spouse gave the survivor their entire estate, and when the survivor died, the combined estates would go to their adopted son.

The husband and wife went to see a solicitor, who drafted the wills for them. There was nothing wrong with the drafting. However, when it came to execute the wills, a mistake was made. The husband signed his wife's will and the wife signed the husband's will. When the wife died, her estate passed to the husband, and no one noticed the error with her will (that it was actually the will intended for her husband). However, when the husband died in 2006, the error was noticed. Mr and Mrs Rawlings' sons challenged the validity of their father's will, recognising that it was actually the will intended for their mother. If it was not valid, they would inherit their father's estate through intestacy. If the will was valid, the adopted son, as intended, would inherit the whole estate.

The adopted son claimed rectification, arguing that Mr and Mrs Rawlings had accidentally signed each other's will due to a clerical error. The rectification asked for was, in effect, to move the husband's signature over to the will intended for him. This naturally raised the question of what was meant by a clerical error. Lord Neuberger, giving the leading judgment, identified that the term 'clerical error' could be given a narrow or wide interpretation. A narrow interpretation would limit the term to drafting errors, where words or phrases were accidentally added or removed from the document. This would clearly not help in this case, since there was nothing wrong with the drafting of the will. A wide interpretation would include drafting errors and extend to other administrative tasks such as preparing the document, filing it, sending it out, or any issue with its execution. In the end, the Supreme Court adopted the wider interpretation of clerical error and allowed Mr Rawlings' will to be rectified. It allowed the adopted son to inherit, as intended.

Dealing specifically with drafting errors, the courts have said that a clerical error is made where the drafter of the will understood the 'significance or effect' of the term added or removed but failed to 'apply [their] mind' to it (*Re Segelman (Deceased)* [1996] Ch 171). If the drafter had applied their mind to the significance or effect of the term, the error would not have been made. This can also be applied to the wider definition of a clerical error, which moves beyond just looking at drafting mistakes. So, in *Marley v Rawlings*, the solicitor clearly understood the significance and effect of the execution. The accidental execution of each other's wills was just that – an accident, a mistake. Whilst unfortunate, as the Supreme

Court sensibly decided, it was not fatal to the wills. As noted above, this has to be distinguished from situations where the drafter did not understand the significance or effect of a term. If the drafter did not know what they were doing, the will cannot be rectified under s 20, but the drafter may be held liable to compensate a disappointed beneficiary on the basis of professional negligence.

The case of *Clarke v Brothwood* [2006] EWHC 2939 (Ch) is illustrative of a drafting error. In her will, the testator left her residue as follows: 1/10 each to two charities and 1/20 each to four godchildren. This amounts to 40% of the residue (since 1/10 equals 10% and 1/20 equals 5%), meaning that 60% of the residue was undisposed of and would pass on intestacy. The executor sought a rectification, arguing that the testator's intention was to give 10% of the residue to each charity and 20% to each godchild, so that the whole residue was disposed of by the will. The court said that if the solicitor drafting the will (who, somewhat embarrassingly, was also the executor) had actually applied his mind to the significance or effect of writing 1/20, he would have pointed this out to the testator before the will was executed. As it stood, the will was drafted based on incorrect note-taking and the solicitor had failed to appreciate the effect of the residue clause. The clause was therefore rectified as suggested. This could possibly have been pleaded as a failure to understand the instructions, but it seems more likely that the solicitor accidentally wrote 1/20 in his notes (and replicated that in the will) given that the testator had said only that the charities should get 1/10.

5.1.2 Failure to understand instructions

The other ground on which a will can be rectified is if the drafter fails to understand the client's instructions. As seen in *Clarke v Brothwood*, this requires an actual misunderstanding of the instructions rather than, as in that case, careless note-taking and a failure to properly proofread the will before it was executed. In *Re Dhalei* the judge noted that it would be beneficial for will-drafters to explain the terms of a will to the testator and have the testator paraphrase it back, to ensure that the testator understands the effect of the clause; this would be particularly helpful where English is not the testator's first language (*Re Dhalei (Deceased)* [2019] EWHC 2763 (Ch)).

The case of *Goodman v Goodman* [2006] EWHC 1757 (Ch) is illustrative of a failure to understand instructions. It involved a husband and a wife, Guy and Jennifer. The husband had a father, Geoffrey. They entered into a property arrangement. For various reasons, Jennifer bought Geoffrey's house. The purchase price was paid in instalments of £3,000 per month. They signed a tenancy agreement, under which Geoffrey paid £1,000 per month rent. He therefore received £2,000 net each month. This was to continue for the rest of Geoffrey's life (meaning that if he lived for a long time, the £3,000 per month he received would eventually surpass the actual purchase price, but if he died sooner, Jennifer would pay less than the actual purchase price). Guy and Jennifer wanted to execute new wills, which would ensure that the property arrangement with Geoffrey remained, even if they both died before him (in that case, the house would be managed by trustees, who would keep paying the £3,000 per month out of the estate). However, the will-drafter misunderstood the arrangement. He thought that they wanted Geoffrey to receive a separate legacy of £2,000 per month. Thus, he inserted a clause (cl 3), which said that Geoffrey was entitled to £2,000 per month for as long as he lived in that house. When Guy died, the result of cl 3 was that Geoffrey kept receiving £3,000 per month from Jennifer (as per the original agreement) and now was to receive an additional £2,000 per month from Guy's estate. This was clearly not the intention. The solicitor had misunderstood the instructions given when Guy and Jennifer had explained their property arrangement. The court therefore rectified Guy's will, by removing cl 3.

5.1.3 Construction instead of rectification

Some cases have been resolved by construction (see below) rather than rectification. The judgment in *Guthrie v Morel* [2015] EWHC 3172 (Ch) is illustrative of this. Here, someone (whose identity was never established) had typed a will on behalf of the testator. The will was validly executed. It gifted a property at 87 Loma Del Rey, Alcadesa, Spain, to a beneficiary. The problem was that the testator did not own No 87. He owned No 81. This was clearly a drafting error, a clerical mistake. That could not be disputed. Nonetheless, the court resolved it through construction. The judge interpreted 87 as meaning 81. This was probably done because the claim was made well after the six-month deadline for a rectification claim, and it would have required a longer court hearing to apply for permission to extend the deadline, before having a hearing on rectification. It was easier to solve the problem though construction. This is problematic as it widens the court's scope for interpretation, but equally it was a quick and pragmatic solution which avoided a lengthier (and more expensive) court hearing.

5.2 Construction

If a PR is not sure what a particular word or phrase in a will means, it will have to be 'constructed' by the courts. This means that the court will interpret the word and determine what it means. There are two aspects to construction. First, definitions of common words and phrases have been established by precedent, so there is uniformity in the law. These technical terms mean what the courts have said they mean. This can become problematic with homemade wills, as testators might not know that particular words are technical terms with a specific meaning. Secondly, the rules on construction have now been supplemented by s 21 of the AJA 1982, which gives the courts the power to interpret words in particular circumstances. This section of the chapter begins by looking at how specific words have been interpreted by the courts, before going on to look at the operation of s 21.

5.2.1 Basic principles of construction

When interpreting a will, the court starts by referring to certain core principles. The will has to be read as written (which is why it might have to be rectified first). The court cannot benignly interpret words to avoid real or perceived injustices. Regardless of the outcome, the judge has to apply what is plainly written in the document. That is, after all, what the testator put their name to.

Let us take the case of *Thorn v Dickens* [1906] WN 54 (a case from Australia) as an example. It concerned what is probably the shortest will ever made; the testator wrote 'All for mother'. At first glance, it seems very straightforward. The testator wants to leave everything he owns to his mother. However, that was not the case. The testator was actually referring to his wife, whom he frequently called 'mother' as, indeed, the two of them had children together. We might take for granted what certain words mean, but that is a dangerous presumption. Words can have many different meanings, both in common usage, as well as with reference to context, as in this case. That is the challenge that PRs might have when figuring out what the testator has instructed them to do, and which is why they may have to go to court for the judge to properly construe the words.

So, how do judges approach construction? In the case of *Abbott v Middleton* (1858) 7 HLC 68, 11 ER 28, Lord St Leonards commented: 'You are not at liberty to transpose, to add, to subtract, to substitute one word for another, or to take a confined expression and enlarge it, without absolute necessity.' However, the court will look at the will as a whole so that each word or phrase is interpreted in context. Further, Lord St Leonards said that a judge is 'at liberty to place yourself in the same situation in which the testator himself stood. You are entitled to inquire about his family, and the position in which he was placed with regard to his property.' This recognises, to an extent, that different people will ascribe different meanings to particular words. Examples, which will be expanded upon below, include words such as 'money' or 'children', which are defined differently by different people.

To this end, in *Boyes v Cook* (1880) 14 Ch D 53, James LJ said that the judge could place themselves in the testator's 'armchair' to help determine what the testator was intending when writing the will. This has sometimes been referred to as the armchair principle. In *Re Cozens* [1903] 1 Ch 138, Swinfen Eady J said that:

> The true rule is to determine by the language and context of each will, including the consideration of the whole instrument and any evidence properly admissible, the meaning of the expressions contained in it …

It again clarifies that the court must start with the specific words used (the words have obviously been chosen for a reason) but also consider the wider context in which the testator used those words.

In *Abbott v Middleton*, Lord Wensleydale similarly stated that the will should be read using:

the ordinary and grammatical sense of the words, unless some obvious absurdity, or some repugnance or inconsistency with the declared intentions of the writer, to be extracted from the whole instrument, should follow from so reading it. Then the sense may be modified, extended or abridged, so as to avoid those consequences, but no farther.

It follows that words should be given their normal meaning, unless that would result in something truly absurd. Then, the court is able to give a different interpretation of that particular word. Today, the courts have moved beyond a dictionary approach and interpret words based not only on their ordinary meaning but also, as appropriate, using the meaning ascribed to them by the testator. Section 21 of the AJA 1982 further allows the court to admit extrinsic evidence to help determine the testator's intentions.

key terminology

Extrinsic evidence: this is evidence that comes from outside the will. This can include witness statements (from people who knew the testator and can explain the testator's intentions), attendance notes written by the solicitor drafting the will, Letters of Wishes written by the testator, and so forth.

More recently, in *Marley v Rawlings* (discussed above), Lord Neuberger explained the modern approach to construction, saying that it is necessary to look at (a) the 'natural and ordinary meaning of those words', as well as (b) the 'facts known or assumed by the parties at the time that the document was executed'. Additionally, it is necessary to consider the purpose of the will, other provisions of the will (meaning one clause can help interpret a different clause), as well as to use 'common sense', which always gives some flexibility to judges. A few examples will be provided below at **5.2.3**.

The same approach is used for technical words. They must be given their technical meaning unless the context clearly shows a different intention (*Re Simcoe* [1913] 1 Ch 552). The case of *Re Cook* [1948] Ch 212 is a good illustration. A testator wrote a will giving 'all [her] personal estate whatsoever' to her nieces and nephews. However, her personal estate was minimal and her major asset was a freehold property. There was nothing on the facts that would allow the court to adopt a non-technical meaning of the phrase 'personal estate' as, in this case, doing so would amount to speculation as to what the testator intended. Despite the fact that the personal estate was very small (compared to the real estate), there was nothing ambiguous about how the will had been written. As such, the freehold estate passed on intestacy outside the will.

In recent times, as noted, the courts have moved beyond a literal approach. Lord Denning MR complained in *Re Rowland* [1963] Ch 1:

I have myself known a judge to say: 'I believe this to be contrary to the true intention of the testator but nevertheless it is the result of the words he has used'. When a judge goes so far as to say that, the chances are that he has misconstrued the will. For in point of principle the whole object of construing a will is to find out the testator's intentions, so as to see that his property is disposed of in the way he wished.

The courts are now more willing to take a purposive approach to wills, looking at the language, the context, but also using extrinsic evidence to determine the testator's wishes, and s 21 of the AJA 1982 has a key role to play here.

Today, the courts take a more lenient approach to the construction of words in homemade wills, given that the testator has not had the benefit of legal advice. In *Harris v Beneficiaries of the Estate of Cooper* [2010] EWHC 2620 (Ch), the court noted that when it comes to construing particular words in homemade wills, precedent has a more limited role, as the court has to consider the individual context in which the testator chose particular words or phrases.

5.2.2 Dual interpretations

Certain words or phrases can be interpreted in several different ways. If there are possible interpretations of a word or phrase, the court adopts the one with the most sensible meaning, bearing in mind that it is the testator's intention that has to be given effect to.

The case of *Re Harrison* (1885) 30 Ch D 390 is illustrative. The testator used a pre-printed form to write her will. Using a pen, she added a few words, which are indicated in italics. The will gave:

> … my estate and effects whatsoever and wheresoever, both real and personal, whether in possession, reversion, remainder, or expectancy, unto _____ to and for *her* own use and benefit absolutely. And I nominate, constitute, and appoint *my niece Catherine Hellard* to be execu*trix* of this my last will and testament.

As you can see, after the word 'unto', where beneficiaries could be added, the line was left blank. The question was whether the testator's niece Catherine Hellard was the intended beneficiary, or whether the will lacked any beneficiaries, meaning that the estate would pass on intestacy to the testator's next of kin. Lord Esher MR, with some flair, explained that 'when a testator has executed a will in solemn form you must assume that he did not intend to make it a solemn farce'. Lord Esher MR referred to a 'golden rule', saying that where there is a will, as far as the language allows it, the court should construct the will on the basis that the testator intended a testate succession, not an intestacy. In this case, the most (and only) sensible interpretation was that Catherine Hellard was the sole intended beneficiary. The testator did not intend an intestacy.

Another example is the case of *Re Rowland* [1963] Ch 1. Here, a husband and wife wrote wills giving their estates to each other, or, if one predeceased the other or if their deaths should coincide, then their respective estates would go to other relatives, with each spouse having different alternative beneficiaries. Dr and Mrs Rowland took up a medical posting in the Solomon Islands. They were travelling on a ship, which sank. It was not known on what day it sank or exactly where or why. The question was whether their deaths had coincided. Lord Denning MR, dissenting, argued that the term 'coinciding' was to be given the meaning it has in common parlance: since Dr and Mrs Rowland died in the same boat accident, their deaths had clearly coincided. The majority, Harman and Russell LJJ, held that not enough was known about the sinking and it could therefore not be said that the deaths coincided, ie that they were simultaneous. Instead, applying the *commorientes* rule (Law of Property Act 1925, s 184), the younger (Mrs Rowland) was said to have survived the older (Dr Rowland), meaning that his estate passed to hers, and then on to her relatives. The majority thus took a strict interpretation of coinciding (the literal approach), whereas Lord Denning advanced a more flexible approach. Russell LJ raised some important factual questions: the boat was fairly large so why did it not launch life boats, why did it not send a distress signal, and why had the only body recovered died from blood loss (eaten by fish) rather than drowning? Nonetheless, Lord Denning's broader interpretation of the word 'coinciding' is surely to be preferred. Given the growing acceptance of contextual and pragmatic interpretations, it is likely that Lord Denning's view would prevail today.

5.2.3 Interpretation of specific words

Case law and legislation have provided definitions of specific words and phrases that are commonly used in wills. This section looks at the construction of the word 'money' and then at the construction of various family terms such as 'children'.

5.2.3.1 Money

Re Cook, above, is a good example of how the courts have approached the phrase 'personal estate', which, in short, means any property other than land. Another word commonly used in wills is 'money'. The testator leaves their money to particular beneficiaries. It may sound simple, but the reality is far from it.

The key case dealing with the definition of money is the House of Lords' decision in *Perrin v Morgan* [1943] AC 399. Here, the testator left all of her 'money' to her nieces and nephews; however, most of her estate was comprised of shares. The question was whether the beneficiaries were entitled to the shares, or just to the small amount of cash held in a bank account. The House of Lords split on the question of how to interpret the word money.

Speaking for the majority, Viscount Simon LC said that money has 'not got one natural or usual meaning. It has several meanings, each of which in appropriate circumstances may be regarded as natural.' The definition of money can therefore change depending on the terms of the will and what the testator is taken to have intended the word to mean. The law recognises that different people will understand the term 'money' differently. On the facts of the case, the majority found that the testator had included her shares within the definition of money, and thus the beneficiaries were entitled to the shares.

The minority agreed that, in this case, the term 'money' included the shares, but argued that the term had to be interpreted within the context of the will. Lord Romer said:

> I think that [the rules of construction] should be strictly observed, but they ought to be applied in a reasonable way. It is, no doubt, of great importance to lawyers and others engaged in the preparation of wills that they should have the certainty of knowing that certain well-known words and phrases will receive from the court the meaning that the court has for generations past attributed to them.

If a term such as money is given a wide definition, which can vary from person to person, as Viscount Simon suggested, there is a real risk that the court will be rewriting the will, based on what the judge thinks the testator intended, as opposed to interpreting what is actually written.

The difference between the majority and minority judgments in *Perrin v Morgan* might seem minor, but it is important. The minority said that money has a technical meaning (generally referring to cash, either coins and notes or money in a bank account) but that technical meaning can, in a reasonable way, be extended if the overall terms of the will allow it. It was relevant here that the will made a specific gift of the testator's freehold property but that the shares were not mentioned at all. Thus, the minority found that the definition of money could, in this particular context, be extended to include the shares. The majority instead simply said that money does not have a technical, legal meaning, and that the court is free to consider the 'popular' meaning of money, which varies from person to person.

This broader approach inevitably led to litigation as the court was asked to determine how specific testators had used the word 'money'. The case of *Re Barnes* [1972] 1 WLR 587 is a good example. In her will, the testator left 'money' to specified beneficiaries and 'any other personal property' to her nieces and nephews. The testator had, in summary, cash in hand (coins and notes), money in various types of savings accounts, government bonds and Premium Bonds, and various household items. The judge had to determine which was which. The household items were clearly personal property and the cash in hand was obviously money. Applying how the word 'money' was used in common parlance, the judge found that the value in the savings accounts and the different bonds was money, and that this was what the testator had intended.

Where the term 'money' is used in relation to a residuary gift (as opposed to a specific gift), the court is freer to give it a broad definition, to include things like shares and bonds. In the case of *Vucicevic v Aleksic* [2017] EWHC 2335 (Ch), the will was home-made by a testator who did not have English as his first language. After leaving some specific gifts, the will simply referred to 'And all the money'. This was taken to include non-money financial assets. The court also took evidence which said that the Serbian word commonly translated in English as 'money' was in Serbian commonly used to include non-money assets, such as shares.

5.2.3.2 'Child', 'issue' and other family terms

Other commonly used words that may require construction are those used to describe particular beneficiaries, such as 'child' and 'issue' as well as other persons such as 'niece' and 'nephew'. Earlier, we considered the case of *Thorn v Dickens* [1906] WN 54, where the phrase 'All for mother' turned out to refer to the testator's wife. Family descriptors, such as 'child', might at first glance appear to have an obvious definition, but that it not always the case.

Let us look first at the terms 'child' and 'issue'. They are generally used synonymously. Traditionally, they refer to the testator's natural born children (including an unborn child *en ventre sa mère* – in the mother's womb). Over time, the definition of child and issue has been expanded by statute.

An adopted child is to be treated as a child of its adoptive parents (Adoption and Children Act 2002, s 67). It is important to note here that, once the adoption is completed, the adopted child is no longer treated as the child of their biological parent. If the biological parent leaves a gift to their 'children' in a will, the adopted child is not a beneficiary, unless there is a clear contrary intention that shows that the adopted child was meant to be a beneficiary. That is a matter of construction (s 67(6)(a)). In *Hardy v Hardy* [2015] EWHC 83 (Ch), an adopted son fell within the class of 'my children' as a contrary intention was found in the wording of the will of his biological parent; namely that the adopted son was one of the appointed executors, and in the appointment clause he was described by the biological parent as 'my son'. The adopted son was therefore able to inherit under his biological parent's will.

The law no longer makes any distinction between a 'legitimate' and 'illegitimate' child, ie a child born to unmarried parents (Family Law Reform Act 1987, s 19).

The Human Fertilisation and Embryology Acts of 1990 and 2008 provide rules as to who is treated as the parent of a child born from artificial insemination, depending on who donated eggs and sperm, who carried the child to birth, and whether consent was given (the details are beyond the scope of this book). Under s 33 of the 2008 Act, the woman who carried the child to term is to be treated as the mother (bearing in mind that if the child is adopted, it will be treated as the child of the adoptive parents).

As a rule, however, stepchildren are not included within the definition of child or issue, unless specifically stated. The case of *Reading v Reading* [2015] EWHC 946

(Ch) is illustrative. Clause 3 of a will established a trust for the testator's wife and his 'issue'. The testator had two children and three stepchildren. Clause 4 then disposed of the residue, which was given to the wife or, if she predeceased the testator, to the five children (who were in cl 4 listed by name and described as either a child or stepchild). The question for the trustees was whether the word 'issue' in cl 3 could be interpreted as including the stepchildren, given that as a matter of technical language, the use of the word 'issue' would exclude the stepchildren. The court interpreted 'issue' as including the stepchildren, based on a number of factors. First, cl 4 clearly referred to the stepchildren, so they were obviously on the testator's mind when preparing his will. Secondly, the testator had a close relationship with the stepchildren and treated them as his own. Thirdly, both one child and one stepchild were appointed as trustees. Finally, the testator had prepared a Letter of Wishes, explaining how the cl 3 trust was meant to operate, and in it he indicated that the stepchildren were beneficiaries. The judge explained that his interpretation was based on common law, but, if necessary, the trustees could have relied on s 21 of the AJA 1982.

This case follows the High Court decision in *Re Davidson* [1949] Ch 670. A testator had left the residue of her estate to her 'grandchildren'. At the time of her death, the only possible beneficiaries were the children of the testator's step-son. The court held that the step-grandchildren were clearly intended to be beneficiaries, as the testator had always treated her step-son as her own. The case of *Wales v Dixon* [2020] EWHC 1979 (Ch) takes the debate to other family members. In this case, the testator left the residue of his estate to the children of his nieces and nephews. The testator had four nieces and nephews by blood, and between them they had seven children, meaning there were seven beneficiaries. The testator also had four living nieces and nephews by marriage (the testator was at the time of his death a widow). There was also a fifth nephew by marriage who had died before the testator, but who had left a child. The nieces and nephews by marriage between them had eight children. The question for the court was whether those eight were also beneficiaries (taking the total number of beneficiaries to 15). Taking the circumstances into account, the court found that all 15 children fell within the class of beneficiaries. The testator had been close to his wife's family; in an earlier will he had left gifts to his wife and her family; there was a continued relationship between the testator and his wife's family after she had died and conversely no evidence that he now wanted them excluded.

In the earlier case of *Re Daoust* [1944] 1 All ER 443, Vaisey J had noted that niece/nephew was a quite expansive term, including blood relatives (ie the child of a sibling) but was also commonly used to refer to relatives by marriage, as well as the spouse/partner of a blood relative (for instance, the husband of a blood niece may well be referred to as a nephew in common parlance). Vaisey J suggested that, as a starting point, the word niece and nephew should be restricted to blood relatives, unless 'compelled by context or circumstances' to decide otherwise, as happened in *Wales v Dixon*.

What happens if the testator leaves a gift to their 'relatives'? Normally, it would refer to all living relatives, however remotely connected to the testator, as was held in *Re Poulton's Will Trusts* [1987] 1 WLR 795. However, the court can refer to extrinsic evidence under s 21 of the Administration of Justice Act 1982 (see further below) to consider whether the testator had a particular definition in mind when using the word 'relatives'. In *Harris v Beneficiaries of the Estate of Cooper* [2010] EWHC 2620 (Ch), a gift to 'my surviving relatives' was construed as only applying to three living first cousins, as those were the only relatives the testator had had a connection with. The court thus excluded another first cousin and multiple remoter cousins (once and twice removed). Despite the court having the ability to construe the word, testators should avoid using a term as vague and broad as 'relatives'.

These cases neatly demonstrate the ambiguity of common words used to describe family members and relatives. Different people will have a different view on what each word means – who is a child, who is a parent, who is a niece/nephew – indeed, who is a relative? If necessary, the court will have to decide, based on the word used and the specific context in which the testator made the will. Of course, to avoid this, a testator should be recommended to list beneficiaries by name or at least specify what they mean by a specific word, such as stating that the word 'child' includes step-children or that 'niece' includes nieces by marriage. That would avoid unnecessary applications to court to seek guidance on the true construction of the word, which takes time and costs money (which is normally paid out of the estate, thus limiting the amount of money left over to distribute to the beneficiaries).

5.2.4 Class gifts and the class-closing rules

A testator may, in their will, leave gifts to specific individuals or to a group of people. The latter is known as a class gift. Specific rules of construction apply to determine whether a gift is an individual gift or a class gift, and if it is a class gift, who is a member of that class. A class is defined as a group of people who fit a 'certain category or description defined by a general or collective formula' (*Pearks v Moseley* (1880) 5 App Cas 714). Common classes are gifts made to 'my children' or 'my grandchildren'.

Using the example will set out in **Chapter 4**, we saw that Dorothy left £20,000 to her niece, Zara. This is an individual gift. As long as Dorothy's estate has £20,000 in it and Zara is alive when Dorothy dies, Zara will get the money.

However, assume that Zara has two children of her own. Dorothy may choose to leave money to them. There are different ways in which she can do so.

(a) 'I leave £10,000 to each of Zara's children.'

Strictly speaking, this is not a class gift, because it is directed at specific individuals. Each of Zara's children will get £10,000 when Dorothy dies.

(b) 'I leave £20,000 to Zara's children.'

This is a class gift. The class, or group, is Zara's children. Because it is a class gift, it is necessary to determine when the class closes. It is only once the class has closed that the PR can distribute the gift. This is because, if Zara has two children, they would get £10,000 each, but if, for example, Zara has a third child, they would get £6,666.67 each, and so on.

The general rule is that the class closes when the testator dies (*Viner v Francis* (1789) 2 Cox 190, 30 ER 88 and *Devisme v Mello* (1782) 1 Brown's CC 537, 28 ER 1285). This is because the gift is immediate, and not postponed (see below). The rule allows the PR to distribute the gift once the testator has died. There is, however, an obvious unfairness to this. What if Zara has another child after Dorothy dies? Unfortunately, such a child would not be entitled to inherit.

The general rule can be displaced by drafting. Dorothy could write in her will, 'I leave £20,000 to Zara's children, whenever they are born.' This would leave the class open even after Dorothy dies. The property would have to be held on trust until the class closes. Technically, this class remains open until Zara dies, because it is possible for her to have a new child up to then. This is, however, hugely inconvenient for everyone. Realistically, the trustee can apply to court to close the class at a convenient time, for instance when Zara reaches an age where it is unlikely she will have more children.

However, what happens if Zara does not have any children at the time Dorothy dies? One option would be for the gift to fail altogether, but that goes against the testator's wishes. Rather, in this situation, the courts have said that the class remains open until Zara dies (or until the trustees apply to close the class) (*Re Bleckly* [1951] Ch 740).

(c) 'I leave £20,000 to Zara's children, who shall attain the age of 21.'

This is known as a conditional gift. This is because the gift imposes a condition that the beneficiary must satisfy before they become entitled; in this case, the beneficiary must turn 21. Regardless of when Dorothy dies, no beneficiary is entitled unless they have reached that age. This is known as the rule in *Andrews v Partington* (1791) 3 Brown's CC 401, 29 ER 610, which says that the class closes either (a) when Dorothy dies if one beneficiary has reached that age, or otherwise (b) when the first beneficiary reaches that age. The application of this rule can also be considered unfair, as it excludes any of Zara's children born after (a) Dorothy dies or (b) the first one has turned 21, as the case may be.

The *Andrews* rule can be displaced by drafting. Dorothy could write in her will, 'I leave £20,000 to Zara's children, who shall attain the age of 21, whenever they are born.' In *Re Clifford's Settlement Trusts* [1981] Ch 63, the court emphasised that the burden of proof to displace the *Andrews* rule is 'high'. Phrases such as 'any child', 'all children' and even 'children now living or hereafter to be born' will not suffice; the class will still close when the first child reaches 21. However, the phrase 'whenever born' has been deemed sufficiently certain and absolute, so it does displace the *Andrews* rule (*Re Edmondson's Will Trusts* [1972] 1 WLR 183).

These rules of construction can be seen as pedantic, but their aim is to ensure consistency between all wills, and they highlight the benefits of seeking legal advice if you want your will to do anything more than just give absolute, individual gifts. When drafting a will, it is of upmost importance to pay close attention to the specific words and phrases used.

(d) 'I give £20,000 to Zara for life and thereafter to Zara's children.'

This is a common example of a trust in succession. Zara obtains a life interest in the property, entitling her to the benefit of the income of the property (such as savings income), but she is not entitled to take the capital itself. When Zara dies, the capital (the actual £20,000) goes to Zara's children. This is known as a deferred, or postponed, class gift. The class closes when Zara dies, not when Dorothy dies (*Re Harker's Will Trust* [1969] 1 WLR 1124). This means that all of Zara's children are entitled to inherit, not just the ones alive when Dorothy died.

What happens if Zara dies before Dorothy? In that case, Zara's children would be immediately entitled to the money when Dorothy dies. This is known as an acceleration, as the children will receive their interest faster than they otherwise would have.

What happens if Zara survives Dorothy but instead disclaims her interest? Zara is, of course, entitled to refuse the life interest and ensure that the property vests immediately in her children. Does the class close when Zara disclaims her interest, or does it remain open until she dies? In English cases, such as *Re Kebty-Fletcher's Wills Trusts* [1969] 1 Ch 339 and *Re Harker's Will Trust* [1969] 1 WLR 1124, the court said that the class remains open until Zara dies, meaning that all of her children are entitled. This is because the rule of construction, as stated, is that the class ordinarily closes on Zara's death. This is what the will means, and the court has to assume that this is what the testator wanted. It would be wrong for Zara to change the effect of the will after Dorothy has died.

Still, this casts doubt on the benefit of such a disclaimer. Whilst the trustee does not have to pay the income to Zara, the trust cannot be distributed until Zara dies and the class closes. The benefit to the beneficiaries is that the interest is accumulated in the trust, rather than being paid out to the life tenant, so there will eventually be more money for the beneficiaries. However, it may require a longer wait before they actually see any of the money. The cases, as said, turn on the testator's intentions, following the ordinary rules of construction.

In the Australian case of *Bassett v Bassett* [2003] NSWSC 691 (New South Wales), the court decided instead to close the class on the date of the disclaimer. There is some merit in this approach, not least since it allows the trustee to distribute the trust fund rather than keeping the trust alive. The downside, as said, is that the court is not following the ordinary rules of construction and is, in effect, rewriting the will. This is because the testator expected the class to remain open until the life tenant died.

5.2.5 Absolute gifts, contingent gifts or life interests

The law presumes that gifts are absolute. This means that the beneficiary takes the property absolutely, free of any restrictions. If the testator only wants to give a beneficiary a life interest, this has to be clearly stated (ie 'I give my house to John for life, thereafter to Amanda').

Gifts of real property are presumed to be absolute by virtue of s 28 of the Wills Act 1837. Gifts of personal property are presumed to be absolute as a rule of construction (*Sherratt v Bentley* (1834) 2 My & K 149, 39 ER 901).

Ultimately, however, it is a question of drafting, and each will must be considered on its own terms. Generally, a gift of property to someone 'absolutely' will be just that, and any subsequent instructions will be void. So, for example, if the will reads, 'I give my house to John absolutely, and when he dies Amanda is entitled to it,' the house will go to John. Amanda has no claim to the house. If the will reads, 'I give my house to John so he can use it when he is alive and after he dies it goes to Amanda,' the court may interpret this as giving John a life interest only. This kind of imprecise drafting will likely only occur in homemade wills, where the courts have a bit more flexibility to determine what the testator intended. However, as discussed above, the court has to give effect to the words actually used.

Since 1983, if the gift is made to a spouse, a more recent rule applies, found in s 22 of the AJA 1982. If the gift appears to be absolute, it will be presumed as such, regardless of whether the gift then purports to give further instructions. Thus, if the will reads, 'I give my house to my spouse and thereafter to my child,' the gift will be absolute. The child will have no claim to the house. To create a life interest, the will must clearly say so. For example, the will could read, 'I give my house to my spouse for life, thereafter to my child.'

Again, these drafting rules may appear pedantic, but they are really important. There is a huge difference between an absolute gift (given to X directly after the testator dies, and with which X can do whatever they want) and a life interest (which has to be held on trust for X for the remainder of X's life, however long, by the will trustees, and after X's death distributed to the deferred beneficiary). Any life interest thus creates an enormous burden for the trustee and conversely greatly limits what X can do with the property (use it and benefit from it, but never sell it). Thus, life interests should not arise unless they are undeniably what the testator wanted.

The testator can also choose to leave a contingent gift. This means that the beneficiary will only inherit if they meet a certain contingency. A common contingency is requiring the beneficiary to reach a certain age. For example, the will may read: 'I leave £10,000 to John, contingent on him turning 21 years of age.'

As seen above, in class gifts, the will may read: 'I leave £10,000 to each of my children as shall attain the age of 21.' Another common condition is the beneficiary getting married. The gift may read: 'I leave £10,000 to John, contingent on him getting married.' Beyond that, the testator can impose any contingency they see fit; this can include the beneficiary obtaining a particular education or qualification, entering a certain profession, or completing some other achievement. The property is held on trust until the contingency is met. If it is not met, the gift fails and returns to the testator's estate, and would pass to the testator's next of kin on intestacy.

5.2.6   The date a will speaks from

The law has provided clear rules on the date a will speaks from. This is important as it helps identify which property or beneficiary the will is referring to. The rule is set out in s 24 of the Wills Act 1837.

5.2.6.1   Property

When it comes to property, the will is interpreted as if it had been executed on the day the testator died. Therefore, the property referred to in the will is taken to mean the property that the testator owned on the day he or she died. Therefore, a gift of 'my jewellery' refers to the jewellery that the testator owned on that day. It does not matter that the testator might have bought, sold or gifted a lot of their jewellery between the date of execution and the date of their death.

Assume there is a testator called Anders. He owns a Volvo car. Anders writes a will, in which he gifts 'my car' to his friend Bert. Later on, Anders sells the Volvo and buys a Land Rover. When Anders dies, Bert will inherit the Land Rover, because the will speaks from the date of death. However, s 24 can be displaced through the drafting of the will. If Anders, in his will, gifts 'the car that I now own' to Bert, Bert is only entitled to the car that Anders owned at the date of execution. It is always a question of interpretation, but generally the word 'now', or any similar word to the same effect, is treated as referring to the item owned at the date of execution (*Re Whitby* [1944] Ch 210). As will be seen in the next chapter, in the section on ademption, this causes a problem if Anders sold his Volvo before dying. If he did that, the gift would fail (adeem), and Bert would not be entitled to anything.

5.2.6.2   Beneficiaries

The identity of individual beneficiaries, however, is interpreted as meaning the person matching the description on the date the will is executed (*Re Coley* [1903] 2 Ch 102). If, for example, Anders in his will gifts his car to Bert's 'wife', the beneficiary is the wife Bert has at the date of execution. If Bert gets divorced and remarries, the new wife is not entitled. If Bert has no wife, the gift fails. As always, the rule can be displaced by drafting. It is always advisable in a will to refer to specific individuals by their full name and current address, to avoid these kinds of problems. The rules on class gifts and the class-closing rules were discussed earlier in this chapter.

5.2.7 AJA 1982, s 21

The common law rules on interpretation have been supplemented by the court's power to interpret wills, now found in s 21 of the AJA 1982:

21 Interpretation of wills—general rules as to evidence

(1) This section applies to a will—

(a) in so far as any part of it is meaningless;

(b) in so far as the language used in any part of it is ambiguous on the face of it;

(c) in so far as evidence, other than evidence of the testator's intention, shows that the language used in any part of it is ambiguous in the light of surrounding circumstances.

(2) In so far as this section applies to a will extrinsic evidence, including evidence of the testator's intention, may be admitted to assist in its interpretation.

Section 21 is not a general power of interpretation; that remains with the common law. Rather, the section allows the court to use extrinsic evidence to help interpret the will, if any of the three circumstances are satisfied. These are if the words used in the will are meaningless; if the words themselves are ambiguous (previously known as patent ambiguity); or if the words, which are otherwise clear, become ambiguous because of the wider circumstances (previously known as latent ambiguity). This is a fairly broad approach to ambiguity. Where there is such ambiguity, extrinsic evidence can be used to clarify what the words actually mean. The extrinsic evidence has to actually help, or 'assist', with the interpretation (*Re Williams (Deceased)* [1985] 1 WLR 905). The same principles apply here as under the general common law rules. First and foremost, the court is looking for the testator's intention. Secondly, terms are given their ordinary meaning. Thirdly, technical terms are given their technical meaning.

The relationship between the common law rules and the court's power of interpretation under s 21 is not exactly clear. *Reading v Reading* [2015] EWHC 946 (Ch), mentioned above, is a good example of this. The court interpreted the word 'issue' in that will to include stepchildren. The judge applied the common law rules, but said that if they had not helped, the stepchildren could have succeeded under s 21(1)(c). This was because the word 'issue' was ambiguous in light of the surrounding circumstances (namely, should it include stepchildren, given the close relationship between them and the testator?).

A key case on s 21 is *Re Williams (Deceased)* [1985] 1 WLR 905. A testator wrote a will, where she appointed two executors. She then listed 25 beneficiaries (some were relatives, some were friends, and three were charities). They were separated into three groups. There was no obvious explanation of why this had been done: the groups were of unequal size, each group consisted of both relatives and friends, and the three charities were split into two of the groups. Before she died, the testator wrote a letter, which suggested a division along the following lines: beneficiaries listed in 'the first, for example, should receive, say £2,000 each, the second £1,000 each, and the third £500'. The Court found that there was ambiguity in the writing itself, following s 21(1)(b). The question was whether the letter should be admitted to court as extrinsic evidence. As s 21(2) says, the extrinsic evidence must 'assist' in the interpretation of the will; the letter did not. It did not explain how the estate was to be divided between the three groups, as it was only suggestive rather than directive. The judge declared that each of the 25 beneficiaries was to receive an equal share of the estate, which was probably the only sensible outcome.

5.2.8 Drawing construction and rectification together

The most important thing to note is that if a clause is vague but cannot sensibly be construed or rectified, the clause is void. Any identified property in the clause would pass outside the will on intestacy. In the case of *Anthony v Donges* [1998] 2 FLR 775, a husband wrote a will, which gave his wife 'such minimal part of my estate … as she may be entitled to under English law for maintenance purposes'. This clause made reference to the Inheritance (Provision for Family and Dependants) Act 1975, under which surviving spouses (and other family members) may claim maintenance support from an estate (see **Chapter 15**). The court held that this clause could not be interpreted in any sensible manner and thus it was void.

The case of *Re Harte (Deceased)* [2015] EWHC 2351 (Ch) is illustrative of how interpretation and rectification can be used together to give effect to a will. Mrs Harte wrote a will. Clause 3 turned out to be problematic. It gave 'all my personal property' to trustees to hold on trust. Ten beneficiaries were listed. Some were entitled to 'one tenth' and others to 'one part'. One charitable beneficiary, a hospital, was mentioned by its colloquial name as opposed to its formal name. One charitable beneficiary, as named, did not exist. The court was asked by the executors to give instructions as to how they should proceed. Matters were complicated even further because the solicitor who drafted the will could not recall the testator (or the instructions given). Only one of the attesting witnesses could be found, but the witness did not recall the testator either.

The executors sought consent to treat all of Mrs Harte's property (including the real property) as part of cl 3, not just the personal property. The term 'one part' was proposed to mean 'one tenth'. The colloquially named hospital was meant to indicate the relevant NHS Trust. The non-existing beneficiary was meant to indicate the local Air Ambulance Trust (rather than the named 'West Berkshire Ambulance Hospital').

The court found that the will was ambiguous on the face of it (a patent defect) and as such that s 21(1)(b) was engaged. The court first interpreted cl 3 to refer to the entire estate, both real and personal. This was clear in context, as the testator was referring to everything she owned after just debts, funeral and other expenses had been paid. The term 'one part' was interpreted as meaning 'one tenth'. In context, this was the only logical outcome. Despite the oddness of using different terms for different beneficiaries, the will had a list of 10 beneficiaries, numbered one to 10. The colloquially named hospital was interpreted as meaning the actual hospital, which was made easy by the fact that the hospital's address was included in the will. Other charities had their correct charity registration number included but their names had been written incorrectly (such as Macmillan Cancer Fund instead of the correct Macmillan Cancer Support).

The last gift was the most problematic. The West Berkshire Ambulance Hospital is a nonsensical term, for starters, and no address or charity registration number was included. This gift had to be rectified as opposed to interpreted, using the court's power under s 20. The solicitor's attendance note indicated a gift to the 'West Berks … Air Rescue'. It was not clear whether the clause in the will was the result of a clerical error or a misunderstanding of instructions, or both. The clause was nonetheless rectified to name the local Air Ambulance Trust as the correct beneficiary.

5.3 Further reading

Law Commission, *Making a Will* (Consultation Paper 231, July 2017), Ch 9 (Interpretation and rectification).

Hamm, Robert, 'Thy Will be Done: Construction and Rectification of Wills in the Supreme Court' (2014) 20 T&T 966–70.

This chapter has outlined the court's powers to rectify a will, under s 20 of the AJA 1982, if it does not accurately reflect the testator's wishes due to a clerical error or a misunderstanding of the testator's instructions. The chapter has then explained how the courts go about constructing ambiguous words or phrases. The old common law rules now operate in conjunction with s 21 of the AJA 1982. Words can be inherently ambiguous (such as money) or become ambiguous because of the circumstances (such as children or issue, which will vary from family to family). If any particular clause in a will cannot be rectified or construed, the clause fails. Any specific property referred to passes outside the will on intestacy instead.

6

Amending Wills, Revoking Wills, Reviving Wills and the Failure of Gifts

It is an ultimate truth in life that we sometimes change our minds. In **Chapters 2 and 3**, we examined the legal requirements for writing a valid will, and it was suggested that one of the reasons behind the formality requirements was to force testators to give serious consideration to what they put into the will. No one should write a will on a whim; the will should be the product of careful and mature deliberation.

Nonetheless, after a testator has executed a will, they might change their minds. The testator might want to change particular terms of a will or even revoke the entire will. Equally, once a will has been executed, the testator's personal circumstances might change. The testator might get married or enter a civil partnership. The testator might sell property which is the subject of a testamentary gift. Such changes in circumstances have an impact on the validity of the will or specific testamentary gifts. The law needs to have clear rules as to what happens in each of these situations. These rules are the focus of this chapter.

This chapter considers the following issues:

- *Amending a will:* the rules for making changes to a will, as set out in s 21 of the Wills Act 1837.
- *Revoking a will:* the rules for revoking a will, as set out in s 20 of the Wills Act 1837.
- *Revoking a will:* the rules determining how a will is revoked by marriage or civil partnership, as set out in ss 18 and 18B of the Wills Act 1837.
- *Reviving a will:* the rules determining how a revoked will can be revived, as set out in s 22 of the Wills Act 1837.
- *Failure of gifts:* the rules determining how individual gifts in a will might fail.

6.1 Amending a will

The first thing to consider are the rules that determine how changes may be made to a will. It is easy to envisage why, after a will has been executed, the testator might want to make changes to it. The change might include adding new beneficiaries, such as new family members or new friends. Conversely, the testator might want to remove beneficiaries, perhaps because there has been a falling out, or because the beneficiary has predeceased the testator, or perhaps because the gift was to a charity or organisation that has ceased operating. The change may relate to a specific gift; perhaps the testator wants to increase or decrease the financial value of a gift to a particular beneficiary. The possibilities are endless.

The rules for making changes are set out below. From the outset, it is important to note that changes can be made before or after the will itself is executed, and the rules differ accordingly.

6.1.1 How to make changes

The rules for amending, or altering, a will are set out in s 21 of the Wills Act 1837. The section is long and could certainly be more succinctly drafted. The whole section is set out below, and thereafter this part of the chapter goes through its constituent parts one by one. Then, at **6.1.2**, a sample will is included, with some changes made to it, illustrating how alterations can work in practice.

> **21 No alteration in a will shall have any effect unless executed as a will**
>
> No obliteration, interlineation, or other alteration made in any will after the execution thereof shall be valid or have any effect, except so far as the words or effect of the will before such alteration shall not be apparent, unless such alteration shall be executed in like manner as herein-before is required for the execution of the will; but the will, with such alteration as part thereof, shall be deemed to be duly executed if the signature of the testator and the subscription of the witnesses be made in the margin or on some other part of the will opposite or near to such alteration, or at the foot or end of or opposite to a memorandum referring to such alteration, and written at the end or some other part of the will.

Section 21 requires a bit of deciphering, but fundamentally it explains that there are four ways of making changes to a will, and that three of those types of changes have to be attested in the same way as provided for by s 9 (that is to say, signed by the testator in the presence of at least two witnesses, who then themselves sign the will). The three changes that have to be attested are obliterations, interlineations and alterations. The fourth type of change, which does not have to be attested, is obliterations where the words are no longer apparent. These four changes are outlined below.

6.1.1.1 Obliteration

To obliterate means to destroy. A clause in a will can be obliterated in many different ways. The text may be drawn over or otherwise scratched out. The words may be covered up by gluing strips of paper over them. The text can also be physically removed, for example by cutting it out of the paper with a pair of scissors. For instance, in the case of *Re Hay* [1904] 1 Ch 317, a testator asked her servant to cross out three legacies with a pen; this obliteration was not valid since it was not signed by either the testator or by two witnesses. If the testator's and the witnesses' signatures are crossed out, the will is treated as revoked in its entirety (*Re Adams (Deceased)* [1990] Ch 601). This will be discussed further below.

6.1.1.2 Interlineation

This means to add new words in between the existing text or next to the existing text.

6.1.1.3 Alteration

Alterations can take many forms, but they include removing or adding particular words, phrases or entire clauses. If the changes are minor (such as crossing out '£1000' and writing '£2000' next to a monetary gift), this can be done in the primary document. If the changes are more major, they can be made through a codicil.

key terminology

Codicil: We have already come across the definition of a codicil in earlier chapters, but reiteration is always good. A codicil is a formally executed document (complying with s 9 of the Wills Act 1837), in which a testator sets out changes that they want to make to their will. Words, phrases or entire clauses can be revoked or added. Once formally executed, the codicil becomes part of the will. They are put into probate together. There is no limit on the number of codicils that a person can execute; at a certain point, however, it will become easier to write a new will from scratch.

6.1.1.4 Execution of obliterations, interlineations and alterations

Once a change has been made, it has to be formally executed, as prescribed by s 9. The courts have confirmed that it is sufficient for the testator and the witnesses simply to write their initials in the margin next to any change (*In the Goods of Blewitt* (1880) 5 PD 116). The same rules apply to these witnesses as to the witnesses who witnessed the will itself, as discussed in **Chapter 3**. Subject to those rules, when making the change, the testator can use any two people as witnesses; there is no need to use the same witnesses who were present when the will was originally executed.

6.1.1.5 Obliteration where the words are no longer 'apparent'

In general, any obliteration has to be executed in compliance with s 9. However, s 21 allows for one exception: where the words are no longer 'apparent', they are treated as validly obliterated, provided that there was an intention to revoke the obliterated text. This naturally raises the question of what is meant by the word 'apparent'.

The test is whether the obliterated words can be read, using any assistance available, such as magnifying glasses, but without the need to resort to extrinsic evidence. In the case of *Townley v Watson* (1844) 3 Curt 761, 163 ER 893, for example, the text had been completely covered over by ink so that the text could not be read, even when the document was held up against the light. The contrary result came about in the case of *Ffinch v Combe* [1894] P 191. Slips of paper had been pasted over particular words, hiding them. This amounted to an obliteration. However, by placing a sheet of brown paper under the will and holding it against a window or other light source, the words underneath the slips of paper could be read. The words were therefore apparent and were admitted into probate.

It is important that the testator also intends to revoke the obliterated words (*Townley v Watson* (1844) 3 Curt 761, 163 ER 893). The case of *Re Itter (Deceased) (No 2)* [1950] P 130 is illustrative. The testator had written a will with various pecuniary gifts. She later covered up the financial value with strips of paper and wrote a new value on top of the strips of paper. This change was not executed and thus the new values could not be admitted into probate. The question was whether the testator had also obliterated the original values, by virtue of them not being apparent. The court found that the original values were not apparent since they could only be read once an infrared photograph of the will had been taken. An infrared photograph is clearly extrinsic evidence. However, the court also found that there was no intention to revoke the gifts. This was because new financial values were added onto the strips of paper. The court asserted that the testator had only intended to revoke the original values if the new ones took effect. Since the new values were not executed, and thus void, there was no intention to revoke the original gifts. The original values were thus admitted into probate with the help of the infrared photograph. *Re Itter* is a good example of the need for intention when words are obliterated or otherwise changed.

6.1.2 Example of a will with changes included

Let us consider a simplified version of the sample will that was discussed in **Chapter 4**, and see how it might look instead with some changes made to it. These changes will be discussed below.

Last Will and Testament

I, Dorothy Smith, of 1 Lincoln Avenue, Lincoln LN30 1AB,

Widow, Being of Sound Mind, **HEREBY REVOKE** all former Wills and testamentary dispositions made by me **AND DECLARE** this to be my last Will and Testament

1. I APPOINT my niece Zara Jones, of 20 London Road, Bristol, BS42 1DW, and Dot Parker, Solicitor, of 12 Bristol Road, Gainsborough, DN21 9TL, or failing her the partners at the date of my death in the firm of Parker and Parker, of the same address, or the firm which at that date has succeeded to and carried on its practice (and in so doing I express the wish that only one of such legally qualified partners shall act as executor and act on its trusts) (hereinafter called 'my Trustees') to be Executors and Trustees of this my Will;

$£50,000$ *DS, AT, DC*

2. I GIVE to my said niece Zara Jones ~~£20,000~~ absolutely;

---

3. I GIVE to my said niece Zara Jones my freehold property, known as 1 Lincoln Avenue, Lincoln LN30 1AB, absolutely;

4. I MAKE the following gifts absolutely;

r ⎯ 1
L ⎯ J

(ii)To Sarah Pike: All Brass and Copper Artefacts in my home;

(iii) ▬▬▬▬▬▬▬▬▬▬▬▬▬▬▬▬▬▬▬▬▬

5. I GIVE DEVISE AND BEQUEATH the whole of my estate of whatsoever kind and wheresoever situate both real and personal **UNTO** my Executors and Trustees **UPON TRUST** to sell call in collect and convert the same into money with power in their absolute discretion to postpone the sale calling in collection and conversion of such part or parts thereof as they shall think fit without being responsible for loss and **TO HOLD** the net proceeds of such sale calling in collection and conversion and my ready money and such part or parts of my estate as shall for the time being remain unsold and unconverted **UPON TRUST** as follows:

(i)To pay thereout my just debts funeral and testamentary expenses;

(ii)As to the residue thereof for my beloved children and my said niece Zara, as shall survive me, and if more than one in equal shares absolutely; *and also to my friend Jane*   *DS, AT, DC*

IN WITNESS whereof I have hereunto set my hand to this my Will this

30th   day of   August   Two thousand and eighteen

SIGNED by the said   *Dorothy Smith*

as and for her last Will in the presence
of us both being present at the same   *Dot Parker* (solicitor)
time who at her request in her presence
and in the presence of each other   *Lucina Xi* (trainee solicitor)
have hereunto subscribed our names
as witnesses:-

What changes has Dorothy made to her will?

In cl 2, there has been an alteration. Clause 2 contains a pecuniary gift to Dorothy's niece, Zara. The original gift was valued at £20,000. However, Dorothy has changed her mind. The value has been crossed out, and a new value, £50,000, has been added above the clause. This alteration is going to take effect, since it has been signed by Dorothy and two witnesses. From the initials, it is clear that these are different witnesses from Dot Parker and Lucina Xi, who witnessed the execution of the will itself. Such a change is permitted. As the law also allows, the new witnesses have initialled next to the change.

Two things have happened to cl 4, both of them obliterations. It would appear that the text of cl 4(i) has been cut out from the document, perhaps using a pair of scissors. The text at cl 4(iii) has been completely covered over. These changes have not been executed, so the validity of the changes turns on whether the text is no longer apparent and whether the change has been made intentionally. This is a question of fact. If the text has been cut out, it is clearly not apparent. Where the text has been covered over, the question is whether the text underneath is still visible, for example, if the will is placed against a light source.

In clause 5(ii), there has been an interlineation. A new beneficiary has been added, namely Dorothy's friend Jane. The addition is a bit vague, but using the rules of construction set out in the previous chapter, the interlineation suggests that Jane should get an equal share of the residue (alongside Dorothy's children and Zara), provided that Jane also survives Dorothy. The interlineation is valid since it has been properly executed.

6.1.3 Changes made before a will is executed

Changes can also be made to a will after it has been written but before it is executed. Words can be added to or removed from the main text. These changes will take effect if they are intended to take effect.

There are two particular rules that must be borne in mind when making changes before the will is executed. If the will is holographic (handwritten), and the text is a mixture of ink and pencil, the law presumes that the text in ink is the intended final version and the text in pencil is only the draft (*In the Goods of Adams* (1872) LR 2 P&D 367). This presumption can be rebutted, either by looking at the text as a whole, or through extrinsic evidence, such as statements from the attesting witnesses. Nonetheless, particular care must be taken with holographic wills, if they are written with different types of pens and pencils.

The most important rule, however, is that if the changes are unattested, ie there are no signatures next to then, the law presumes that they were made after the will as a whole was executed, and thus the changes have no effect (*In the Goods of Adamson* (1872-1875) LR 3 P&D 253). Again, the presumption can be rebutted by looking at the text as a whole or through extrinsic evidence. Good practice is thus to ensure that both the testator and the two witnesses sign next to the change, as well as at the end of the will.

The rules for pre-execution changes may not be so relevant today. Where a will is professionally drafted on a computer, and the testator wishes to make a change before the will is executed, the change can be made on the computer, and a fresh copy can be printed out for execution. However, the rules are still relevant where a person uses a pre-printed will form and fills in the blanks with a pen. In this situation, if the testator changes their mind, they may still have to cross out specific words and add new ones next to them. In this case, the testator and the witnesses should sign next to the change as well as at the end.

6.2 Revoking a will

Just as a testator may wish to make changes to their will, the testator may also wish to revoke it in full. There are two statutory grounds through which a will can be revoked. The first ground, the focus of this part of the chapter, is s 20 of the Wills Act 1837. The second ground, which is considered at **6.3** below, is revocation through marriage, found in ss 18 and 18B of the Wills Act 1837.

Section 20 reads as follows:

> **20   No will to be revoked but by another will or codicil, or by a writing executed like a will, or by destruction**
>
> No will or codicil, or any part thereof, shall be revoked otherwise than as aforesaid, or by another will or codicil executed in manner herein-before required, or by some writing declaring an intention to revoke the same, and executed in the manner in which a will is herein-before required to be executed, or by the burning, tearing, or otherwise destroying the same by the testator, or by some person in his presence and by his direction, with the intention of revoking the same.

The section provides three different ways in which a will can be revoked:

(a)   revocation by a later will;

(b)   revocation by a document executed in accordance with s 9 of the Wills Act 1837;

(c)   revocation by intentional destruction.

These three different ways to revoke a will are discussed in turn below.

6.2.1 Revocation by a later will

Despite what s 20 might suggest, a later will does not automatically revoke a former will. Section 19 of the Wills Act 1837 also holds that a change in the testator's personal circumstances (other than marriage or civil partnership) does not revoke an existing will.

Rather, a prior will should be revoked by an express revocation clause. An example of a revocation clause was seen in **Chapter 4**. It is generally insufficient to write, 'This is my last will.' Rather, the revocation clause must stipulate something along the lines of, 'I hereby revoke all my previous wills and codicils and declare this to be my last will.' In the case of *Re Hawksley's Settlement* [1934] Ch 384, a testator executed a will in 1922. She then wrote 'Cancelled' over it and executed a new will in 1927, which referred to the 'cancelled will'. The court said that this, on its own, was not sufficient to expressly revoke the 1922 will (though most of the 1922 will was revoked by implication, which is discussed below).

All professionally drafted wills are likely to include an express revocation clause. Although s 9 of the Wills Act 1837 does not require a will to include a date, it is good practice to date the will, to avoid confusion in case an executor finds several undated wills, each containing a revocation clause. Even if the testator is preparing their first will, it is still good practice to include a revocation clause (even though there is nothing to revoke), again, to avoid any confusion – the executor might not know that this is the first and only will executed by the testator.

A later will does revoke a former will by implication, but only insofar as there are inconsistencies between them. It is a matter of construction (interpretation) whether the later will or codicil is inconsistent with the former and thereby revokes it (*Hearle v Hicks* (1832) 1 Cl & F 20, 6 ER 823).

In the case of *Re Bund* [1929] 2 Ch 455, the testator executed a will, leaving his real and personal property on trust for the benefit of his sister, for the duration of her life, and thereafter to other beneficiaries. He later executed a codicil, leaving parts of his freehold and certain household items on trust for his stepdaughter, for the duration of her life. The question was whether the codicil had revoked the will. If not, the court would have to determine the extent of the sister's and the stepdaughter's respective interests in the estate. The codicil was much more restrictive in its scope, and therefore did not revoke the will in its entirety. Rather, the stepdaughter was entitled to the parts of the freehold and other household items specifically mentioned. The sister was still entitled to the remainder of the estate, as per the original will.

The judge, Luxmoore J, identified a number of key rules. The will and the codicil(s) have to be read and constructed together. The codicil should interfere as little as possible with the will. This means a restrictive reading of the codicil. For example, if a will refers to both real and personal property, and a codicil just to real property, the codicil beneficiary is entitled only to the real property and the will beneficiary remains entitled to the personal property. The codicil beneficiary should only obtain the personal property if that is clearly intended from the words used.

The restrictive approach to revocation through implication highlights the need to have a proper express revocation clause in each new will.

6.2.2 Revocation by a document executed in accordance with s 9

A will can be revoked by another document, not in itself a will or codicil, but which has been executed like a will, ie complying with the requirements set out in s 9 of the Wills Act 1837.

In the case of *In the Goods of Durance* (1869-72) LR 2 P&D 406, a testator had executed a will. He later moved to Canada where he fell ill. He wrote a letter to his brother, asking the brother to burn the will. This letter was signed in the presence of two witnesses, who also signed the letter. The testator then died. The court decided that his will had been revoked through the letter.

6.2.3 Revocation by intentional destruction

A testator can revoke a will through destroying it. The destruction has to be intentional, that is to say, there has to be an intention to revoke the will. To be able to demonstrate intention, the courts have said that testamentary capacity is required (*Re Sabatini* (1969) 114 SJ 35). As a lifetime act, it is arguable that the Mental Capacity Act 2005 applies here to determine if mental capacity was present, though that has not been established by the courts.

It is clear from the case law that this is not an easy way in which to revoke a will. Given the importance of a will, the courts seem reluctant to find that a will has been revoked by destruction unless that is clearly the only rational decision.

Destruction is nonetheless broadly defined. Section 20 provides a good starting point, as it says: 'burning, tearing, or otherwise destroying'. Nonetheless, the document has to be destroyed. In the case of *Cheese v Lovejoy (No 2)* (1877) 2 PD 251, a testator crossed out parts of his will, wrote 'This is revoked' on it, and threw it into the trash. His maid picked it up and kept the document in the kitchen. The Court of Appeal held that the will had not been destroyed, nor did s 21 assist, since the words crossed out were still legible (hence, apparent) and the obliteration had not been done in the presence of two witnesses. Further, the Court of Appeal found that there was no intention to revoke; on the facts of the case, throwing the will into the trash seems to have been more symbolic, rather than a demonstration of a genuine intention to revoke.

In the case of *Hobbs v Knight* (1838) 1 Curt 768, 163 ER 267, a testator cut out his signature from his will, and the court held that this amounted to a valid revocation by destruction. This case was applied in *Re Adams (Deceased)* [1990] Ch 601. There, a testator used a pen to scratch out her and her witnesses' signatures, to the point that they were no longer apparent. Applying the 'no longer apparent' test from s 21 of the Wills Act 1837, the court found that the testator had revoked her will by destruction. Similarly, in the case of *In the Goods of Morton* (1887) 12 PD 141, a testator had scratched out her signature with a knife. Even though the paper itself was intact, the signature was gone, and the will was revoked.

If the will is successfully revoked, the revocation also applies to any formally executed copies that the testator might have (*Rickards v Mumford and Freemans* (1812) 2 Phil 23, 161 ER 1066). It is certainly possible for a testator to execute two copies of the will and leave one copy with a third party for safekeeping (it is common for law firms to store their clients' wills).

The will is not revoked if the destruction has not been completed. In the case of *Doe d Perkes v Perkes* (1820) 3 B & Ald 489, 106 ER 740, a testator became enraged at one of his beneficiaries. He took out his will and ripped it into four pieces. At this point, he was restrained by another person. The beneficiary apologised and the testator calmed down. He then put the four pieces together again, noting with approval that the text was still legible. The court found that the destruction had not been completed, given that the testator was restrained, and thereafter there was no intention to revoke. Further, if only a part of the will is destroyed, only that part of the will is revoked and the remainder is admitted into probate. In the case of *In the Goods of Woodward* (1869-72) LR 2 P& D 206, a testator had torn off the first eight lines of his will. The remainder of the will was held to be unrevoked.

The destruction has to be done with the intention to revoke. Tearing or cutting the will in and of itself is not sufficient. This is because documents can easily be lost or damaged by accident. The case of *Singh v Vozniak* [2016] EWHC 114 (Ch) is illustrative. A testator wrote a will in which he gave his estate to his grandchildren. The testator had a wife, who was not a beneficiary. The wife claimed that in April 2012, following a row between her and the testator, the testator tore up the will, stating that he was going to write a new one, with her as the beneficiary. The executors denied that any of this had happened, because even after April 2012, the testator kept saying that his grandchildren were his beneficiaries. The testator died in July 2012. The court rejected the claim that the will had been torn up; on the balance of probability, this was simply a claim invented by the wife, so that she could benefit through intestacy. The court also found that, if the will actually had been torn up as alleged, it had not been done with an intention to revoke, but merely with an intention to end the domestic row.

In *Singh v Vozniak*, the court did reiterate a general and important presumption. If a will is known to have been in the testator's possession before their death, but it cannot be found after their death, it is presumed to have been intentionally revoked. However, the court will determine, on a balance of probability, whether the will has been intentionally revoked or if it has been lost or destroyed by accident or carelessness. The Privy Council in the case of *Welch v Phillips* (1836) 1 Moore 299, 12 ER 828 said that the presumption of an intentional revocation is 'founded on good sense; for it is highly reasonable to suppose that an instrument of so much importance would be carefully preserved'. However, in the case of *Rowe v Clarke* [2005] EWHC 3068 (Ch), the court rebutted the presumption of an intentional revocation by finding that, most likely, it was the testator's general carelessness as to his property that was at fault for the will going missing. There was no intention to revoke.

Singh v Vozniak and *Rowe v Clarke* also confirm another rule, a so-called presumption against fraudulent abstraction.

key terminology

Fraudulent abstraction: A fraudulent abstraction occurs where one party knowingly destroys a will after the testator has died, with the aim of thereby benefiting through intestacy or an earlier will.

The case of *Finch v Finch* (1867) LR 1 P&D 371 is illustrative, even though later judgments have argued that the judge misapplied the rule (consider the comments in *Allan v Morrison* [1900] AC 604 and *Sykes v Sykes* (1907) 23 TLR 747). A father had a will, leaving everything to his daughter, to the exclusion of his son. Both daughter and son knew that the father kept the will in his bedside cabinet. The father died. In the morning, the daughter witnessed the son leaving the father's room, apparently hiding something under his coat. Later, the will was not found in the cabinet, and the son challenged his sister to find the will if she wanted to inherit anything. On the facts, the presumption against fraudulent abstraction should have been rebutted – clearly, the son had removed and destroyed the will. (Instead, the judge, for some reason, asked the son to disprove the existence of the will – a near impossibility; the daughter was successful at trial because the son did not attend to give evidence.) Today, it is for the claimant alleging that a will has been fraudulently removed to prove that has happened, on the balance of probability. In *Finch*, the daughter had done so, and the case should have been decided on that evidence alone.

If the will has been destroyed and the destruction was intentional, then the will is treated as revoked. If the testator had made an earlier will, that earlier will is admitted into probate. If not, the testator has died intestate.

6.2.4 Conditional revocation

A testator can also conditionally revoke a will. This means that the will is only revoked if a particular condition is met. Otherwise, the will remains valid. Four examples illustrate the principle.

example 1

In the case of *Re Carey* (1977) 121 SJ 173, a testator had a will, leaving everything to his sister-in-law. However, the testator did not own anything, and he stated that he was destroying his will because he had nothing to leave. Then, the testator's sister died, leaving him £4,000. When the testator died, his original will could not be found; however, a copy was admitted into probate. This was because, on the facts, he had only revoked his will because he had nothing to leave to the beneficiary; once he had inherited the £4,000, the situation changed.

example 2

In the case of *In the Estate of Southerden* [1925] P 177, a testator had a will leaving everything to his wife. He then burnt the will, on the assumption that his wife would anyway inherit everything through intestacy. This was a misunderstanding of the then rules of intestacy. On that basis, the court found that the will had only been conditionally revoked, and since the condition had not been met, the will was admitted into probate.

example 3

In the case of *Re Jones (Deceased)* [1976] Ch 200, a testator destroyed her will, as she had changed her mind as to who should inherit her estate. However, she died before she was able to write a new will. The court decided that merely having an intention to write a new will was not sufficient to make the revocation conditional. The testator was therefore deemed to have revoked the will and she died intestate.

example 4

In the case of *Re Finnemore (Deceased)* [1991] 1 WLR 793, a testator wrote three successive wills. Each had an express revocation clause, thus revoking the earlier wills. In each of the three wills, the testator left his freehold estate and ¾ of the residue to a friend. However, the second and third wills were witnessed by the friend's husband. Therefore, under s 15 of the Wills Act 1837, the gifts to the friend in the second and third wills failed (s 15 is discussed further below). The question was, when the third will was admitted to probate, what happened to the freehold estate and the ¾ of the residue. The court found that the revocation was conditional on the clauses being valid. Thus, the friend could benefit under the first will (since the revocation in both the second and third wills was conditional). The remaining ¼ of the residue was left to the beneficiaries mentioned in the third will, since the disposition of the ¼ residue in the earlier wills had been validly revoked.

6.3 Revocation by marriage

A will is automatically revoked if the testator marries or enters into a civil partnership. This rule is set out in ss 18 and 18B of the Wills Act 1837. Professional will-drafters should advise their clients about this rule.

Some marriages are voidable, which means they can be nullified by either party petitioning the family court. The definition of what marriages are voidable is set out in s 12 of the Matrimonial Causes Act (MCA) 1973. It includes marriages that are not consummated due to lack of capacity or the refusal of one party; marriages entered into where one party has a communicable STI; marriages entered into where one party is already pregnant by a third party; and a few other circumstances. Where a person enters into a voidable marriage, their will is revoked. For example, in the case of *Re Roberts* [1978] 1 WLR 653, a testator got married, which revoked his will. The will-beneficiary sought to admit the will to probate, on the basis that the testator had lacked the requisite mental capacity to marry, and that the marriage therefore was voidable. The court found that the will had been revoked.

Some marriages are void. That means they are unlawful and have no legal effect at all. The definition of what constitutes a void marriage is set out in s 11 of the MCA 1973. It includes marriages between close relatives or where one party is under the age of 16. A void marriage does not revoke a will. For example, in the case of *Mette v Mette* (1859) 1 Sw & Tr 416, 164 ER 792, a widowed man wrote a will and thereafter married his half-blood sister-in-law. This was an unlawful marriage in England, on the ground of 'consanguinity', ie marriage within a family (though permitted in their home country, Frankfurt am Main (then a city state, now part of the German Federation)). This did not revoke his will.

The rationale for this rule is that a void marriage never legally existed and so has no effect on the testator's existing will. A voidable marriage, however, is legally valid and is only voided if one party petitions the court to end the marriage. Accordingly, as a valid marriage, it does revoke the testator's will.

The exception to the rule is now found in s 18(3). The exception was first created by s 177 of the Law of Property Act 1925, and was later inserted into s 18 when the Wills Act was amended by the Administration of Justice Act 1982. Older cases will therefore refer to the Law of Property Act. The exception says that a will is not revoked by marriage if it had been written in contemplation of marriage or civil partnership to a particular person and the testator intended the will to remain valid.

The will has to be made in contemplation of an actual marriage to a particular person. It is not sufficient to be thinking about marriage in abstract. In the case of *Sallis v Jones* [1936] P 43, a man wrote a will, stating that it was written 'in contemplation of marriage'. A few months later he proposed to his partner and they later married. The court found that the will had been revoked as it was not written in contemplation of an actual marriage. At best, the testator was hoping that his partner would agree to his intended proposal. This outcome was replicated in the case of *Court v Despallieres* [2009] EWHC 3340 (Ch), [2010] 2 All ER 451. A testator wrote a will, declaring in cl 2 that 'this, my last Will and Testament shall not be revoked by neither subsequent marriage, Civil Union Partnership nor adoption'. The court found that the will was revoked when the testator entered into a civil partnership. There was nothing in the wording of cl 2 that suggested that the will was written in contemplation of an impending civil partnership to a particular person.

In the case of *Pilot v Gainfort* [1931] P 103, a testator wrote a will leaving his entire estate to a woman he referred to as his wife. They later married. The court found that the will had not been revoked, as it was made in contemplation of an upcoming marriage to that particular person. This outcome has been challenged, as there are many instances of people referring to their partners as 'wife' or 'husband' without being married and without necessarily contemplating a marriage to that person (see Megarry J's observations in *Re Coleman (Deceased)* [1976] Ch 1).

In the case of *Re Coleman (Deceased)*, a testator wrote a will leaving his freehold and some particular property to his fiancée, but he left the residue to other beneficiaries. He later married the fiancée. The court found that the will had been revoked. This was because the will as a whole had not been written in contemplation of marriage; only the freehold and some gifts were given to the fiancée. In the case of *Re Langston* [1953] P 100, a testator left his entire estate to his fiancée, and the court found that the will had not been revoked, suggesting that using the word fiancée was sufficient to show that the testator was contemplating an intended marriage to that particular person. *Re Coleman* is therefore distinguished on the facts, since that will only left a part of the estate to the fiancée, and it was therefore not a will written in contemplation of marriage; it was merely a will which included some gifts to the fiancée.

These cases all appear to be very fact-specific. The only rule that can be stated with certainty is that s 18(3) applies where the testator is about to marry or enter into a civil partnership with a particular person. It has to actually be about to happen; it cannot be something hoped or wished for.

6.4 Revival

As noted, people change their minds. This is why they are allowed to change and revoke their wills. What happens if a testator has executed a will, then changed their mind and revoked it, but then changes their mind again? The law does actually provide an answer to this. If a will has been revoked, a testator is allowed to revive it, namely bring it back to life as a valid and enforceable will. This is provided for in s 22 of the Wills Act 1837. The testator must execute the document again, complying with the requirements in s 9 of the Wills Act 1837. The will can also be revived through a codicil, if an intention to revive the will is clearly stated in the codicil.

In the case of *In the Goods of Steele* (1865-69) LR 1 P&D 575, the court found that there are three ways in which a will can be revived, in addition to re-executing the document. Either an express intention to revive is found in a codicil, or the codicil disposes of property in a way which is inconsistent with any intention other than to revive the primary will, or there is sufficient surrounding evidence to prove an intention to revive. Nonetheless, it appears that if the will has been physically destroyed, it cannot be revived, because s 9 requires the will to be in writing (*Rogers v Goodenough* (1862) 2 Sw & Tr 342, 164 ER 1028). In that case, the will had been burnt and the court held that it had not been validly revived by a later codicil.

In the case of *Re Davis (Deceased)* [1952] P 279, a testator wrote a will, leaving everything to his girlfriend. The will was revoked when he married his girlfriend. Having learnt about its automatic revocation through marriage, the testator made a note on the envelope containing the will that the beneficiary was now his wife. The note on the envelope was witnessed, in accordance with s 9. Using the third of the three revival methods identified in *In the Goods of Steele*, the court found that the handwritten note on top of the envelope showed a sufficient intention to revive the will, and it was admitted into probate.

In the case of *Hoare Trustees v Jaques* [2008] EWHC 2022 (Ch), a testator executed a will and later a codicil. She then executed a second will, expressly revoking the first will and its codicil. Later on, she executed a second codicil. This second codicil referred to her first will, and made some changes to its terms. These were terms not included in the second will. The court found that the second codicil had revived the first will, with the amendments included in the codicil, and the second codicil therefore revoked the second will. The first will, together with the two codicils, was admitted into probate.

Date	Action	Effect
1999	T executes the 1999 Will	The 1999 Will is valid
2000	T executes the 2000 Codicil to the 1999 Will	The 1999 Will is valid, as amended by the 2000 Codicil
2000	T executes a 2000 Will, expressly revoking the 1999 Will and the 2000 Codicil	The 1999 Will is revoked, and the 2000 Will is valid
2004	T executes a 2004 Codicil referring to the 1999 Will, making changes to terms not mentioned in the 2000 Will	The 1999 Will and 2000 Codicil are revived, with a clear intention to revoke the 2000 Will

The earlier case of *In the Goods of Chilcott* [1897] P 223 had similar facts. A codicil, executed after a second will, revived the first will. However, in *Chilcott* there was nothing in the drafting which suggested that the second will had been revoked. Therefore both wills and the codicil were admitted into probate together. If necessary, there could be a later hearing to construct the combined terms.

Each of these cases will turn on the particular drafting of each document and what intentions can be obtained from that drafting. What has to be clear is an intention to revive an earlier will which has been revoked. The revived will takes effect from the date of revival (Wills Act 1837, s 34). This can be relevant as the identity of beneficiaries is decided based on the date of execution.

6.5 Failure of gifts

In an existing will, there are likely to be a few gifts, perhaps to different beneficiaries. Examples of gifts were seen in the sample will in **Chapter 4**, which you can quickly revisit if necessary. Because life moves on after the will is executed, there are circumstances in which those gifts will fail. If a gift has failed, the intended beneficiary will not be entitled to the gift. This section of the chapter looks at a number of key reasons why gifts fail and outlines the legal response to those situations. The following failures will be looked at:

* failure under s 15 of the Wills Act 1837;

- failure due to divorce or dissolution of a civil partnership;
- lapse;
- failure due to the testator not being allowed to dispose of the property;
- ademption;
- abatement;
- void for uncertainty;
- void for breaching the perpetuity rule;
- Forfeiture Act 1982.

The law provides different justifications as to why gifts fail for each of these circumstances. Unlike amendments and revocations, which are done deliberately by the testator, a failure of a gift is unlikely to be what the testator intended. Rather, the gift fails because of particular legal rules or changes in circumstances which mean that the gift is no longer permissible or possible. It is important for a solicitor, advising on the execution of a will, to explain this to the testator. Unfortunately, with homemade wills, ignorance of the law might produce unfair outcomes and disappointed beneficiaries. This is why the law has to justify these failures.

6.5.1 Failure under s 15 of the Wills Act 1837

Section 15 is, in many ways, an extension of the formality requirements under s 9. Section 9 requires that the execution of the will is witnessed by at least two witnesses. The witnesses are there to ensure that the testator is signing the will freely and is not being subjected to external pressure, such as undue influence. They can also provide evidence to this effect, and as to the testator's testamentary capacity, to court when the will is submitted to probate.

The witnesses therefore serve a very important function. Section 15 is a necessary extension of this. Section 15 says that any gift in a will to a witness or to a witness's spouse or civil partner is void. It is important to emphasise that the will itself remains valid; it is merely the gift to the witness or their spouse/civil partner that fails. All other beneficiaries are entitled to inherit as per the will. Without s 15, the risk is that a witness, desiring to inherit under the will, decides to testify in court that the execution of the will was valid or that the testator had testamentary capacity, even if neither of those statements are true. Section 15 emphasises the need for witnesses to be independent and impartial; they should have no personal interest in whether the will is found valid or not.

At the moment, s 15 only encompasses a witness and their spouse or civil partner. It therefore excludes other people close to the witness, such as their cohabitants, fiancé(e)s, or close family and relatives. The Law Commission in its 2017 Consultation has suggested the idea of extending s 15 to also encompass these other people (Law Com 231, [5.58–5.59]). This is because, if a will benefits a witness's cohabitant or parent, the witness may still be inclined to swear to the will's validity, even if that is not true. Given the falling marriage rates and increase in cohabitation, it seems sensible to extend the rule as the Law Commission suggests.

There are some exceptions to s 15. First, if the witness signed as the fiancé(e) of a beneficiary, and later married the beneficiary, s 15 does not apply. This current exception seems to be completely at odds with the purpose of s 15 and, in itself, suggests that the scope of s 15 should be extended as proposed by the Law Commission.

A further exception is that of superfluous witnesses. A new rule was introduced by s 1 of the Wills Act 1968, applying to testators dying after the Act came into force that year. If there are more than two witnesses, and there is a gift to one of them, the gift remains valid, because that witness is superfluous. Section 9 of the Wills Act 1837 only requires two witnesses for the will to be valid, so if there are three witnesses, and one of them is also a beneficiary, there is no reason for that third witness to lose their entitlement. However, s 1 does not apply if two witnesses are beneficiaries and only one is not. Then both of them would lose out on their inheritance. There have to be two independent witnesses.

So, the starting point is that if a beneficiary witnesses the execution of a will, their gift fails. However, if the gift is confirmed in a later will, or if the will is republished or revived, or if the gift is confirmed in a codicil, which is executed with different witnesses, then the gift to the beneficiary remains valid. This is because the gift is confirmed in the later document, which is validly executed with two independent witnesses (*Re Trotter* [1899] 1 Ch 764). Similarly, if a beneficiary in a will acts as a witness to a later codicil, and the codicil does not affect the will gift to them, that gift remains valid. In the case of *Gurney v Gurney* (1855) 3 Drew 208, 61 ER 882, a residuary beneficiary witnessed a codicil. The codicil revoked various specific gifts. The consequence was that the residue became bigger. Nonetheless, the beneficiary was entitled to the residue, as he had not witnessed the document giving him that gift (namely the will).

Section 15 does not apply if the beneficiary signs the will other than as a witness. This is always a question of fact, and the beneficiary may be asked to give evidence to court, explaining why they signed the will. In the case of *In the Goods of Smith* (1889) 15 PD 2, a beneficiary signed the will to confirm the contents, not as an attesting witness (there were two independent witnesses who had already signed). The beneficiary was entitled to inherit. The same outcome was reached in *Kitcat v King* [1930] P 266, where two beneficiaries signed a codicil 'to make it legal'; they were entitled to inherit since there were two independent witnesses and the beneficiaries did not sign with the intention of witnessing the codicil. In the case of *In the Goods of Sharman* (1865-69) LR 1 P&D 661, one of the witnesses, ignorant of the law, thought that it would be good if the sole beneficiary also signed the will, believing this to be the best course of action. On that evidence, the court ignored the beneficiary's signature and she was entitled to inherit. The same occurred in the case of *In the Estate of Bravda* [1968] 1 WLR 479. A testator, having made a homemade will which was signed by two witnesses, asked the two beneficiaries to sign as well, as this would 'make it stronger'. Again, the court overlooked the beneficiaries' signatures and they were entitled to inherit.

Section 15 also does not apply if the witness benefits only indirectly. The case of *Re Ray's Will Trusts* [1936] Ch 520 is illustrative. The testator was a Franciscan nun, residing in a nunnery. She wrote a will, leaving her property to whoever should be abbess of the nunnery when she died. The will was signed by two fellow nuns. One of those witnesses was then elected abbess and served in that capacity when the testator died. The court held that the gift was valid, since it was a gift to the community (to be administered by the abbess), rather than a personal gift to the abbess.

If the will is prepared by a solicitor, they have a duty of care to warn the testator about the effect of s 15. If they do not, the solicitor may be liable to compensate a witness/beneficiary for the value of the gift they should have received (*Ross v Caunters* [1980] Ch 297) (the rule therein has been clarified by the House of Lords in *White v Jones* [1995] 2 AC 207 – see **Chapter 16**).

6.5.2 Failure due to divorce or dissolution of a civil partnership

If a testator has died after 1995, the applicable rules are those set out in ss 18A and 18C of the Wills Act 1837, introduced by the Law Reform (Succession) Act 1995. They deal, respectively, with the consequences of divorce or dissolution of a civil partnership being made final (by the court issuing a decree absolute). A spouse or civil partner is to be treated as having died on the day of the divorce or dissolution of the civil partnership. This means that they lose any entitlement under a will. The property will instead pass either to a substitute beneficiary or it will pass outside the will on a partial intestacy (see **Chapter 8**).

Let us take an example. Say that Sarah writes a will leaving her estate to her husband Roger for the duration of his life and thereafter to their child Blake. If Sarah divorces Roger, he is treated as having died on the day of the divorce being made final. Therefore, when Sarah dies, Blake will inherit her estate. Alternatively, Sarah writes a will leaving all of her money to her sister Rebecca and gives Roger the residue. If Sarah divorces Roger, he is treated as having died on the day of the divorce. Therefore, when Sarah dies, Rebecca will inherit Sarah's money. The residue is now undisposed of. It passes outside the will on intestacy and will therefore go to Sarah's child, Blake.

Between 1982 and 1995, a different s 18A was in effect. It held that a gift would lapse on a divorce. This was deemed unsatisfactory. In the example above, if Sarah left her estate for life to her husband Roger and thereafter to their child Blake, and she later divorced Roger, the gift would fail altogether. Blake would not be entitled, as held in *Re Sinclair (Deceased)* [1985] Ch 446. In *Sinclair*, a testator gave his estate to his wife, or if she predeceased him, to a charity. The testator and his wife divorced. On his death, the charity sought to inherit but was unable to do so, since the gift had lapsed in its entirety. Rather, the testator's estate passed according to the intestacy rules. After the 1995 reform and the new s 18A, the charity would be entitled, which seems a more satisfactory outcome.

Sections 18A and 18C do not apply if a contrary intention is apparent in the will. The testator can clearly state in the will that even if there is a divorce or dissolution of a civil partnership, their former spouse/civil partner should still inherit as per the will.

6.5.3 Lapse

A gift can lapse in a number of different circumstances. This means that the gift itself fails. The property in question will generally pass outside the will on intestacy.

An example of lapse is if a beneficiary predeceases the testator. The gift fails because the beneficiary is no longer alive when the testator dies and cannot therefore inherit. In the case of *Re Bailey (Deceased)* [1951] Ch 407, a testator left her residue to her trustee on trust, to pay the income to her daughter, and then to give the capital to her sister-in-law if the sister-in-law survived the daughter; otherwise the capital should go to the testator's nephew. Both the daughter and the sister-in-law predeceased the testator. The court had to determine what should happen to the residue. The court found that the gift had failed when the sister-in-law, having met the condition of surviving the daughter, then predeceased the testator. It could therefore not be saved for the nephew. Rather, the residue passed on intestacy. The outcome would have been different if the sister-in-law had died before the daughter. Then the nephew, as the alternative, would have taken in lieu of the daughter.

Re Bailey followed on from the decision in *Re Graham* [1929] 2 Ch 127. A testator left a life interest in her property to her parents, and thereafter her estate would pass to her husband, or, if he predeceased her parents, to her husband's children. The husband survived the testator's parents but predeceased the testator. Since the condition was not met, the husband's children could not inherit. The testator's estate passed on intestacy.

Whether a gift lapses because a condition is not met or the beneficiary predeceases the testator is a matter of construction. In the case of *Re Bowen* [1949] Ch 67, with similar facts, the court interpreted the will in favour of the alternative beneficiaries. There was a life interest to the testator's mother, and thereafter the property would go to the testator's uncle, but if the uncle predeceased the mother, the property would go to the testator's cousins. The uncle survived the mother but predeceased the testator. Nonetheless, the cousins were able to inherit. *Re Graham* was distinguished based on the wording of the respective wills.

An exception to this rule is found in s 33 of the Wills Act 1837. If the testator leaves a gift to their child or further descendants, and the beneficiary predeceased the testator, leaving children of their own, then those children will inherit, rather than the gift lapsing. So, assume that Sarah leaves her entire estate to her son Blake, and Blake has his own son, Ronan. Then, Blake dies. Later, Sarah dies. Ordinarily, under the lapse doctrine, the gift would fail, and it would pass on intestacy. However, using s 33, Ronan would inherit in Blake's stead. Assume, instead, that Blake has three children, Ronan, Zara and Nadine. Here, the three children would all inherit, *per stirpes*, that is to say, in equal shares.

key terminology

***Per stirpes*:** in practice, *per stirpes* means that children of a parent take equally if the parent predeceased the testator. For a discussion of the rules, see the Privy Council decision in *Sammut v Manzi* [2008] UKPC 58, [2009] 1 WLR 1834.

Section 33 can be disapplied by the will, though this must be clearly stated. For example, in *Hives v Machin* [2017] EWHC 1414 (Ch), a will left the residue in equal shares to the testator's three children who were living at the time of the testator's death. One son pre-deceased the testator, leaving children of his own. The wording of the will, leaving the residue in equal shares to the children who survived the testator, suggested that the residue should be divided equally between the two surviving sons. However, the court found that the wording used was insufficient to displace s 33, meaning that the grandchildren of the son who pre-deceased the testator could take his one-third share of the residue.

Where a gift comes with a contingency (that is to say, the beneficiary must satisfy some criterion before they can inherit), that contingency applies equally to the beneficiary's children, if they seek to inherit under s 33 (*Naylor v Barlow* [2019] EWHC 1565 (Ch)).

6.5.4 Failure of a gift – no entitlement to dispose of property through a will

A gift will also fail if the testator did not have the right to dispose of it through a will. This can occur when the property has been jointly owned with another person. The details of joint ownership are set out in, for example, Glover and Campbell-Pilling, *Land Law*, 2nd edn (Hall & Stott Publishing, 2021). Only a summary is provided here.

Any property can be owned by two or more people together. The co-owners will always hold the property on trust for themselves. The legal title must be held as a joint tenancy (Law of Property Act 1925, s 1(6)). The equitable interest can be held either as joint tenants or as tenants in common. The key distinguishing feature of a joint tenancy is that each party has a 100% interest. In a tenancy in common, each person has an individual equitable interest in the property. In a joint tenancy, where there are no individual shares but everyone has a 100% interest in the property, the doctrine of survivorship applies. The survivorship doctrine states that on the death of one joint tenant, the remaining joint tenant simply continues on with their pre-existing 100% interest. As such, no title or interest passes from the deceased. Following key decisions such as *Jones v Kernott* [2011] UKSC 53, [2012] 1 AC 776, the law presumes that co-owners of private property (holding legal title on joint tenancy) are equitable joint tenants (the situation for commercial property is more ambiguous, but an equitable joint tenancy might now be presumed there as well – see *Marr v Collie* [2017] UKPC 17, [2017] 3 WLR 1507). With the survivorship doctrine in place, a co-owner can therefore not gift that property to anyone. If the equitable interest is held as tenants in common, where each person has an individual equitable interest, the equitable interest can be passed to someone else through a will or on intestacy. It must be emphasised that only the equitable interest, held as a tenancy in common, can pass. The legal title is always held on joint tenancy and cannot pass (Law of Property Act 1925, s 36(2)). Any gift of property held on a joint tenancy in equity will therefore fail as it is legally impossible for it to pass to a beneficiary.

6.5.5 Ademption

The date a will speaks from was discussed at **5.2.6**. Section 24 of the Wills Act 1837 says that when it comes to property, the will speaks from the date of death. The beneficiaries are entitled to the property that the testator owned on that day. When it comes to general gifts (such as 'my money', 'my shares', 'my jewellery'), the rule is very straightforward and easy to apply. However, there is a problem with specific gifts.

Let us go back to the example of Anders leaving his car to his friend Bert. Anders writes in his will that he leaves 'his car' to Bert. At the date of execution, Anders owned a Volvo, but he then sold it and bought a Land Rover. When Anders dies, Bert will inherit the Land Rover. This is because it is a general gift and Anders did own a car on the day he died. However, what happens if Anders sells the Volvo, but does not buy a new car. In this situation, the gift has adeemed. Bert is not entitled to anything. Most importantly, Bert is not entitled to the proceeds of sale.

It was also said at **5.2.6** that s 24 can be displaced through drafting. Anders could, in his will, gift 'the car that I now own' or 'the car that I currently own' to Bert. This will be interpreted by the court as referring to the car Anders owned on the date of execution, namely the Volvo (*Re Whitby* [1944] Ch 210). If Anders sold the Volvo, the gift would adeem. Even if Anders later on bought a Land Rover, Bert would not be entitled to it. This is a matter of construction and each will must be looked at with reference to its particular language, as explained in **Chapter 5**.

Ademption does not depend on the testator having any intention to make a change to the subject matter or any intention to disentitle the beneficiary. In *Rokkan v Rokkan* [2021] EWHC 481 (Ch), the testator had gifted her son all the money in a bank account she held with a Norwegian bank (where the testator had lived). After she executed the will, she closed the account and moved the money to a bank in Wales (where the testator now lived). After the testator's death, it was established that she did not have mental capacity at the time she made the money transfers, using the MCA 2005 test. The beneficiary argued that this meant that there was no ademption and that he should be entitled to the money in the Welsh bank account. However, the court held that the gift had adeemed, despite the lack of mental capacity, as the Norwegian bank account identified in the will was closed and ademption did not depend on intention.

Ademption also occurs where the testator, having gifted property in his will, thereafter enters into a contract to sell the property, even if the testator has not completed the sale at the time of his death (*Re Edwards* [1958] Ch 168). Because there is a contract for sale, the purchaser can apply for specific performance against the estate, to complete the sale. Where land is concerned, specific performance is always granted. In the case of *Watts v Watts* (1873) LR 17 Eq 217, the court held that the beneficiary of a gift of land, which was subject to a contract for sale, was entitled to the rent collected from the tenant between the date of the testator's death and the date the purchase was completed. However, since the gift had adeemed due to the sale, the beneficiary was not entitled to the proceeds of sale.

Ademption does not occur when the will is executed after the contract for sale has been signed. In the case of *Re Calow* [1928] Ch 710, a testator signed a contract to sell his land. He thereafter gifted the land in his will. On his death, the court held that the beneficiary was entitled to the proceeds of sale. This was because the will had been executed after the contract for sale had been signed; the testator obviously knew that the land was being sold, and thus clearly intended the beneficiary to take the proceeds of sale.

Ademption does not occur where there is a simple change in name or some other inconsequential change to the property. The cases of *Re Clifford* [1912] 1 Ch 29 and *Re Leeming* [1912] 1 Ch 828 can be considered together. In both cases, testators owned shares in companies and gifted these shares in their wills. The companies then underwent change (in *Clifford* the company changed its name and in *Leeming* the company reconstructed itself) and issued new shares (in *Clifford* the existing shares were subdivided so that each shareholder held four smaller shares and in *Leeming* new shares were issued by the reconstructed company). In each case, the court found that the new shares were, in substance, the same as the old, and the gift was valid. In the case of *Re Dorman* [1994] 1 WLR 282, a testator left money in a specific bank account. Later, the testator closed that account and moved all the money to a new account, which had a better interest rate (though compare this case to *Rokkan v Rokkan* (above), where *Re Dorman* was not mentioned in the judgment). Again, the court found that the new bank account was, in substance, the same as the old, and the gift was held to be valid.

key rule

Section 24 of the Wills Act 1837 provides the following rule:

- **Property:** property is defined on the date of death (unless expressly stated otherwise).
- **Beneficiaries:** beneficiaries are defined on the date of execution (unless expressly stated otherwise).

6.5.6 Abatement

Abatement occurs when the property in the estate is required for the payment of the estate's debts. This will be looked at in more detail in **Chapter 13**. A short summary is set out here.

Where a testator dies leaving debts, these debts have to be paid by the PR, using the assets (if any) contained in the estate. Common debts will include a mortgage on the testator's home, outstanding tax liabilities, utility bills, credit card debts and other contractual debts (if, for instance, the testator had bought a car or computer on credit and was paying it off in monthly instalments). The PR must also pay funeral expenses and other administrative expenses associated with probate. This means that even though a testator leaves their house, car, cash and other personal property to specific beneficiaries, those beneficiaries may be disappointed because the property is needed to repay existing debts.

Which assets are used for the payment of debts depends on whether the estate was solvent (there are enough assets to pay all debts) or insolvent (there are insufficient assets to pay all debts). The payment of debts for solvent estates is governed by s 34(3) and Sch 1, Pt II of the Administration of Estates Act 1925. The payment of debts for insolvent estates is governed by s 231 of the Insolvency Act 1986 and the Administration of Insolvent Estates of Deceased Persons Order 1986 (SI 1986/1999).

The beneficiaries of an estate, whether testate or intestate, may therefore lose out on the property they have been promised. The payment of probate expenses and the testator's debts have priority. If the estate is solvent, the beneficiaries will receive a payout subject to further rules on priority. If the estate is insolvent, the beneficiaries are unlikely to receive anything.

6.5.7 Void for uncertainty

A testamentary trust can be void on the grounds of uncertainty. This is a topic that is generally covered in an Equity & Trusts module and a more detailed explanation of these rules may be found in, for example, Farran and Davies, *Equity & Trusts*, 2nd edn (Hall and Stott Publishing, 2019). A testamentary trust, like any trust, has to satisfy the so-called three certainties: *Knight v Knight* (1840) 3 Beav 148, 49 ER 58. In that case, a testator gave his estate to his brother, writing further that: 'I trust to the liberality of my successors to reward any others of my old servants and tenants according to their deserts, and to their justice in continuing the estates in the male succession.' In short, he hoped that his brother would pay a fair share to the servants employed in the family home and, after his death, leave the estate to male descendants within the family. The court found that the words used were not sufficiently imperative so as to bind the brother. The brother was therefore free to do whatever he wanted with the inheritance.

The three certainties in trust law are certainty of intention, certainty of subject matter and certainty of objects/beneficiaries.

6.5.7.1 Intention

There must be evidence of a clear intention to create a trust and to bind the trustee to the terms of the trust. Precatory words, such as 'I hope' or 'I desire', are generally not sufficient to give rise to a trust. It is generally straightforward to prove intention for a testamentary trust, given that it has been written down in the will, but the language must still be imperative. As seen in *Knight v Knight*, the use of precatory words meant that the brother inherited the estate free from any restrictions; he did not take the property as a trustee himself.

6.5.7.2 Subject matter

It must be sufficiently clear what property is meant to be held on trust (*Re London Wine Co (Shippers)* [1986] PCC 121). If a testator leaves 'a fair share of my estate' to a particular person, the gift fails due to uncertainty. It is not clear what is meant by a fair share. In the case of *Palmer v Simmonds* (1854) 2 Drew 221, 61 ER 704, the testator left her residue to her nephew, asking him, if he died without heirs, to leave the 'bulk' of her estate to specified individuals. The court found that this was uncertain, and the nephew took the residue absolutely. In the case *Re Golay's Will Trust* [1965] 1 WLR 969, a testator granted a 'reasonable income' to a beneficiary. The court found that this was sufficiently certain, as the court could objectively ascertain what was reasonable. The judgment, however, did not specify what it thought reasonable income was, on the particular facts of that case. In the case of *Re Steel (Deceased)* [1979] Ch 218, the testator left cash gifts to 25 beneficiaries, ranging from £25 to £250. The will then stated that the residue was to be divided amongst the beneficiaries who had received a 'small amount'. The court saved the residue gift, assuming that the testator meant all of the 25 beneficiaries. This was because the residue was £14,000, and if it had been divided only between the beneficiaries gifted, say, £25, they would have received a sum significantly larger than those gifted £250. This was probably not what the testator intended.

In the unfortunate case of *Boyce v Boyce* (1849) 16 Sim 476, 60 ER 959, the testator left his houses to his two daughters. One of them, Maria, was to choose the house that she wanted. The second, Charlotte, would then receive all the others. Maria died before the testator and had therefore not made a choice. Since it was not clear which houses Charlotte was meant to get, the gift failed entirely. A slightly different example is the case of *Re Knapton* [1941] Ch 428. The testator owned a number of houses and left one each to her nieces, nephews and four other people. Other than one each, it was not clear which freehold was meant for which beneficiary. Drawing on old Roman law principles, the judge held that if the beneficiaries could not sort it out themselves, they would have to draw lots to determine who got to choose a freehold title first. It is an unusual case, but the outcome is pragmatic and based on the fact that much of succession law derives from ecclesiastical law, which in turn was based on Roman law.

6.5.7.3   Objects/beneficiaries

Thirdly, it must be certain who the beneficiaries are (*Re Baden's Deed Trusts (No 2)* [1973] Ch 9). In *Re Baden*, the court found that terms such as 'relatives' and 'dependants' were sufficiently certain. Questions remain about other general descriptors. A gift of property to 'my friends' or 'my associates' is unlikely to be successful, because it is not clear to whom the testator is referring. The testator is allowed to designate a person to make decisions on whether a claimant is or is not within the class of beneficiaries. In the case of *Re Tuck's Settlement Trusts* [1978] Ch 49, a trust required beneficiaries to be Jewish. The court said this was sufficiently certain, as it was possible to ask the Chief Rabbi to make a decision (based on Jewish law) as to whether a claimant met the requirements.

If any of the certainties are missing, no trust arises. The property in question either becomes an absolute gift to the beneficiary mentioned, such as in *Palmer v Simmonds*, or it goes back to the estate. The property then passes outside the will on intestacy.

6.5.8   Void for breaching the perpetuity rule

A testamentary trust can also fail if it breaches the perpetuity rule. The perpetuity rule says that a private trust cannot exist indefinitely (however, a charitable trust can); it has to come to an end within a specific period. After the introduction of the Perpetuities and Accumulations Act 2009, the perpetuity period is 125 years. Prior to that, the rules were rather more complex. For trusts created between 1964 and 2009, the perpetuity period was generally 80 years. For trusts created prior to 1964, the perpetuity period was generally measured in a life plus 21 years. The life chosen was often a Royal life. For example, a trust could run for the life of Prince Charles, plus 21 years. Whilst the current period is 125 years, the trust itself could specify a shorter timeframe.

However, if a testamentary trust reads, 'my residue to trustees to hold on trust and pay the income derived from it to my children and further descendants indefinitely', the trust will fail. To avoid the perpetuity period, testamentary trusts usually give a life interest to one person, and thereafter give the property absolutely to another on the life tenant's death. For instance, a will can leave 'my residue to my child for life and thereafter to my grandchild absolutely'. The child has the benefit of the residue for their life, and then the grandchild inherits absolute legal title when their parent dies.

6.5.9 Forfeiture Act 1982

English law has long recognised, as a matter of public policy, that a person cannot inherit if they have unlawfully killed the deceased. This rule is now set out in s 1 of the Forfeiture Act 1982. This rule extends to people who aid, abet, counsel or procure the unlawful killing of the deceased. The Forfeiture Act 1982 applies both to entitlements under wills and to an entitlement on intestacy.

The rationale for the rule is quite obvious, as no person should stand to gain from committing a crime. If a killer could inherit, it is certainly possible that some may be tempted to kill to speed up their inheritance. Sir Samuel Evans P stated, in *In the Estate of Crippen* [1911] P 108, that the 'human mind revolts at the very idea that any other doctrine could be possible'. Still, the fact is that human nature is unpredictable, and it is accepted that the application of the forfeiture rule may be unjust in some cases.

This has led to two exceptions. First, the court accepts that the forfeiture rule might not apply in some situations. This may include circumstances such as a suicide pact, where one party reneges and seeks to benefit from the party that committed suicide (*Dunbar v Plant* [1998] Ch 412). It may also include circumstances where the death is accidental and no criminal culpability arises. In such cases, the inheritance can go ahead without interference. Secondly, s 2 of the Forfeiture Act 1982 gives the court the power to grant relief from forfeiture in certain circumstances.

To begin with, s 5 of the 1982 Act says that where a person has been convicted of murdering the deceased, the forfeiture rule applies without exceptions. Where a person has otherwise unlawfully killed the deceased, such as through manslaughter, their inheritance is forfeited; however, s 2 gives them the right to apply to court for relief from forfeiture, which the court has discretion whether or not to grant. The test, set out in s 2(2), says that the court must consider 'the justice of the case' in the broadest sense, taking into account the conduct of the offender and the deceased, as well as any other facts that the court finds relevant.

Where a person is convicted in court of an unlawful killing, such as manslaughter, they have three months in which to make their application for relief (s 2(3)). In *Challen v Challen* [2020] EWHC 1330 (Ch), [2020] 3 WLR 440, the court held that 'conviction' meant the day the defendant was sentenced in court (noting, as a matter of criminal procedure, that the defendant may enter a guilty plea at a much earlier date).

Each case turns on its own facts, and a few recent examples can be given to illustrate the court's power to grant relief from forfeiture. The case of *Henderson v Wilcox* [2015] EWHC 3469 (Ch), [2016] 4 WLR 14 is illustrative of where the court declined to grant relief from the forfeiture rule. The offender was suffering from depression, learning disabilities and autism. He was convicted of manslaughter, having killed his mother in a violent assault. He was the sole beneficiary in his mother's will, which was now forfeited. The court declined to vary the forfeiture rule. Clearly, the absence of mental capacity is a relevant factor, but in this case, the offender had been declared mentally competent to stand trial and it was shown that he did understand what he was doing during the assault (indeed, there had been several earlier assaults on his mother). He had not pursued a defence of diminished responsibility at trial and the medical evidence was lacking.

The case of *Macmillan Cancer Support v Hayes* [2017] EWHC 3110 (Ch) is illustrative of where the court appropriately granted relief from the forfeiture rule. An elderly husband, suffering from serious illnesses, killed his wife, who also was suffering from a serious illness. It was, in essence, a so-called mercy killing. He then committed suicide. If the husband was allowed to inherit, then their combined estates would, under his will, pass to various charities, which is what both of them wanted. However, if the husband was not allowed to inherit (by an application of the forfeiture rule), the wife's estate would pass on intestacy to remote family in Australia. This is a clear example of where the forfeiture rule would not serve the public interest, and the court was right to grant relief from the forfeiture rule. One further point is important from this case. The husband, having committed suicide, was never charged with or convicted in court of murder. However, the absence of a criminal conviction is irrelevant; the forfeiture rule applies anyway once it has been shown (on the civil standard) that the offender unlawfully killed the deceased.

The case of *Challen v Challen* (above) received much press attention when it was decided, given the tragic underlying story. Sally Challen killed her husband in 2010 and was later convicted of his murder. An appeal was heard in 2019, which quashed the conviction and ordered a retrial, where the Crown accepted a plea of manslaughter on the basis of diminished responsibility. This was on the basis that Mrs Challen had suffered long-term domestic abuse through what the law now terms 'coercive control' on the part of her husband. In terms of the criminal law, the case opened a serious debate around the impact of domestic violence and the criminal culpability of people in Mrs Challen's circumstances who kill their abusers. In terms of the inheritance issue, the High Court granted relief from forfeiture. The judge did issue a general warning that anyone who kills their abuser as a result of coercive control could not expect automatic relief from forfeiture, but clearly such circumstances would, in general, weigh in favour of granting relief.

An unfortunate outcome was reached in *Re DWS (Deceased)* [2001] Ch 568. Two grandparents were killed by their son. They both died intestate, and ordinarily the son would inherit on intestacy. The intestacy rules further provided that if the son died before the grandparents, then the grandson would inherit instead. In this case, the son forfeited his inheritance. The grandson argued that he should therefore inherit. However, the court ruled against him, saying that the grandson could not inherit because the son had forfeited the inheritance. Instead, the estate passed to the grandfather's sister. This outcome was deemed to be unfair, as there was no obvious reason why the innocent grandson should not inherit just because the son had forfeited his inheritance.

As a result, a new rule was created through the Estates of Deceased Persons (Forfeiture Rule and Law of Succession) Act 2011. Where a person disclaims their interest (saying they do not want it) or forfeits their interest under the Forfeiture Act 1982, they are deemed to have died before the deceased. For wills, the rule is found in s 33A of the Wills Act 1837 and, for intestacy, the rule is found in s 46A of the Administration of Estates Act 1925. This rule is important as it helps the court determine who should inherit instead. Thus, today, in the *DWS* case, the grandson would inherit on intestacy.

6.5.10 Void for being a capricious gift

The court can invalidate a gift if it is capricious or otherwise nonsensical. In *Brown v Burdett* (1882) 21 Ch D 667, the testator ordered through a codicil that her house (save a few rooms in which her housekeeper would live) should be boarded up for 20 years, before being transferred to certain beneficiaries. The judge called the instructions 'useless', ignored the gift, and determined that the house instead passed on intestacy.

This power was explored by Mark Pawlowski in his article, 'Testamentary trusts and capricious testators' (2020) 26 Trusts & Trustees 222–26, where he refers to various examples from other jurisdictions. There are no other English examples and it is unlikely that many testators would make such peculiar gifts. There was no discussion of testamentary capacity in *Brown v Burdett*, though clearly such odd directions could raise suspicions about the testator's state of mind when executing the will (or, as in that case, a codicil).

6.6 Further reading

Law Commission, *Making a Will* (Consultation Paper 231, July 2017), Chs 10 (Ademption), 11 (Revocation).

summary

This chapter has covered the rules for amending wills, using s 21 of the Wills Act 1837. It has looked at how a will can be revoked under s 20 of the Wills Act 1837, and how a will is revoked by marriage or civil partnership under ss 18 and 18B of the Wills Act 1837. Finally, the chapter has looked at various reasons why a gift in a will might fail.

Mutual Wills

In **Chapters 2** through to **6**, the textbook has shown how one person can dispose of their property through a will. Everyone is entitled to write an individual will. However, many people enter into lifelong relationships and form families. They might want to enter into a joint agreement on how their property is to be disposed of, meaning that it is irrelevant which of them dies first. The outcome would be the same. Such arrangements have given rise to the doctrine of mutual wills.

This chapter will address the following issues:

- What is a mutual will?
- Why are mutual wills used?
- What are the problems associated with mutual wills?

7.1 The requirements for a mutual will

The doctrine of mutual wills differs somewhat from the rest of English succession law. As explained in **Chapter 1**, most of succession law was historically developed by the common law courts and the ecclesiastical courts, before it was all brought together into the Probate Court in 1857. Mutual wills, however, was a doctrine developed by equity. At its heart, therefore, lies the equitable notion of unconscionability.

The basic idea for the mutual wills doctrine is simple. Assume there is a family, consisting of a mother, father and a child. The mother and father each write a will, in which they give their entire estate to the survivor for life, and thereafter to the child. If the mother dies first, the father takes her entire estate and can use it for his lifetime, and when the father dies, both parents' estates pass to the child. The same happens in reverse if the father dies first.

The mutual wills doctrine may therefore seem like a good way of managing property within a family. In the scenario above, the child is guaranteed to inherit both of the estates when the surviving parent dies. There are, however, some problems. If the two parents have valid and enforceable mutual wills, the survivor is bound by the agreement to pass both the estates to the child. The survivor cannot change their mind. Reality, on the other hand, is not always that simple. The survivor may have genuine reasons to change their mind. They might remarry and have more children. They might get closely involved with a charity they want to benefit when they die. The survivor might genuinely want to benefit other people or organisations, such as a carer or a doctor. However, they cannot benefit any of these people, because they are bound by the mutual will. The end result is that mutual wills are not commonly used, and serious caution should be exercised before executing a mutual will.

Within a family, testators do, however, commonly execute so-called mirror wills. Mirror wills are simply wills that contain similar, if not identical, terms, but which are not formally mutual wills. Mirror wills can be revoked by each testator at any time, meaning that the survivor is not bound by the terms of it. For the reasons given above, a simple mirror will might therefore be advantageous.

There are two requirements needed to make a valid and enforceable mutual will. First, there has to be an agreement between the two testators about how they are to jointly dispose of their respective property. Secondly, the agreement has to be binding on both testators and they have to intend it to be binding. The consequence of the agreement being binding is that the survivor cannot change their mind but has to carry out the joint agreement. These two requirements will be expanded upon below.

7.1.1 There has to be an agreement between the testators

The first requirement is that the testators have to come to a joint agreement which stipulates how they are to dispose of their property. In the scenario suggested above, the mother and father have to jointly agree that they will leave their estate to the survivor, for use during their lifetime, and thereafter both estates will go to the child.

The courts have said that the agreement has to be something akin to a contract (*Goodchild v Goodchild* [1997] 1 WLR 1216). This does not mean an actual contract, in the formal sense, but an agreement which is sufficiently clear, authoritative, and one which neither party could change on their own. In the case of *Lord Walpole v Lord Orford* (1797) 3 Ves Jr 401, 30 ER 1076, the two testators had only arrived at what the Lord Chancellor called an 'honourable engagement'; this was not sufficiently strong to give rise to a mutual will.

A few key points about the nature of the agreement were laid down in the case of *Dufour v Pereira* (1769) Dickens 419, 21 ER 332. The Lord Chancellor stated that the agreement was a 'contract' between the parties. It followed that they were bound by it. Neither party could, by themselves, change their minds. However, whilst both testators were still alive, they could jointly agree to revoke the mutual wills or to jointly agree to amend them. It has to be a joint decision whilst both testators are alive. The Lord Chancellor emphasised that once the first testator has died, the survivor cannot, on their own, change the terms of the agreement.

The use of the word 'contract' has led to some debate. It is unlikely that any judge in the older cases actually referred to a legal contract. Rather, the reference was to an agreement that both sides considered to be binding. The problem is that if the mutual will agreement is an actual contract, then any mutual will concerning land would have to satisfy s 2(1) of the Law of Property (Miscellaneous Provisions) Act 1989, which states that contracts concerning land have to be in writing and set out all the agreed-upon terms. This is what the court suggested in the case of *Healey v Brown* [2002] EWHC 1405 (Ch). However, in the case of *Legg v Burton* [2017] EWHC 2088 (Ch), [2017] 4 WLR 186, the judge said that it would be 'capricious, even unprincipled' for mutual wills to operate differently depending on whether or not the estate consisted of land. Because the requirement is for an agreement which both parties consider to be binding and therefore rely on, the judge in *Legg v Burton* queried whether the 'agreement' is actually a form of proprietary estoppel. This, however, also seems unlikely. There is a desire amongst some lawyers and academics for everything to be neatly classified into separate boxes. So, mutual wills have to be either a legal contract or fit within proprietary estoppel. However, there is no need for that kind of shoehorning. Mutual wills is its own doctrine. The only requirement is that the two testators have entered into an agreement that they both consider to be binding. When the first one dies, the survivor is bound by the agreement as a matter of conscience; since it would be unconscionable for the survivor to change their minds, the agreement is enforced through a constructive trust (*Re Walters (Deceased)* [2008] EWCA Civ 782, [2009] Ch 212).

7.1.2 The parties have to intend the agreement to be binding

The second requirement is that the parties have to intend their agreement to be binding. In the scenario given, where two parents agree to give their estates to the survivor for life and thereafter to their child, the starting point is that the two testators have what are called mirror wills. The wills are identical and therefore mirror each other. What turns mirror wills into mutual wills is that the agreement is binding on the survivor. If the parties have only mirror wills, they remain free, on their own, to amend or revoke them.

Cases such as *Re Hagger* [1930] 2 Ch 190 and *Re Green (Deceased)* [1951] Ch 148 make it quite clear that the wills should, in some way, stipulate that they are, in fact, mutual wills. This should be included in the opening recital or in an explanatory clause near the top of the will. The recital or explanatory clause should explain that this is a mutual will and that the testator therefore cannot independently amend or revoke it.

For example, in *Re Walters (Deceased)*, cl 2 of the wife's will read: 'This [will] is made pursuant to an agreement made between my husband and me for the disposal of our property in a similar way by mutual testamentary dispositions.' Clause 2 of the husband's will read the same, but using the word 'wife' instead. (They were actually two codicils, but that makes no difference here.) This clause was sufficient to prove a mutually binding agreement.

The absence of such a clause is not necessarily fatal, but it is going to be much more difficult to prove that there is a mutual will. However, it can be done. In the case of *Charles v Fraser* [2010] EWHC 2154 (Ch), two sisters had entered into mirror wills, which did not have any clause suggesting that the wills were mutual wills. However, looking not only at the terms of the wills (which were the same) but also at the surrounding evidence, such as the close relationship between the sisters (they were both widowed without children and lived together in a house they co-owned), the court decided that the wills were, in fact, mutual wills.

The case of *Re Oldman* [1925] Ch 75 is illustrative. A husband and a wife executed mirror wills. They gave the survivor an absolute interest in their estate and identified the same beneficiaries when the survivor died. The husband died. Thereafter, the wife remarried and sought to execute a new will, to reflect her new family circumstances. The wills executed by the husband and the wife were clearly mirror wills because they had identical terms and the two wills were executed on the same day. Astbury J said:

> Of course it is a strong thing that these two parties came together, agreed to make their wills in identical terms and in fact so made them. But that does not go nearly far enough.

Merely executing mirror wills at the same time does not, on its own, make them mutual wills. The wills have, in some way, to stipulate that they are binding on the survivor. In *Re Oldham*, a key problem was that the survivor received an absolute interest in the property. This suggests that the survivor is, in fact, free to dispose of that property as they see fit. For it to be a mutual will, the survivor should receive only a life interest in the property, which means that they can enjoy the property but do not have an unfettered right to dispose of it.

7.1.3 The effect of the first testator's death

The mutual will comes into effect once the first testator dies. As seen, until this point, the two testators can jointly agree to amend or revoke the mutual wills. Once the first testator dies, the survivor is bound by its terms.

Why did the Chancery hold the survivor to the terms of the mutual will? It was essentially justified on the basis of equitable fraud. The survivor perpetrates fraud on the first testator if the survivor changes their will after the first testator has died (*Re Dale (Deceased)* [1994] Ch 31). This is because the first testator dies with the expectation that the mutual will agreement is going to be adhered to. It is fraud if the survivor then starts to make changes to the agreement. It makes no difference if the survivor does not benefit from the will. For instance, in the scenario above, the mutual will agreement might say that both parents give their entire estate to the child, not to each other first. The surviving parent is still bound by the agreement, even though they do not benefit from the first testator's death. In *Re Dale (Deceased)*, Morritt J said:

> I see no reason why the doctrine should be confined to cases where the second testator benefits when the aim of the principle is to prevent the first testator from being defrauded.

The practical consequence of the first testator's death is that the survivor holds that property on constructive trust for the ultimate beneficiary (*Re Cleaver (Deceased)* [1981] 1 WLR 939). This means that the ultimate beneficiary (such as the child, in the scenario above) can hold the survivor to account in court if the survivor starts dealing with the property in a way that is contrary to the mutual will agreement. For example, the ultimate beneficiary can object to the survivor selling off property.

The mutual will, and the constructive trust that arises when the first testator dies, applies only to the property specified in the agreement. In the scenario above, with a mother and father giving each other a life interest in their estate before it goes to the child, the mutual will applies to the whole estate. The parties can, of course, agree that the mutual will agreement only covers certain parts of their respective estates. In that case, the survivor can freely dispose of the remainder of their estate and can change their mind about that even after the first testator has died. Because the mutual will doctrine applies through a constructive trust, which attaches itself only to the relevant property, the survivor is free to make other changes to their will. The survivor can, for example, appoint new executors (*Charles v Fraser* [2010] EWHC 2154 (Ch)). Such changes have no impact on the ultimate beneficiary, whose property is protected through the constructive trust. Ultimately, what the survivor can and cannot do with the property is subject to the terms of the mutual will itself, and is thus fact-specific (*Legg v Burton* [2017] EWHC 2088 (Ch), [2017] 4 WLR 186).

7.2 Problems with mutual wills

There are many problems with the mutual wills doctrine. Key amongst them is the fact that the survivor cannot change their mind, no matter what changes occur in their personal circumstances. The survivor might remarry, have more children, form new friendships or become involved in charities or other organisations. Equally possible is that the survivor falls out with the ultimate beneficiary and no longer wants to benefit them. If a survivor is bound by a mutual will, they cannot do anything in response to any of these changes. This is undoubtedly the main reason why mutual wills are not common in practice and, quite possibly, why they should be discouraged.

Another practical problem is proving the existence of a mutual will, if there is no explanatory clause in the will itself (though, as seen in *Charles v Fraser*, it can be done). Related to that is the question of what rights the ultimate beneficiary actually has against the survivor, for example, if the survivor starts disposing of assets. The ultimate beneficiary, as a beneficiary under a constructive trust, is entitled to bring a complaint to court. However, this presupposes that the ultimate beneficiary is actually aware of their status. If not, there might be very little they can do once the survivor also dies and the ultimate beneficiary inherits the survivor's estate. Assets from the first testator might have been sold off years before, and there is no chance of recovering them or in any way claiming compensation from the survivor.

The problems with mutual wills have led some to call for the complete abolition of the doctrine, but this has not been accepted by the Law Commission in its 2017 consultation (Law Com 231, [12.31]). This is on the basis that, whilst not commonly used and despite the problems, it is a disproportionate response simply to abolish the doctrine. It is one way in which testators can agree to dispose of their property. As much as it might be a problem where a survivor remarries and has more children, a mutual will agreement at least ensures that the child from the first marriage is protected and will inherit; this might provide some peace of mind to the first testator (Law Com 231, [12.28]).

The Law Commission also rejected any suggestion of clarifying the mutual wills doctrine by placing it on a statutory footing in any new Wills Act (Law Com 231, [12.32]). This is because doing so might raise the profile of mutual wills, meaning more people enter into them, which might exacerbate the problems already identified. In short, given the rarity of mutual wills in practice but respecting the fact that they might be useful in some circumstances, the Law Commission simply proposes to leave the current law in peace.

7.3 Further reading

Law Commission, *Making a Will* (Consultation Paper 231, July 2017), Ch 12 (Mutual wills)

Liew, Ying Khai, 'The Ambit of the Mutual Wills Doctrine' (2016) 132 LQR 664–77.

Pawlowski, Mark and Brown, James, 'Problems with Mutual Wills – A Study of Probate Practice' [2012] Conv 467–83.

This chapter has covered the doctrine of mutual wills. These arise where two testators form a binding agreement about how they will dispose of their property. The most common form of mutual will gives the survivor a life interest in the first testator's estate, and thereafter the two estates will go to an identified ultimate beneficiary. The survivor holds the first testator's estate on constructive trust for the ultimate beneficiary. The doctrine comes with several practical problems, such as the inability of the survivor to benefit any new people in their life, such as after a new marriage. Because mutual wills are rare in practice, the Law Commission has suggested that the best course of action is to do nothing, and simply to leave the law in its current state.

8 Intestacy

In the previous chapters, we considered the rules relating to wills. We set out the legal requirements for making a valid will, how wills are interpreted, and how wills can be changed and revoked. Finally, we looked at the mutual wills doctrine. All of that falls under the category of testate succession.

It is now time to look at what happens when a person dies without having a valid will. They are said to have died intestate. On intestacy, it is the law that decides who inherits the deceased's property. The Law Commission has suggested that some 40% of adults in England and Wales do not have wills (Law Com 231, [1.1]). The rules of intestacy are therefore extremely important.

This chapter addresses the following issues:

- What is the difference between total and partial intestacy?
- Who inherits an estate when the deceased has died intestate?
- What is the effect of the revised s 46 of the Administration of Estates Act 1925?
- What is the position of a surviving spouse/civil partner?

8.1 Definitions: total and partial intestacy

Before looking at the intestacy rules in detail, it is important to understand the difference between a total and a partial intestacy.

A total intestacy arises when the deceased does not dispose of their property through a valid will. This can be because there is no will at all; or an existing will might have been revoked; or an existing will is declared invalid (for example, because it fails to comply with the formality requirements or the deceased lacked mental capacity); or there are no valid gifts made in an existing will (for instance, because all of the beneficiaries have predeceased the testator). In the case of *Re Skeats* [1936] Ch 683, a testator left a will which included no gifts at all, and his property passed on intestacy. In the case of *Re Edwards* [1906] 1 Ch 570, a testator left her estate on a contingent gift to her children, who would inherit if they turned 21. Only one child survived the testator (who died in childbirth) but the child died soon thereafter, therefore not meeting the contingency. The Court of Appeal held that the testator's estate passed on intestacy. Thus, on a total intestacy, no property at all is disposed of by a will. Rather, after the payment of debts and expenses, the property is distributed to the statutory next of kin. Section 46 of the Administration of Estates Act (AEA) 1925 sets out who receives the property.

A partial intestacy arises where the deceased does leave a valid will, but some of their property is not disposed of by that will. As discussed in **Chapter 6**, a will gift can fail or lapse for a variety of reasons. Unless that property is captured by the residuary clause, it will pass outside the will on a partial intestacy. Section 46 of the AEA 1925 also applies to this property, as confirmed in s 49 of the AEA 1925. As will be shown below, if the testator leaves a surviving spouse or civil partner, they will most likely be entitled to anything passing on a partial intestacy.

The remainder of this chapter proceeds on the basis of a total intestacy.

8.2　Administration of intestate estates

As discussed in the previous chapters, where a person leaves a will, they ordinarily appoint an executor to administer their estate. The testator therefore has a choice in the appointment of their personal representative (PR). Where a person dies intestate, however, the court is responsible for making that choice. The court will appoint an administrator to administer the estate. This process is explained in detail in **Chapter 9**. What follows is a brief summary.

Rule 22 of the Non-Contentious Probate Rules 1987 determines who will be appointed as administrator. In short, r 22 mirrors s 46 of the AEA 1925. There is an order of priority, and whoever has priority will be appointed as the administrator, unless they disclaim the position. In the first instance, the surviving spouse or civil partner will be appointed. Thereafter, it is the child or, if the child has predeceased the deceased, grandchildren. Thereafter, it is the deceased's parents, siblings and their issue (nieces/nephews), grandparents, then aunts and uncles and their issue (cousins). If the deceased dies without a next of kin, the Treasury Solicitor will be appointed as administrator because the Crown will claim the property through *bona vacantia*. Alternatively, if the deceased dies owing money, a creditor can apply to be the administrator, but a creditor will have to ask the Treasury Solicitor to step aside.

Once appointed, the administrator must take control of the deceased's property. The administration process will be explained in more detail in **Chapters 11** to **14**. Section 33(1) of the AEA 1925 states that the administrator holds all of the deceased's property on trust, with a power to sell it. Out of the money available or raised from selling off property, the administrator must first pay 'all such funeral, testamentary and administration expenses, debts and other liabilities as are properly payable' (AEA 1925, s 33(2)). The administrator only has to sell the estate property to the extent necessary to pay off the debts and expenses.

Funeral expenses must be paid first, to cover reasonable costs of the funeral. Thereafter come all of the administration expenses. They include any costs associated with the administration procedure (such as getting court documents) and any costs involved in selling the estate assets. They also include all taxes, including inheritance tax, if applicable (see **Chapter 10**). Thereafter, the administrator must pay off all legal debts. This might include a mortgage on a house (which will often be paid off by selling the house), credit card debt, bank account overdrafts and paying off any items that had been bought on credit.

Once all of that has been paid off, any remaining money and unsold property is called the residue. The residue will be distributed to the statutory beneficiaries. Their entitlement is governed by s 46 of the AEA 1925.

8.3   The statutory beneficiaries

Section 46 of the AEA 1925 was amended in 2014. The new rules apply to anyone who dies intestate on or after 1 October 2014. For clarity, this chapter will focus on the new rules (and only briefly mention the key differences). Section 46 lists potential beneficiaries in a hierarchical order. Thus, if the deceased has next of kin with priority over you, it is unlikely that you will inherit anything. The only time that there will be two classes inheriting at the same time is if the deceased left both a surviving spouse and children, and then only if the estate is of a large enough size.

Section 46 is based on a presumed intention; this is most likely what the deceased would have wanted to happen to their property, had they exercised a choice by making a will. Not everyone might intend for the Crown to claim property through *bona vacantia*, where there is no next of kin, but it is nonetheless the easiest and most practical outcome.

8.3.1   The rights of a surviving spouse or civil partner

The person with top priority to inherit is a surviving spouse or civil partner. A spouse or civil partner remains entitled to inherit even if divorce or dissolution proceedings have been initiated (and the Family Court has issued a decree nisi) but have not been completed (through a decree absolute) at the time of death (*Re Seaford* [1968] P 53). A voidable marriage is still valid unless the parties void it, and a spouse will be entitled to inherit (Matrimonial Causes Act 1973, s 12 and Civil Partnership Act 2004, s 50). If the marriage is void, it is taken as never having existed, and the party cannot inherit through intestacy (Matrimonial Causes Act 1973, s 11 and Civil Partnership Act 2004, 49). The definitions of a void and voidable marriage were set out at **6.3**.

English law does not allow for polygamous marriages, but the law does recognise that such marriages are lawful in other countries; therefore, if the deceased had several spouses, all of the spouses will be entitled on intestacy in equal shares (*Official Solicitor to the Senior Courts v Yemoh* [2010] EWHC 3727 (Ch)).

Exactly what the surviving spouse or civil partner is entitled to depends on the size of the net estate.

key terminology

Net estate: The financial value of the estate after all expenses, taxes and debts have been paid.

8.3.1.1 Entitlement where the deceased leaves no issue

If the deceased does not leave any children (or further issue), the surviving spouse or civil partner is entitled to the whole estate (s 46(1)(i)(1)), and the administrator will hold it on trust for them.

8.3.1.2 Entitlement where the deceased leaves issue

If the deceased leaves children, other rules apply, set out in s 46(1)(i)(2). The estate will be divided into three parts. First, the surviving spouse/civil partner is entitled to the deceased's personal chattels. Secondly, the surviving spouse/civil partner is entitled to a so-called statutory legacy, namely a financial payment out of the estate assets. For anyone dying on or after 6 February 2020, the statutory legacy is an award of up to £270,000 (set out in the Administration of Estates Act 1925 (Fixed Net Sum) Order 2020 (SI 2020/33)). The previous statutory legacy, in force since 2009, was an award of up to £250,000. Thirdly, the remainder of the estate is divided equally between the surviving spouse/civil partner and the deceased's children. These three entitlements will be expanded upon below.

The surviving spouse or civil partner is entitled to all personal chattels (s 46(1)(i)(2)(A))

First, the surviving spouse or civil partner is entitled to the deceased's personal chattels. The AEA 1925, s 55(1)(x) defines personal chattels as 'tangible movable property' which is either: (a) not 'money or securities for money'; (b) not used 'solely or mainly for business purposes'; or (c) not held 'solely as an investment'. In short, it refers to everyday household items.

This definition was inserted into the AEA 1925 by the Inheritance and Trustees' Powers Act 2014 and is an improvement on the old definition. Prior to 2014, the definition in the old s 55(1)(x) listed a wide range of particular items, leading to litigation to see whether or not this or that thing was captured by the definition. The old case law can still be valuable today, to determine whether or not something is used mainly for business purposes or is held as an investment. In the case of *Re Reynold's Will Trusts* [1966] 1 WLR 19, the court held that a valuable stamp collection was a personal chattel. Similarly, in the case of *Re Crispin's Will Trusts* [1975] Ch 245, a valuable collection of clocks was interpreted as personal chattels. In the case of *Re Chaplin (Deceased)* [1950] Ch 507, a 60-foot pleasure yacht was interpreted as a personal chattel, since it was used only for personal pleasure.

Despite its broader wording, the new definition may nevertheless give rise to dispute. What if some items were used for business purposes (for example the pleasure yacht was rented out every so often for a profit)? Valuable collections, whether they are stamp collections or collections of valuable clocks, also raise questions as to whether or not they are investments. If they are used at home, it is unlikely that they are held 'solely' for investment purposes. In *Re Reynolds* and *Re Crispin*, the stamp and clock collections were the hobbies of the deceased. Thus, they were clearly not investments. However, this is always going to be fact specific.

The surviving spouse or civil partner is entitled to a lump sum payment (s 46(1)(i)(2)(B))

Secondly, the surviving spouse or civil partner is entitled to a lump sum payment out of the estate. This lump sum is known as the statutory legacy. For anyone dying on or after 6 February 2020, the statutory legacy is £270,000, which is set out in the Administration of Estates Act 1925 (Fixed Net Sum) Order 2020. Prior to that date, the statutory legacy was £250,000.

The method for determining the statutory legacy is set out in Sch 1A of the AEA 1925, inserted by the Inheritance and Trustees' Powers Act 2014. It says that the Lord Chancellor must by a statutory instrument confirm the statutory legacy at least every five years. The first review following the 2014 Act was due in the autumn of 2019; however, it was delayed due to the December 2019 General Election, meaning the new statutory legacy of £270,000 only came into effect on 6 February 2020. The next review of the statutory legacy must be made by February 2025.

If the net value of the estate is below that sum, the surviving spouse or civil partner is entitled to the entire estate. The surviving spouse or civil partner is also entitled to interest on the lump sum, calculated from the date of death until the date of payment.

If there are assets remaining in the estate after the statutory legacy has been paid, the remainder is divided into two parts: (a) one half to go on trust absolutely to the surviving spouse or civil partner; and (b) one half to go on trust for the deceased's children, in equal shares if more than one (s 46(1)(i)(2)(C))

Thirdly, the surviving spouse or civil partner is entitled to one half of the remainder, once they have received the personal chattels and the statutory legacy. The children are entitled to the other half of the remainder.

The key difference prior to 2014 was that the surviving spouse or civil partner did not take an absolute interest in half of the remainder, but only a life interest, with the remainder to the children. This was potentially complicated, as that half would have to be held on trust for the surviving spouse or civil partner for the remainder of their life. Also, prior to 2014, if there were no children but the deceased was survived by parents or whole-blood siblings and their issue, the wife took half of the remainder and the other half went (in the stated order) to those other relatives.

The rules show that the surviving spouse or civil partner is in a good position where the deceased dies intestate, even more so post-2014. This could explain why some people choose to die intestate, as they are content to leave their estate to their spouses or civil partners.

8.3.1.3 Entitlement to the family home

Commonly, a person's main asset is their home. In most cases, it is also where the surviving spouse remains living. Therefore, the question of who is entitled to the family home is of great importance.

Many family homes are co-owned by the two partners and generally held on a joint tenancy in both law and equity. Where property is held on a joint tenancy, the doctrine of survivorship applies. This means that the surviving co-owner acquires sole ownership when the first co-owner dies. This is an operation of land law rather than succession law. If a surviving spouse obtains sole ownership of the family home through survivorship, they will still be entitled to the full distribution as detailed in s 46.

Other provisions apply where the surviving spouse did not have a joint tenancy in equity in the family home. This may be because the partners (whilst legal co-owners) were tenants in common in equity (thus having their own, individual shares of the beneficial interest) or because the family home was solely owned by the deceased.

Section 41 of the AEA 1925 allows the PR to appropriate and use any property owned by the deceased. In effect, the PR can use the statutory legacy and half of the remainder to effectively purchase the matrimonial home for the surviving spouse.

Section 41 grants the PR discretion only. However, an additional rule was added by the Intestates' Estates Act 1952. Schedule 2, para 1 of that Act states that the surviving spouse can 'require' the PR to exercise their appropriation power in s 41, if the following conditions are met:

- The residue of the deceased's property must include an interest in a 'dwelling-house'. In practice, this will mean the matrimonial home, but technically it can include any dwelling-house owned by the deceased. Both a freehold and a leasehold are included within the definition of an 'interest' (see Law of Property Act 1925, s 1(1)). However, Sch 2, para 1(2) excludes leases with less than two years to run or a lease which the landlord can determine (bring to an end) within two years of the deceased's death.

- The surviving spouse or civil partner must be resident in that dwelling-house at the time of death. In most cases, this means that Sch 2, para 1 is addressing the family home. However, for instance, if the deceased and the surviving spouse had separated, and the surviving spouse was living in a separate dwelling-house owned by the deceased, it is that house that the surviving spouse can claim.

- The dwelling-house will be valued at the date of appropriation (not the date the deceased died) (Sch 2, para 3(2); *Re Collins (Deceased)* [1975] 1 WLR 309). If the value of the house exceeds what the surviving spouse is entitled to, both under the statutory legacy and half of the remainder, the surviving spouse can personally pay the difference, so that the dwelling-house can be appropriated into their name.

- The surviving spouse or civil partner has 12 months in which to require the PR to appropriate the dwelling-house.

- The right does not apply in some circumstances, outlined in Sch 2, para 2. This includes where the dwelling-house forms part of a larger building and the deceased owned the whole building; where the dwelling-house was attached to agricultural land; and where the dwelling-house was, in whole or in part, used as a hotel or a lodging house. In these situations, the court will only consent to the appropriation of the dwelling-house if it is 'not likely to diminish the value of assets in the residuary estate … or make them more difficult to dispose of'.

These rules show a great discrepancy in terms of the entitlement of a surviving spouse or civil partner depending on whether the property was co-owned as joint tenants or not. As a joint tenant, the surviving spouse is entitled to the property as a matter of land law and then, as a matter of intestacy law, entitled according to s 46. If they are not a joint tenant, the surviving spouse or civil partner will have to use their s 46 entitlement towards purchasing the property. If there are insufficient funds in the estate to purchase the property, the surviving spouse or civil partner will have to put up their own money to cover the difference. Of course, if they cannot afford that, the house will have to be sold by the PR. This demonstrates the huge importance of co-ownership in land law and why, generally, it is advisable for spouses and civil partners to co-own the family home as joint tenants.

8.3.1.4 Survivorship requirement

There was one important proviso added in 1995 to s 46 of the AEA 1925, and it applies to people dying intestate after that year (Law Reform (Succession) Act 1995, s 1). Section 46(2A) states that the surviving spouse or civil partner has to survive the deceased by at least 28 days. If the surviving spouse or civil partner dies within the 28 days, they are to be treated as having predeceased the deceased.

8.3.1.5 Cohabitant

Under the current law, only a spouse or civil partner can inherit on intestacy. However, today, more and more couples are living together as a family, and having children, but without marrying or entering into a civil partnership. This is generally referred to as cohabitation. The exclusion of cohabitants from inheriting on intestacy presents serious problems when one of the cohabitants dies intestate. The surviving partner has no legal protection and will not inherit anything.

If the family home was co-owned on a joint tenancy, the survivorship principle applies, and the survivor becomes the sole owner of the house. If the house was co-owned with an equitable tenancy-in-common, the deceased's share passes to the next of kin. If the house was owned solely by the deceased, the whole house passes to the next of kin. The surviving partner has no right under s 41 to have the property purchased on their behalf. Of course, using their own money, they can try to purchase the house from the PR.

If the cohabitation has lasted for at least two years, the surviving cohabitant has the right to apply to court for a financial award out of the estate, which the court has discretion whether or not to grant. The right to make an application for a financial award under the so-called family provision rule is set out in the Inheritance (Provision for Family and Dependants) Act 1975, which will be explained in **Chapter 15**.

Given the increase in cohabitation and decrease in marriage, there is a strong argument that the intestacy rules are in need of reform. However, common law courts have even recently upheld the exclusion of cohabitants on intestacy. In the Canadian case of *Jackson Estate v Young* [2020] NSSC 5, a court in Nova Scotia found that the exclusion of cohabitants was permitted under the Canadian Charter of Fundamental Rights. The Court held that the exclusion violated Article 15 (which guarantees equal rights and prohibits discrimination) but was saved by Article 1, which holds that all rights can be subject to 'reasonable limits prescribed by law' that are 'demonstrably justified in a free and democratic society'. Many countries, including the UK, do provide various legal rights to married couples or those in a civil partnership that are not available to cohabitants, including the right to inherit on intestacy and a wide range of tax advantages. The Canadian court found the policy to favour marriage over cohabitation to be a valid justification under Article 1 for infringing the claimant's right to equal treatment under Article 15. The same arguments could be made in an English court, referring both to Article 8 of the European Convention on Human Rights (the right to a private and family life without disproportionate state interference) and Article 14 (the right to equal treatment under the law). However, as s 46 is set out in primary legislation, an English court could not go beyond issuing a declaration of incompatibility, leaving it to Parliament to decide whether s 46 should be reformed.

The general merits of providing additional legal rights to married couples over cohabitants is obviously a significant social debate that will continue to go on. For the time being, cohabitants must take care to consider how the family home (and other assets, including bank accounts) is owned – ie is the family home owned on a joint tenancy with the right of survivorship? – and, to avoid having to rely on the Inheritance (Provision for Family and Dependants) Act 1975, cohabitants are strongly recommended to write a valid will.

8.3.2 Entitlement on intestacy if the deceased does not leave a spouse or civil partner

8.3.2.1 Children

If the deceased does not leave a spouse or civil partner, but leaves children, the intestate estate will be held on statutory trust for the children (s 46(1)(ii)). The details of the statutory trust are set out in s 47.

To be entitled, the child has to be alive when the parent dies (or *en ventre sa mère*). If there is only one child, that child is entitled to the entire estate. If there is more than one child, they will be entitled in equal shares. If the child dies before the parent, any child of the child is entitled, known as an entitlement *per stirpes*. The grandchild will take the child's interest. If there are several grandchildren, they will share the child's interest equally.

The entitlement to inherit is conditional on the child (or further descendants taking *per stirpes*) either (a) turning 18, or (b) getting married (which a child can do, with parental consent, from the age of 16). Until the child turns 18 or marries below that age, the estate is held on trust for them. If the child dies before they meet either of the conditions, the estate will instead be held on trust for any child of their own *per stirpes* or for their siblings. In the absence of either, the deceased will be deemed to have died without issue. In accordance with ss 31 and 32 of the Trustee Act 1925, the PR, as trustee, can use any interest accrued from the trust for the maintenance of a minor (such as covering the costs of school) and also advance their capital entitlement if the PR deems that is the right thing to do. The powers of maintenance and advancement are covered in more detail in an Equity & Trusts textbook. Section 47(1)(iv) also states that the PR can allow the minor to use and enjoy the personal chattels held in the estate (the definition of personal chattel was set out above).

The current law defines children quite broadly (see **Chapter 5**). The law no longer distinguishes between legitimate and illegitimate children (Family Law Reform Act 1987, s 18). An adopted child is to be treated as a child of its adoptive parents (Adoption and Children Act 2002, s 67) rather than its biological parents. The Human Fertilisation and Embryology Acts of 1990 and 2008 provide a legal framework as to who is treated as the parent of a child born from artificial insemination, depending on who donated eggs and sperm, who carried the child to birth, and whether consent was given (the details are beyond the scope of the book). The starting point, under s 33 of the 2008 Act, is that the woman who carried the child to term is to be treated as the mother (bearing in mind that if the child is adopted, it will be treated as the child of the adoptive parents).

Stepchildren remain excluded from the definition of children in intestacy law. This exclusion is a potential problem in modern society, given the increase in divorce and remarriage as well as the increase in cohabitation. More and more people die intestate leaving stepchildren. It can be considered unfair for the stepchild to be excluded from inheriting and, on a more personal level, can cause unnecessary upset and hurt within families. As with the exclusion of cohabitants, mentioned above, the law may be in need of reform to bring stepchildren into the class of people entitled to inherit on intestacy. Some jurisdictions have addressed this. In California, for example, the law recognises the doctrine of 'equitable adoption', which arises where an adult assumes responsibility for a child, without formally adopting them; the child has a right to inherit on intestacy (California Probate Code 6455). In English law, it will be necessary to amend s 46 if it is felt that bringing stepchildren into the class of beneficiaries is the right way forward.

The above rules can be demonstrated with an example. Assume that the deceased parent left two children, who were alive at his or her death, and three grandchildren. The estate would be distributed as follows:

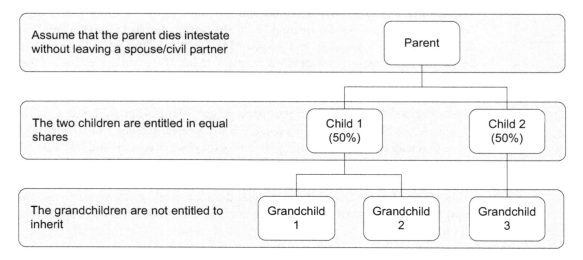

If a child predeceased the deceased, leaving their own children, those children (the deceased's grandchildren) would inherit the share that the deceased's child was entitled to. This is known as an entitlement *per stirpes*:

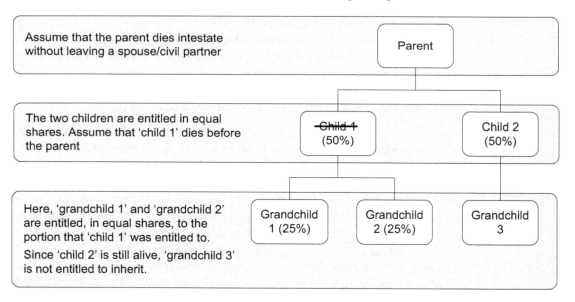

Particularly since people are living longer, it is certainly possible that both a child and grandchild may predecease the deceased. If the grandchild left their own children (great-grandchildren), they will inherit the grandchild's portion, in equal shares:

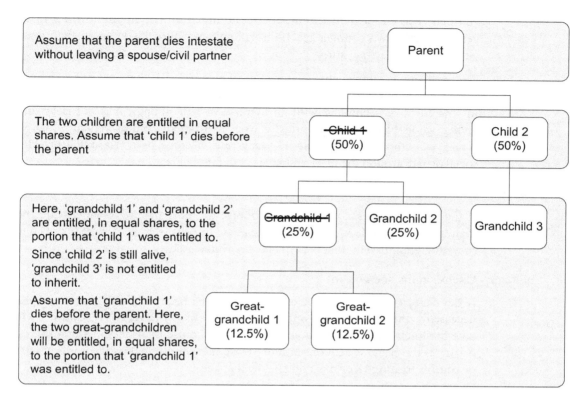

8.3.2.2 Parents

If the deceased does not leave a spouse or civil partner and leaves no children or further descendants, the estate will be held on trust for the deceased's parents (s 46(1)(iii) and (iv)). If both parents are alive, they will take the estate in equal shares. If only one parent is alive, that parent will be entitled to the entire estate.

There is one remaining exception to this. If a child was born 'illegitimate' (that is to say, the parents were not married at the time), the father is presumed to have died before the child (Family Law Reform Act 1987, s 18(2)). This means that the father will not be entitled to inherit. This exclusion does not apply where the father is registered as the father on the birth register (s 18(2ZA)) (which refers to the birth registry system governed by the Births and Deaths Registration Act 1953). If the father is not on the birth register, he will have to rebut the presumption that he predeceased the child in order to inherit, for example by proving that there was a relationship between him and the child.

8.3.2.3 Brothers and sisters and their issue

If the deceased does not leave parents, their estate will be held on statutory trust for their siblings or their issue (nieces and nephews) (s 46(1)(v)). If there is more than one sibling, they take the estate in equal shares. The same conditions apply as for children. The entitlement to inherit is conditional on the sibling turning 18 or getting married at a younger age. If the sibling dies before the deceased, their issue will take their share *per stirpes*.

The entitlement begins with siblings of the whole blood. If there are none, siblings of the half blood will take. Again, given ongoing social changes, where parents split up and form new families, with an increase in half-siblings, it is not clear that giving whole-blood siblings priority over half-blood siblings remains logical. Again, as with cohabitants, the intestacy rules become part of a much broader social debate around the modern make-up of family life.

8.3.2.4 Grandparents

If the deceased does not leave any siblings, the next in line to inherit are the grandparents (s 46(1)(v)). They take the estate in equal shares. If there is only one surviving grandparent, that person take the whole estate.

8.3.2.5 Uncles, aunts and cousins

If the deceased does not leave any grandparents, next in line to inherit are the deceased's uncles and aunts, and their issue (cousins) (s 46(1)(v)). Cousins will take the uncle or aunt's share *per stirpes* and, if more than one, in equal shares. Again, as the estate is held on statutory trust, it is conditional on the aunts, uncles or cousins turning 18 or marrying below that age.

Again, family of the whole blood take priority over family of the half blood.

8.3.2.6 *Bona vacantia*

If the deceased does not leave behind any family member in the classes listed above, s 46 provides that the estate passes to the Crown (or, as applicable, to the Duchy of Cornwall or the Duchy of Lancaster), putting on a statutory footing the rule of *bona vacantia* (s 46(1)(vi)).

key terminology

Bona vacantia: the Latin term means 'ownerless goods' or, more literally, 'vacant goods'. It is an ancient legal principle, stemming from Roman law, that property cannot be ownerless; in default of an owner, it passes to the Crown.

The Crown is entitled under s 46 to distribute the estate to persons for 'whom the intestate might reasonably have been expected to make provision'. As discussed above, this can include people who are excluded from s 46, such as cohabitants and stepchildren.

In all instances, those excluded from s 46 might be entitled to make an application for maintenance support out of the estate under the Inheritance (Provision for Family and Dependants) Act 1975, which will be discussed in detail in **Chapter 15**.

8.4 Further reading

O'Sullivan, Kathryn, 'Distribution of Intestate Estates in Non-Traditional Families: A Way Forward?' (2017) 46 Common Law World Review 21–41.

This chapter has shown how a deceased's estate is distributed when they die intestate. The rules are said to be based on a presumed intention – this is most likely what most people want to happen to their property when they die. Having said that, it is clear from the above discussion that s 46 of the AEA 1925 is outdated and can lead to unfair results. It makes no provision for cohabitants, an increasingly common scenario today with a corresponding decline in marriage over the past two decades. Stepchildren remain excluded. The rules still draw a distinction between whole-blood and half-blood relatives. There is also a potential unfairness to a surviving spouse when it comes to the family home, depending on whether the house was co-owned on a joint tenancy or not. Nonetheless, the rules are clear and relatively straightforward.

chapter 9

Personal Representatives

The role of the personal representative (PR) has been referred to many times in the previous chapters. This chapter looks at PRs in much greater detail. To summarise, it is the role of the PR to deal with the estate of the deceased. This chapter looks at the role of a PR and how they come to be appointed. The duties and powers of PRs will then be looked at in the subsequent chapters.

This chapter addresses the following issues:

- What are the different types of PRs?
- Who can be appointed an executor?
- Who can be appointed an administrator?
- What is the difference between a grant of probate, a grant of letters of administration, and a grant of letters of administration with the will attached?
- How can a PR be removed and replaced?

9.1 Two types of personal representatives

To begin with, it is important to distinguish between the two types of PRs. There are executors and there are administrators. As mentioned in **Chapter 1**, historically, a female executor was known as an executrix and a female administrator as an administratrix. This distinction is rarely used today, but since those terms are found in the case law, it is important to be aware of it.

An executor deals with a testate estate. They are appointed by the testator in the will. The testator has almost complete free rein to choose whom they want as their executor; commonly the testator will either choose a professional (such as their solicitor) or a trusted family member or friend. An administrator is appointed by the court. They will deal with either (a) a testate estate where there is no executor, or (b) an intestate estate. The court has to follow a fixed, hierarchical list of people when appointing an administrator, and there is limited discretion allowed. There are two separate lists, one for a testate estate and one for an intestate estate.

Below, the chapter looks first at executors and then at administrators for testate and intestate estates.

9.2 Executors

This section of the chapter sets out how executors are appointed to their office, what eligibility requirements there are, and finally how they don the cloak of executorship after the testator has died.

9.2.1 Appointment

In short, there are three different ways in which an executor can be appointed to their office:

(1) They can be appointed through the will.

(2) The will can authorise someone to appoint an executor on the testator's behalf.

(3) In limited circumstances, the court can appoint an executor.

9.2.1.1 Executors appointed through the will

This is undoubtedly the most common way for an executor to be appointed. The testator can, and should, specify in the will whom they want to act as their executor. There will always be an appointment clause in a professionally drafted will. There is strictly speaking no limit on how many executors a testator can appoint in the will. However, when the testator dies and the executors go to court to seek probate, no more than four executors will actually receive probate (Senior Courts Act 1981, s 114(1)). Large or complicated estates can be split into different parts, and then no more than four executors will get probate for each part of the estate. This might be relevant if the testator has both significant personal assets and business assets: here, up to four executors can be appointed to handle the personal estate and up to four executors can be appointed to handle the business assets.

The appointment of an executor can be straightforward: the appointment clause names a particular person, such as 'I appoint John Burke as my executor'. The appointment can also be substitutional in nature: 'I appoint John Burke as my executor, but should John Burke predecease me, I appoint Claire Burke as my executor.' This type of substitution is also useful if the testator appoints a professional to be the executor, such as a solicitor. Here, the appointment clause can stipulate that another solicitor/partner in the same firm will be the executor if the named solicitor has retired or moved jobs. These substitutional appointments can be very practical, especially if the testator is expected to live for a long time after executing the will. The appointment can also be conditional in nature: for example, the appointment might be conditional on the person turning 18. An example of an appointment clause was seen in **Chapter 4**, and you might want to quickly revisit the sample will at this point.

An executor can also be appointed through the will by implication. This can occur, in particular in homemade wills, if there is no express appointment clause, but the words used suggest that a particular person is meant to handle the estate. The courts have referred to this as being appointed 'according to the tenor of the will'.

For example, in the case of *In the Goods of Brown* (1877) 2 PD 110, a homemade will read: 'I appoint my said sister Susannah Brown my executrix, only requesting that my nephews Frederick Poynder and John Arthur Beddome, will kindly act for or with this dear sister.' Both Susannah Brown and John Arthur Beddome predeceased the testator. The court held that Frederick Poynder was the executor, having been appointed by implication.

Another example is the case of *In the Estate of Fawcett* [1941] P 85. A homemade will gave various specific gifts to named individuals, before concluding: 'All else to be sold and proceeds after debts, etc, Barclays Bank will do this to Emily Thompson and any money I may have in bank.' It is obviously not crystal-clear what is meant here, but the court decided that Barclays Bank had been appointed the executor and that Emily Thompson was the intended beneficiary (as it happened, Barclays renounced probate and the court appointed Emily Thompson as administrator instead).

It is, of course, preferable to appoint an executor directly, but the courts have to allow some leeway for the fact that many wills are still written by testators at home without the benefit of professional advice.

9.2.1.2 The will authorises a person to appoint an executor

The second way in which an executor can be appointed is by someone who has been authorised by the testator to make such an appointment. This can be of particular relevance to larger estates, where the probate process might take a long time.

This is illustrated by the case of *In the Goods of Deichman* (1842) 3 Curt 123, 163 ER 676. Here, the will appointed two executors. The will also specified that if one of the executors died during probate, the survivor had the authority to appoint a replacement, so that there would always be two executors. As it happened, the first executor died during probate. As envisaged, the surviving executor appointed a replacement. However, the surviving executor died himself before the replacement had gone to court to seek probate. The question was whether the replacement would be given probate of the estate, or whether the court should appoint one of the beneficiaries as administrator. The court gave probate to the replacement and authorised him to appoint a second executor, so that there would be two of them.

This is different from an express appointment by substitution, mentioned above, since there the testator would nominate the substitute. In this type of case, however, it is the executor who names the substitute, not the testator.

9.2.1.3 Executors appointed by the court

There are some legislative provisions that allow the courts to appoint executors, but this may be done in very limited circumstances. For example, at any point, a PR (both executors and administrators) can apply to court to have another PR removed and replaced (Administration of Justice Act 1985, s 50). This is usually granted if, for instance, two co-executors have fallen out and are unable to keep working together. This is detrimental to the beneficiaries, and it is therefore appropriate to remove one executor and, possibly, appoint a replacement.

Section 114(4) of the Senior Courts Act 1981 allows the court to appoint an additional executor in two prescribed circumstances. If there is only one executor appointed in the will, but either (a) one of the beneficiaries is a minor, or (b) one of the beneficiaries has a life interest under a trust, then the court can appoint an additional executor, so that there are at least two executors in total.

key terminology

Life interest under a trust: a beneficiary has a life interest in property if they are given the enjoyment of the property for their lifetime, but not the ownership; rather, when they die, ownership to the property passes to a third party. A typical example would be a testator providing: 'My house to my spouse for life, and thereafter to my child.' The spouse can remain living in the house for the rest of their life, but they are not the owner of it; the testator's child gets ownership when the surviving spouse dies. The beneficiary with a life interest is called a **life tenant**. During their lifetime, ownership of the property is held by the testamentary trustee (commonly the same person who was the executor).

The reason why two executors might be useful here is that they will be asked to hold the property on trust for a longer period of time. There is a risk that one of them may die before the testamentary trust comes to an end.

9.2.2 Eligibility to be an executor

Having discussed the ways in which an executor can be appointed, the next question to ask is who is eligible to become an executor. The short answer is that anyone can be an executor. In practice, however, there are some important considerations to bear in mind. Although a minor can be named an executor in a will, they will not be given probate over the estate until they turn 18 (Senior Courts Act 1981, s 118; Non-Contentious Probate Rules (NCPR) 1987, rr 32, 33). It may be imprudent to appoint a minor as an executor in the will, unless the will also appoints a second executor who is an adult. The testator can also appoint a trust corporation to be the executor (Senior Courts Act 1981, s 115; NCPR 1987, r 36).

The key requirement is that the executor has mental capacity. The court will not grant probate to a person who has lost mental capacity (NCPR 1987, r 35). Again, this suggests that it might be prudent to appoint at least two executors in case one of them (perhaps through illness or old age) loses capacity. Mental capacity for executors is assessed using the test in the Mental Capacity Act (MCA) 2005, which was explained in **Chapter 2**. Thus, regardless of whether the MCA 2005 replaces the test in *Banks v Goodfellow* for testators, any student or practitioner of succession law must have an understanding of that test. If an executor loses capacity after they have been granted probate, they will be removed by the court (*In the Estate of Shaw* [1905] P 92; *In the Goods of Galbraith* [1951] P 422).

English law does not impose any restriction on foreign nationals or companies owning property in the UK. It follows that nationality is not a bar to being an executor (Status of Aliens Act 1914, s 17). (Alien is an old word for a foreign national that is no longer used in England; it is still used in that capacity in other countries, such as the United States.) There is also no restriction on being appointed as an executor if the executor has been made bankrupt or has a criminal record. However, this might present grounds for a beneficiary to object to them being granted probate, which will be expanded upon later in this chapter.

9.2.3 Accepting the office of executor after the testator has died

More will be said about the grant of probate and the duties of PRs in later chapters. A few words will suffice at this point. An executor gets their power to deal with the estate through the will, meaning that they get ownership of the estate directly after the testator's death. They can immediately start dealing with the property. However, the common procedure is to put the will into probate, which is to say, present it to a probate judge. A grant of probate is the court's authorisation for the PR to deal with the estate. Many institutions (such as a bank) will normally require the probate document before they allow a PR to access the deceased's property (eg through a bank account).

When the testator dies, the named executor can either accept the position or they can decline it. The court can summon the named executor to court, so that the executor can accept or decline the position in front of the probate judge (Senior Courts Act 1981, s 112). If the named executor declines the position, they will immediately lose all legal rights of ownership over the estate (Administration of Estates Act 1925, s 5). If they accept the position, they cannot thereafter change their minds but must see the full administration process through to the end (*In the Goods of Viega* (1862) 3 Swabey & Tristram 13, 164 ER 1176). However, as mentioned above, an appointed executor can be removed from office for a reason such as a loss of mental capacity.

9.3 Administrators

Administrators are PRs who are appointed by the court. Whereas an executor gets their authority to deal with the estate through the will (even though in many instances they will need a grant of probate from the court), an administrator receives their authority from the court. This means that if an administrator deals with the estate (by taking control of it, selling or transferring assets, or the like) before their court appointment, they are acting unlawfully and are personally liable to the beneficiaries. Liability for wrongdoing will be considered in **Chapter 16**.

When the court appoints an administrator, the court is granting 'letters of administration' over the estate. There are two types of letters of administration, which differ depending on whether or not there is a will. Administration is granted over a testate estate (where there is a will) in a number of different circumstances: the will might not appoint an executor, the appointed executor might decline the position, or the appointed executor might have predeceased the testator. In this type of situation, the court grants 'letters of administration with the will annexed' (Senior Courts Act 1981, s 119). Where administration is granted over an intestate estate (where there is no will), the court grants, simply, 'letters of administration' (also referred to as 'simple administration').

It is very important to distinguish what type of administration the court is granting. This is because there are two different lists of who is entitled to administration, depending on whether it is simple administration or administration with the will annexed. These two lists are presented in a hierarchical order. This means that the person at the top of the list has priority over everyone below. If a person further down the list wants to be appointed as an administrator, they have to 'clear off' anyone with priority over them. In practice, this means that anyone with priority has to waive their right to be appointed as an administrator. Alternatively, if there is an objection against someone with priority being appointed, they can be 'passed over' (Senior Courts Act 1981, s 116). This will be returned to below.

9.3.1 Order of priority for letters of administration with the will annexed

The order of priority for a grant of administration with the will annexed is set out in r 20 of the NCPR 1987.

Rule 20(a) – 'the executor'

The person who has first priority is the named executor. As mentioned above, the rest of the list only becomes relevant if either (a) there is no named executor, or (b) the named executor declines probate, has predeceased the testator, does not have mental capacity, or for any other reason is unable to accept probate.

Rule 20(b) – 'any residuary legatee or devisee holding in trust for any other person'

In short, this means any person who takes the residue of the estate as a trustee, thereby holding it on behalf of someone else. A devise is a gift of real property (ie land), and a devisee thus is someone who receives real property in the will. A legacy is a gift of personal property, and a legatee thus is someone who receives personal property in the will. Using different terminology for real and personal property is less common today.

Rule 20(c) – 'any other residuary legatee or devisee (including one for life) or where the residue is not wholly disposed of by the will, any person entitled to share in the undisposed of residue (including the Treasury Solicitor when claiming bona vacantia on behalf of the Crown)'

In short, this means anyone who is absolutely entitled to the residue of the estate (rather than taking it as a trustee, as in r 20(b) above). It also includes a beneficiary who has only a life interest in the residue rather than receiving it as a gift outright. Further, it includes anyone entitled on intestacy to an undisposed of part of the residue, using the rule in s 46 of the Administration of Estates Act 1925 (see

Chapter 8). Should all the beneficiaries predecease the testator, or there is no one to take on intestacy, the Crown takes the residue through *bona vacantia*.

If there are several beneficiaries with different entitlements to the residue, the court will prefer a beneficiary with an absolute interest rather than a beneficiary who has a contingent interest (ie an interest which is contingent on the beneficiary achieving some goal, such as turning 21 years old, or getting married) (NCPR 1987, r 20(c)(i)).

Rule 20(d) – 'the personal representative of any residuary legatee or devisee (but not one for life, or one holding in trust for another person), or of any person entitled to share in any residue not disposed of by the will'

This class follows r 20(c), and encompasses the PRs for any of the beneficiaries entitled to the residue, who have predeceased the testator, or who would take on intestacy. However, it excludes the PRs of those beneficiaries who have only a life interest in the residue or who take the residue as a trustee.

Rule 20(e) – 'any other legatee or devisee (including one for life or one holding in trust for any other person) or any creditor of the deceased'

This class encompasses anyone left, namely any beneficiaries entitled to specific gifts (whether real or personal property), and it includes beneficiaries who have only a life interest in property or those who take the property as a trustee. In this class, any of the testator's creditors (anyone the testator owed money to) can also be appointed as an administrator.

Rule 20(f) – 'the personal representative of any other legatee or devisee (but not one for life or only holding in trust for any other person) or of any creditor of the deceased'

This final class encompasses the PRs of any beneficiary who receives a specific gift, but excludes PRs of those with a life interest or who take the property as trustee. The class also encompasses the PRs of any of the testator's creditors.

9.3.2 Disputes over the order of priority for administration with the will annexed

As mentioned, the list in r 20 is in a strict hierarchical order. Any person who seeks administration over an estate must prove to the court that they have priority over anyone else. There are some minor exceptions to the hierarchy, which are set out in r 27(5). The court will generally prefer an adult beneficiary over the guardian of a minor beneficiary (even if the minor beneficiary is in a higher class than the adult beneficiary). The court will also prefer a living beneficiary over the PR of a deceased beneficiary. Rule 32 also states that, whereas administration can be granted to a parent or guardian of a minor, if the minor has no interest in the residue of the estate, administration should be granted to whomever takes the residue, unless the probate registrar or district judge directs otherwise.

Indeed, ultimately the probate registrar or district judge has a fair amount of discretion to make a decision as to whom will be granted administration under r 27(5).

Where there are several potential administrators in the same class, one of them can seek administration without notifying the others in the same class (r 27(4)). This might be of practical relevance if, for instance, another beneficiary in that class cannot easily be located or is living abroad. Nonetheless, it also has the potential to cause upset. If there is a dispute over who should be appointed, the court follows certain rules.

An obvious solution is to appoint several people as co-administrators, but this is not always a practical solution. The court will not force people to serve as co-administrators against their will, and there may be several reasons (such as a family dispute) why beneficiaries do not want to serve together. As seen, the court will prefer someone with an absolute interest over someone with a contingent interest. If necessary, the court will make a decision based on who has the larger beneficial interest (*Dampier v Colson* (1812) 2 Phill Ecc 54, 161 ER 1076). The court will also not appoint someone who is involved in a legal dispute against the estate (as seen, creditors can be appointed administrators). The court will also not appoint someone who is of 'bad character' (*Budd v Silver* (1813) 2 Phill Ecc 115, 161 ER 1094).

key case

Budd v Silver (1813) 2 Phill Ecc 115, 161 ER 1094

There were nine beneficiaries equally entitled through a will. Two of them sought to be appointed administrator. Four beneficiaries supported Budd, three supported Silver. The court thus favoured Budd, since he and his supporters had the larger beneficial interest (five out of nine shares). One of the objections to Budd was that Silver had a 'superior' station in society: Silver was an alderman of the City of Winchester whereas Budd was 'only a small shopkeeper'. Now, it is true that Britain in 1813 had a much more rigid class system than today. However, the court sensibly held that Budd's 'inferior' station in life was not a valid reason to favour Silver's appointment. Further, one of Silver's sons was 'likely' to raise an objection to the validity of one of the gifts in the will, and thus it was inappropriate to appoint Silver as administrator. Budd was therefore appointed administrator.

A person can also be 'passed over', which will be expanded upon below at **9.5**.

9.3.3 Order of priority for simple administration

The order of priority for simple administration is set out in r 22 of the NCPR 1987. This applies for intestate estates. The hierarchical order mirrors the entitlement to the estate on intestacy set out in s 46 of the Administration of Estates Act 1925 (see **Chapter 8**). To be considered as an administrator, the person must have a beneficial interest in the estate by virtue of s 46.

Rule 22(1)(a) – 'the surviving spouse or civil partner'

The person with priority is any spouse or civil partner who survives the deceased. Remember that, according to s 46(2A) of the Administration of Estates Act 1925, the surviving spouse or civil partner must outlive the deceased by 28 days; otherwise they are treated as not having survived the deceased. The spouse or civil partner is still entitled if divorce proceedings have been initiated but not yet concluded by a decree absolute.

Rule 22(1)(b) – 'the children of the deceased and the issue of any deceased child who died before the deceased'

The second class includes the deceased's children. It also includes the deceased's grandchildren if the deceased's children died first. If the child or grandchild so entitled is still a minor, administration can be granted to their parents, anyone acting as their parent, a legal guardian, or a relevant adoption agency or local authority that has responsibility for the minor (NCPR 1987, r 32).

Rule 22(1)(c) – 'the father and mother of the deceased'

The third class is the deceased's parents. The parents would ordinarily be appointed together and become co-administrators, though if it is necessary, letters of administration will only be given to one parent (*Re JS (Disposal of Body)* [2016] EWHC 2859 (Fam), [2017] 4 WLR 1).

Rule 22(1)(d) – 'brothers and sisters of the whole blood and the issue of any deceased brother or sister of the whole blood who died before the deceased'

The fourth class includes brothers and sisters of the whole blood, that is to say, having the same parents as the deceased. If the siblings predeceased the deceased, the fourth class also includes the deceased's nieces and nephews.

Rule 22(1)(e) – 'brothers and sisters of the half blood and the issue of any deceased brother or sister of the half blood who died before the deceased'

The fifth class is the same as the fourth, except that it deals with half-blood siblings, that is to say, where they share only one parent with the deceased. Again, if the half-blood siblings predecease the testator, the fifth class also includes the deceased's nieces and nephews.

Rule 22(1)(f) – 'grandparents'

The sixth class is the deceased's grandparents.

Rule 22(1)(g) – 'uncles and aunts of the whole blood and the issue of any deceased uncle and aunt of the whole blood who died before the deceased'

This class encompasses whole-blood aunts and uncles and, should they predecease the deceased, it also includes the deceased's cousins.

Rule 22(1)(h) – 'uncles and aunts of the half blood and the issue of any deceased uncle and aunt of the half blood who died before the deceased'

Again, it is the same as group (g) above, but making the distinction between whole-blood and half-blood relatives.

Rule 22(2) – The Treasury Solicitor if the Crown is claiming the estate through *bona vacantia*

If the Crown is claiming the estate through *bona vacantia*, the Treasury Solicitor can apply for simple administration.

Rule 22(3) – Any creditor of the deceased

The last person entitled to simple administration is a creditor of the deceased. The creditor might not have a beneficial interest in the estate but is entitled to administration if everyone else renounces administration.

9.3.3.1 Determining the order of priority for simple administration

Rule 27(5) applies also to simple administration. This means that an adult is preferred over the guardian of a minor, and a living beneficiary is preferred over the PR of a deceased beneficiary. Nonetheless, r 22(4) says that the PR of any person mentioned in r 22 is entitled to the administration of the deceased's estate. Any disputes will be resolved by the court.

9.4 Chain of executors and administration *de bonis non*

Another issue that must be addressed is what happens if an executor or administrator dies whilst they are still in the process of administering the estate. The law states that the administration should, ideally, be completed within a year. However, this is not always possible, especially for larger and more complex estates. There is, therefore, a very real risk that the PR might die in office.

Where there are two executors, and one dies, the other remains to continue the work. This, therefore, does not present any problems. However, if there is only one executor, and this person dies, a so-called chain of executors can arise (Administration of Estates Act 1925, s 7). The chain is illustrated in the example below.

example – a chain of executors

Assume that Amit has died. In his will, Amit appointed Kabir to be his executor. Whilst administering Amit's estate, Kabir dies. In his will, Kabir has appointed Nadine to be his executor. Nadine will take on the role of executor over Kabir's estate as well as becoming the executor of Amit's estate. Nadine will be Amit's executor by representation. Nadine will either have to be executor for both Kabir and Amit or for neither of them. She cannot choose to be only Kabir's executor. The chain can continue on as long as it is necessary. If Nadine dies before finishing the administration of Kabir's and Amit's estates, and appoints Amira to be her executor, Amira will be Nadine's executor and executor by representation for Kabir and Amit.

The chain of executors is broken in three circumstances (Administration of Estates Act 1925, s 7(3)):

(1)   It is broken if any executor dies intestate.

(2)   It is broken if any executor dies without appointing their own executor.

(3)   It is broken if an executor renounces probate or fails to get probate, perhaps because the will is invalid.

Where the chain of executors is broken, administrators will have to be appointed over all of the relevant estates instead. Here, there is no chain, and each estate will get an administrator using the NCPR 1987 rules. These administrators will be given letters of administration *de bonis non*. The court will apply the hierarchical lists in r 20 or r 22 of the NCPR 1987, as appropriate, for each estate to find the next appropriate administrator.

Letters of administration *de bonis non* are also granted if an administrator dies whilst still administering the estate. Unlike for executors, there is no chain for administrators. The court will return to r 20 or r 22 and find the next appropriate person to appoint as administrator.

9.5   Passing over a PR

As seen above, a testator can freely choose whom they want as their executor, and the courts have to follow fixed lists when they are appointing administrators. Reality is always more complicated than that. Circumstances can arise where beneficiaries have legitimate complaints against either a named executor or a person with priority over them to obtain administration. To address such concerns, the law allows the court to 'pass over' any PR, if it is deemed necessary. The test for passing over a PR is set out in s 116 of the Senior Courts Act 1981:

116 Power of court to pass over prior claims to grant

(1)   If by reason of any special circumstances it appears to the High Court to be necessary or expedient to appoint as administrator some person other than the person who, but for this section, would in accordance with probate rules have been entitled to the grant, the court may in its discretion appoint as administrator such person as it thinks expedient.

...

The legislative provision requires two things to be shown. The first is that there are 'special circumstances', and the second is that it would be 'necessary or expedient' to pass over the PR. The court has wide discretion to determine whether the two requirements have been met (*Khan v Crossland* [2012] WTLR 841 (unreported)). Different judgments have suggested that the court's discretion is either broad or more limited, which is unfortunate. The discretion is likely to be broader when objecting to administrators rather than executors, given that executors have been consciously chosen and appointed by the testator (*AB v Dobbs* [2010] EWHC 497 (Fam)). That choice should be respected, which might mean that the court should be more reluctant to exercise its power under s 116. Nonetheless, each case will turn on its own facts.

A good example of the operation of s 116 is the case of *Re JS (Disposal of Body)* [2016] EWHC 2859 (Fam), [2017] 4 WLR 1. A teenage girl, dying of cancer, wanted her body to be cryogenically frozen. The idea of cryogenic freezing is that one day, when a cure has been discovered for whatever illness killed the individual, they can be reanimated and cured. Cryogenic freezing is something that divides the scientific community. As JS was a minor, both her parents would ordinarily be appointed joint administrators of her estate, which would include deciding what to do with the body (NCPR 1987, r 22(1)(c)). The mother agreed to cryogenic freezing but the father objected to it. The court agreed that the circumstances were special and that it was expedient to pass over the father. As such, the mother became the sole administrator of JS's estate.

In the case of *In the Estate of S* [1968] P 302, a wife killed her husband and was convicted of manslaughter on the grounds of diminished responsibility. The wife was the named executor in the husband's will. She was passed over in favour of the husband's daughters, who were granted letters of administration with the will annexed. A similar situation arose in the case of *In the Estate of Crippen* [1911] P 108. This might be one of England's most infamous murder cases. Dr Crippen killed his wife, Cora Crippen. Dr Crippen and his mistress, Ethel Le Neve, went on the run but were captured. Dr Crippen was sentenced to death for the murder; Ethel Le Neve was also charged with murder but was acquitted. Dr Crippen wrote a will, naming Ethel Le Neve as his executor. After his execution, Ethel Le Neve sought probate of Dr Crippen's estate but also of Cora Crippen's estate, as the PR of Cora Crippen's husband who had survived her (today, NCPR 1987, r 22(1)(a) and r 22(4)). Cora Crippen's sisters objected to her appointment. The court passed over Ethel Le Neve, saying that the circumstances were special, and gave letters of administration over Cora's estate to Cora Crippen's sisters.

In other cases, PRs have been passed over on the grounds of convenience more than anything. In the case of *In the Goods of Cholwill* (1865-69) LR 1 P&D 192, a testator died leaving a working farm. The named executor lived in New Zealand. At the time, it would take many months for news of the testator's death to reach New Zealand by post and for the executor to return to England to seek probate. This kind of delay is not appropriate for any estate, especially for a working business, which needs someone to take legal ownership immediately. The court therefore passed over the executor in favour of the testator's sister, who, as administrator, could immediately take over the running of the farm.

As a matter of course, rr 20 and 22 of the NCPR 1987 apply here, and administration will be granted to whomever is next in line, or to some other person whom the court finds most appropriate. There may be cases where, due to a family dispute, it might not be appropriate to appoint the people with immediate priority, in case they might be biased against each other in the administration of the estate (consider *Adepoju v Akinola* [2016] EWHC 3160 (Ch)).

9.6 Further reading

Munro, Philip, 'The Passing Over of Executors Following *Khan v Crossland*' [2012] PCB 217–20.

This chapter has looked at personal representatives. It is important to distinguish between executors, who ordinarily are appointed through the will, and administrators, who are appointed by the court. It is important to understand the hierarchical lists in rr 20 and 22 of the Non-Contentious Probate Rules 1987, which outline who will be appointed administrator over the estate. The chapter then considered the chain of executors. Lastly, the chapter looked at how PRs can be passed over where, in special circumstances, it is necessary or expedient to do so.

chapter 10 Taxation

In the previous chapter, we saw how a PR is chosen and how they are appointed to the office. Once appointed, they are subject to a number of key duties. One of the fundamental issues that the PR has to deal with is tax. The purpose of this chapter is to outline the PR's tax obligations.

This chapter will therefore only look at those aspects of tax law that are relevant to the administration of estates. It must be stressed from the start that tax law is inherently complex, and this chapter can only present a general overview. In particular, there are many tax exemptions and reliefs that cannot be covered here. There are also many ways to engage in (lawful) tax planning, which allows a person to structure their affairs in the most tax efficient way possible. In practice, a PR will have to carefully follow the HMRC guidance and, especially for larger and more complex estates, they may need to seek professional advice.

The chapter starts by looking at income tax and capital gains tax before turning to inheritance tax. The chapter covers the following issues:

- What duties does a PR have in relation to paying tax?
- Income tax (IT): what is it and how does it relate to the administration of estates?
- Capital gains tax (CGT): what is it and how does it relate to the administration of estates?
- Inheritance tax (IHT): what is IHT and when does a PR have to pay IHT?
- What is the difference between paying IHT on death, on a potentially exempt transfer and on a lifetime chargeable transfer?
- What are the main exemptions and reliefs from IHT?

This chapter is written based on the tax rates for the 2021/22 tax year. These rates were announced by the Chancellor of the Exchequer on 3 March 2021. It is important to emphasise that tax law is dynamic, and many tax rates are changed on an annual basis (through the Budget, which results in the annual Finance Act). Always check the latest tax rates on www.gov.uk.

10.1 Tax and the PR's duty to pay it

There is no specific definition of a tax. It is a sum of money that individuals or businesses have to pay whenever they obtain taxable income or provide taxable goods or services. It is normally calculated based on a percentage of that income or based on the value of the goods or services provided. Taxes are imposed each year by Parliament in the annual Finance Act, which puts onto a legal footing the government's annual financial plan (generally known as the budget). Taxes are paid to HMRC (Her Majesty's Revenue and Customs), which is the government department responsible for collecting taxes. There are a lot of different taxes, but the ones with the most relevance to the administration of estates are income tax, capital gains tax and inheritance tax. Trustees of a trust, including a testamentary trust, will be subject to further taxes when investing the trust fund, such as stamp duty (a tax on the value of a share, paid by the purchaser of the share) or stamp duty land tax (a tax on the value of a legal estate in land, paid by the purchaser of the estate).

The tax year runs from 6 April–5 April each year. Changes to the tax code, including changes to the tax rates, generally take effect from 6 April. In general, any tax due must be paid to HMRC by 31 January the following year. Thus, tax accrued between 6 April 2021 and 5 April 2022 must be paid to HMRC by 31 January 2023. However, employment income tax and National Insurance contributions are generally paid automatically by the employer through a system called PAYE (Pay as You Earn), which means that many people have no need to concern themselves with the tax system. However, anyone who has tax liabilities that are not covered by PAYE must account for tax each year to HMRC and pay it on time. HMRC can impose penalties for late payment.

A PR can be liable to pay tax in three specific circumstances:

(1) The first thing that the PR has to investigate is whether the deceased had any outstanding tax liability to HMRC, which needs to be paid. This can include income tax not yet paid on income generated before death. As noted, the tax year runs from 6 April to 5 April each year. If the deceased died in, for example, October, the deceased might have accrued tax liabilities between 6 April and the date of death.

(2) The second is to account for inheritance tax (IHT) on the estate and, where necessary, pay the IHT. The date by which IHT must be paid is different from the norm, and is explained in more detail below.

(3) The third is to pay any tax liability that arises during the administration of the estate, such as income tax on income generated during the administration process.

The PR will have to check for all three potential tax liabilities, though whether tax does need paying will depend on the particular estate. For example, not all estates will have income-generating assets (such as a savings account or shares in a company) on which income tax must be paid. However, the PR is under a duty to check. Dealing with tax is therefore a key duty that the PR has to perform. As such, when studying succession law, it is vital to obtain a basic understanding of the relevant tax law. Again, it is emphasised that what follows is a general overview of three key taxes (income tax, capital gains tax, and inheritance tax), but it is not a comprehensive guide. Furthermore, other taxes apply, which are not covered here.

10.2   Income tax

Income tax is a tax levied on all money that a person earns. Perhaps the most obvious form of earning is employment income, namely your salary, wages or other job benefits, such as bonuses (Income Tax (Earnings and Pensions) Act 2003, s 62). Income tax is also levied on other earnings, such as interest paid on cash savings; investment income, such as share dividends; or rental income, if you are a landlord and let out a property.

10.2.1   The general income tax rates

The tax rates for income tax are set by the Income Tax Act 2007. For the 2021/22 tax year, there are three income tax rates, set out in s 6. They are the basic rate, taxed at 20%; the higher rate, taxed at 40%; and the additional rate, taxed at 45%.

The tax brackets are set out in s 10, and they are usually varied each year with the annual budget:

- A person is entitled to a 'personal allowance', where income tax is not paid. For the 2021/22 tax year, the personal allowance is £12,570. The government announced in the 2021 Budget Statement that the personal allowance would remain at that value until 2026, though that could, of course, change in future budgets. However, this allowance is reduced if the person earns more than £100,000 per year – the allowance goes down by £1 for every £2 a person earns above £100,000. This means that once a person earns £125,140, the personal allowance has been reduced to zero.
- The 'basic rate' bracket (taxed at 20%) is charged on the first £37,700 above the personal allowance. The government announced that this would also remain until 2026, though that could, of course, change in future budgets.
- The 'higher rate' bracket (taxed at 40%) is charged on income above the basic rate bracket and up to £150,000.
- The 'additional rate' (taxed at 45%) is changed on income above £150,000.

income tax – example 1

Assume Hannah is 25 and works 40 hours per week on the National Living Wage (in 2021 it is £8.91 per hour). Over a 52-week period, Hannah will earn £18,532. What is Hannah's income tax liability?

- Personal allowance: the first £12,570 is tax exempt.
- Hannah's taxable income is therefore £18,532 – £12,570 = £5,962.
- £5,962 is within the basic rate bracket (which is £37,700) so it is taxed at 20%.
- Hannah's pays £1,192.40 in tax.

(Note that this calculation does not take into account National Insurance payments or any pension fund contributions that Hannah might make, which might affect how the income tax is calculated.)

income tax – example 2

Assume that Phoebe is a solicitor and earns £65,000 per year. What is Phoebe's income tax liability?

- Personal allowance: the first £12,570 is tax exempt.
- Phoebe's taxable income is therefore £65,000 – £12,570 = £52,430.
- The basic rate bracket covers only the first £37,700 – this is taxed at 20%, which amounts to £7,540.
- Phoebe's remaining income (£52,430 – £37,700 = £14,730) is in the higher rate bracket – this is taxed at 40%, which amounts to £5,892.
- Phoebe's total income tax liability is therefore £7,540 + £5,892 = £13,432.

(Again, this calculation does not take into account National Insurance payments or any pension fund contributions that Phoebe might make, which might affect how the income tax is calculated.)

10.2.2 Income tax on savings

When it comes to interest paid on savings, such as from money held in a savings account at the bank, the starting point is the personal allowance. Beyond that, a person who only pays income tax in the basic rate bracket is entitled to earn £1,000 in interest per year tax free. A person who reaches the higher rate bracket is entitled to earn £500 in interest per year tax free. A person who reaches the additional rate has no allowance.

Where a person earns less that £17,570 from their other income, they can get up to £5,000 in savings income taxed at 0%. The 0% savings income band reduces by £1 for each £1 the person earns above their personal allowance. Thus, assume that Emma earns £16,000 in employment income and £400 in savings income. The personal allowance is £12,570, meaning that Emma has earned £3,830 above it. The £5,000 0% income tax band has thus been reduced by that amount. Her £400 savings income fits within the remaining £1,170 0% band, so Emma pays no income tax on her savings.

10.2.3 Income tax on dividends

When it comes to dividends paid out on shares, the tax brackets are different. The starting point, again, is the personal allowance. Beyond that, a person has an additional £2,000 dividend allowance. Thereafter, any dividend income that falls within the basic rate bracket (the first £37,700 above the personal allowance) is taxed at 7.5%. Dividend income that falls within the higher rate bracket is taxed at 32.5%. Dividend income that falls within the additional rate bracket is taxed at 38.1%. Note that dividend income is taxed as the 'top slice', namely after other income (from wages or savings) has been counted.

income tax on dividends – example 3

In example 1 above, we identified that Hannah is paying £1,192.40 in income tax. Assume that Hannah has inherited some shares. This year, the company paid out £700 to Hannah as dividends. This falls within the £2,000 allowance, so Hannah pays no additional dividend income tax. However, let us say that the company was very successful, and paid out £3,000 in dividends. The first £2,000 falls within the allowance. The remaining £1,000 is added to her wages income. It still falls within the basic income tax bracket. Therefore, the dividend income is taxed at 7.5%, which is £75. This means that Hannah's total income tax liability is £1,192.40 (wages) + £75 (dividends), which amounts to £1,267.40.

income tax on dividends – example 4

In example 2 above, we identified that Phoebe pays £13,432 in income tax. Assume that Phoebe has invested her money in shares. This year, the company paid out £6,000 to Phoebe as dividends. The first £2,000 falls within the allowance. The remaining £4,000 is taxable. We saw in this scenario that Phoebe has reached the higher rate bracket. This means that the £4,000 is taxed at 32.5%, which amounts to £1,300. Phoebe's total income tax liability is therefore £13,432 (wages) + £1,300 (dividends), which amounts to £14,732.

10.2.4 Relevance to a PR

The PR administering an estate has to consider two things. The first is that the deceased might have earned money in the tax year in which they died. The tax year runs from 6 April each year. If the deceased earned savings income and received dividend payments before dying in, say, November, the PR will have to account for that income. The second is that the estate might generate income after the deceased has died. The PR has to account for that income as well and pay the relevant income tax (Taxes Management Act 1970; Income Tax (Trading and Other Income) Act 2005, s 649ff). This has to be settled before the estate assets are transferred to the beneficiaries. Once the assets have been transferred to the beneficiaries, it becomes their property, and they must start paying the income tax on any income generated.

10.2.5 Relevance to a trustee

If money is held on trust, such as a testamentary trust invested for a minor beneficiary, income tax must be paid on any earnings made. In general, the tax rate for a fixed trust is linked to the beneficiary. If the income is paid directly to the beneficiary, the beneficiary might pay income tax rather than the trustees.

In accumulation trusts (where the income is not paid out, but is simply accumulated into the trust fund) or in a discretionary trust (where the trustees have discretion whether or not to pay out the income or capital), the trustees are tax liable. The first £1,000 of income is tax exempt (Income Tax Act 2007, s 491).

Thereafter, the 'trust rate' applies, which is 45% or, for dividends, 38.1%. These high rates are designed to ensure that trust property is actually paid out to beneficiaries, rather than kept 'hidden' in trust funds as a means of avoiding tax. One might query, however, whether these high rates have incentivised the use of offshore trusts in so-called tax havens.

Where money is paid from the trust fund to the beneficiaries, the beneficiaries can get relief from any tax that the trustees have already paid, which ensures that there is no double taxation on the property. Viscount Cave noted that 'if the Income Tax Acts are examined, it will be found that the person charged with the tax is neither the trustee nor the beneficiary as such, but the person in actual receipt and control of the income' (*Williams v Singer* [1921] 1 AC 65). Thus, whether it is the trustee or beneficiary who pays income tax depends on the type of trust.

10.3 Capital gains tax

Capital gains tax (CGT) is levied on the increase in the capital value of an item, measured from the purchase price to the sale price. For instance, Lara might buy shares worth £3,000 and, a few years later, sell them at profit for £5,000. The capital gain is the difference between the purchase price and the sale price, ie the amount of value that the asset has increased by or has 'gained'. In this instance that is £2,000. It is the capital gain that is subject to CGT. CGT is governed by the Taxation of Chargeable Gains Act 1992 and, as with income tax, the rates and exemptions will vary from year to year.

CGT is levied on chargeable gains. It follows that some gains are not chargeable, that is to say, they are exempt. This includes the purchase and sale of personal chattels worth less than £6,000 (s 262(1)). Personal chattels include things such as jewellery, paintings and collectibles, such as coins or stamps. CGT may be levied if the personal assets are sold for more than £6,000. Gifts to spouses (s 58), gifts to charities (s 256), the sale of the main residential home (s 222) and the sale of a personal motor vehicle (s 263) are also CGT exempt. However, CGT is applied for the sale of second homes or homes used as investments and on cars used for business purposes.

It is important to note that, whilst gifts to spouses and civil partners are themselves CGT exempt, the recipient spouse may have to pay CGT if they later sell that gift. The acquisition value of the property is the value when the first spouse obtained the property, not the value on the date of transfer from one spouse to the other. In the case of *Godfrey v HMRC* [2010] UKFTT 611, a husband inherited a house in 1986, valued at £40,000. This is the acquisition value. In 2005, he transferred a half-share in the property to his wife. The property was then valued at £450,000, and the wife's half-share was thus worth £225,000. In 2006, the property was sold and the wife obtained £232,500 for her half-share. The wife erroneously paid CGT on the increase from £225,000 to £232,500; rather she should have paid CGT on the increase from £20,000 (half of the original acquisition value) to £232,500. This, obviously, makes a huge difference; her CGT liability went up from the £90 she erroneously paid to £39,000 which she should have paid, using the applicable tax rates at the time.

As with income tax, there is an annual personal allowance for CGT. For CGT, this is referred to as the annual exempt amount. In 2021/22 it stands at £12,300 (ss 1K and 1L). The annual exempt amount applies in the same way to a PR when disposing of the estate assets. The PR is entitled to the full exemption for the tax year in which the deceased died and for the next two years (s 1K(7)). There is no exemption if the administration process takes longer than that. A trustee is entitled to only half of that exemption when disposing of trust assets (for example if shares are sold to make a cash payment to a beneficiary). However, if the beneficiary has a disability, the trustee is entitled to the full exemption. Various other reliefs may be available for CGT, but it is beyond the scope of this textbook to consider them here.

If a person makes chargeable gains above the annual exempt amount, they must pay CGT (s 1I). Unfortunately, this is where CGT gets complicated. The CGT rates are linked to the person's income tax liability. In short, a basic rate income tax payer will pay 10% CGT on all gains except for residential homes, where 18% CGT is levied. A higher or additional rate income tax payer will pay 20% CGT on all gains except for residential homes, where 28% CGT is levied. A PR or a trustee pays only the higher rates (20% and 28%). However, the CGT rates are, as said, linked to income tax. A basic rate income tax payer pays 10% or 18% CGT on gains that are within the balance of the basic rate income tax bracket. For gains that exceed the basic rate bracket, the higher CGT rates are levied.

If a person makes a loss, perhaps because shares were sold for less than they were purchased for, that loss can generally be offset against corresponding gains from other property. For example, if Sara sells one set of shares at a £5,000 profit (a chargeable gain) and sells another set of shares at a £2,000 loss (an allowable loss), her taxable gains are £3,000. Losses can also be carried forward to future tax years. If a person has made a large loss in one year, with some careful tax planning they can spread it out over future years and stay within the annual exempt amount. However, this rule has also been abused, with people trying to create artificial losses in order to reduce their tax liability. Such schemes are clamped down on by HMRC wherever possible; consider the case of *Schofield v HMRC* [2012] EWCA Civ 927.

To understand CGT, it is best to look at a couple of examples.

CGT – example 1

Assume that Lara earns £25,000 in income and, through good investments, makes £14,000 in chargeable gains by selling shares. What is Lara's tax liability?

- Income tax
  - The personal income tax allowance is £12,570. This means that Lara has a taxable income of £12,430. This is within the basic rate bracket of £37,700. This means that Lara pays income tax at 20%, which amounts to £2,486.
- Capital gains tax
  - The annual exempt amount is £12,300. This means that Lara is CGT liable for £1,700.
  - Go back to the basic rate income tax bracket. It is £37,700. Lara's taxable income is £12,430. This means that there is £25,270 left in the basic rate bracket (£37,700 − £12,430).
  - The chargeable gains of £1,700 fit within the balance of the basic rate income tax bracket. This means that the CGT rate is 10%, which amounts to £170.
- This means that Lara's total tax liability is £2,486 (income tax) + £170 (CGT), which amounts to £2,656.

(Again, this calculation does not take into account National Insurance, any pension fund payments that Lara might make, or various other reliefs that might be available to offset CGT.)

CGT – example 2

Assume that Alicia earns £45,000 in income and also makes £18,000 in chargeable gains. What is Alicia's tax liability?

- Income tax
  - The personal income tax allowance is £12,570. This means that Alicia has a taxable income of £32,430. This is within the basic rate income tax bracket of £37,700. This means that Alicia pays 20% income tax, which amounts to £6,486.
- Capital gains tax
  - The annual exempt amount is £12,300. This means that Alicia is CGT liable for £5,700.
  - Go back to the basic rate income tax bracket. It is £37,700. Alicia's taxable income was £32,430. This means that there is £5,270 left in the basic rate bracket (£37,700 − £32,430).
  - Of the £5,700 of gains that are subject to CGT, the first £5,270 is levied at 10% (£527).
  - The balance of the chargeable gains exceeds the basic rate income tax bracket. The balance, £430, is levied at 20% (£86).
  - The total CGT is £527 + £86, which is £613.
- Alicia's total tax liability is therefore £6,486 (income tax) + £613 (CGT), which amounts to £7,099.

(Again, this excludes National Insurance, pension fund contributions, or other CGT reliefs.)

10.3.1 Relevance to a PR

The PR's responsibility is the same as for income tax. The PR has to account for CGT on chargeable gains made by the deceased in the tax year in which the deceased died. The PR must then account for CGT on estate assets which are sold during the administration process. There is no CGT payable because of death; even though the property devolves on the PR, this does not qualify as a chargeable transfer (s 62).

There is no CGT levied if an asset is transferred *in specie* to the beneficiary. For instance, instead of selling shares to pay cash to the beneficiary, the shares themselves are transferred to the beneficiary. The beneficiary must then pay CGT when they sell the shares. The acquisition value of the property is the deceased's date of death, not the date the property was transferred from the PR to the beneficiary. This could make a difference if the value has changed noticeably between these two dates.

10.4 Inheritance tax

The final tax to consider is inheritance tax (IHT). It has a lot of components to it, but at the same time, there is a logical process to follow in order to calculate it. IHT is governed by the Inheritance Tax Act 1984. The short version of IHT is that estates worth more than £325,000 are taxed at 40% on the value above that threshold. However, unsurprisingly, the reality is more complex than that.

'Inheritance tax' is really a bit of a misnomer. IHT is actually a transfer tax, and it applies when property is transferred from one person to another in the applicable circumstances. IHT is applicable in three circumstances:

(a) on death, when the estate is devolved on the PR;

(b) on lifetime gifts made within seven years of the deceased's death, known as a 'potentially exempt transfer' (PET);

(c) on lifetime gifts into a trust or to a company, known as a 'lifetime chargeable transfer' (LCT). Half the tax is due when the LCT is made; the other half becomes due only if the donor dies within seven years.

The reason why IHT is levied on PETs and LCTs is quite logical. If not, it would be very easy to avoid IHT by simply giving away all of your assets before you died. Indeed, before LCTs, this was probably quite common. A person would transfer all of their assets into a discretionary trust, ostensibly giving the trustees 'discretion' whether or not to pay it back to the settlor (and perhaps the settlor's family) – in practice, there was no discretion; it was understood by everyone that the trustee would make payments back to the settlor. Tax reforms in the past decades have put a stop to such schemes and, unsurprisingly, discretionary trusts are not very popular today.

IHT is therefore levied on transfers on death and on certain lifetime gifts. Once a person has died, or has made an LCT, the following steps have to be followed:

(1) Value the estate (adding up its total value and deducting allowed liabilities).

(2) Deduct any exemptions.

(3) Deduct any reliefs.

(4) If applicable, add together the cumulative total (by including previously made chargeable PETs and LCTs).

(5) Calculate what IHT is payable.

Two additional steps may become relevant where LCTs have been made and IHT was immediately payable. This will be demonstrated in the examples later in the chapter.

(6) Apply taper relief.

(7) Account for tax already paid.

10.4.1 Step one: value the estate

The first thing that has to be done is to value the estate. At a basic level, this simply means identifying the financial value of each item owned by the deceased and adding them together. The value is the 'price which the property might reasonably be expected to fetch if sold in the open market at that time' (s 160). For some items, such as money in a bank account, valuation is very straightforward. For other items, a market value will have to be arrived at. When it comes to freeholds or leaseholds, for instance, the Valuation Office Agency may be instructed to provide a valuation. For practical reasons, so that the administration process does not become prohibitively complicated, the HMRC guidance states that if the estate is estimated to be valued at less than £250,000, the PR can rely on a 'best guess' using the s 160 test. If the estate is estimated to be valued above £250,000, the PR should engage a professional valuer.

Certain specific rules apply.

10.4.1.1 Joint property

It is quite common for family assets, such as a house or bank account, to be jointly owned between two spouses or civil partners. If the property is owned on a joint tenancy, the value of the deceased's share is simply half. Thus, if Patrick and Sandra were married and jointly owned a family home valued at £400,000, Patrick's share is £200,000. If Patrick jointly owns property with someone who is not a spouse or civil partner, the value of the house is half and then less 10%. So, if Patrick and Sandra were in a relationship (but not married), Patrick's share would be £180,000 (£200,000 – 10% (£20,000)).

10.4.1.2 Related property

Section 161 states that where two spouses jointly own property as tenants in common or separately own part of a collection of items, the valuation is based on the aggregate value, not the individual value of each share or item.

For example, let us consider a simplified version of the facts in *Price v HMRC* [2010] UKFTT 474. A husband and a wife owned a family home as tenants in common, meaning that the beneficial interest was split. The wife died, leaving her beneficial interest to her children. The house was worth £1.5 million. The husband remained living in the house. Now, if the husband, as his wife's PR, tried to sell the wife's beneficial interest on the open market, it would not be worth much (using the s 160 test). Why would anyone buy a 50% interest in a house where the husband remained living? However, since the husband's beneficial interest and the wife's beneficial interest were in the same house, the two assets (the beneficial interests) are related. Therefore, the valuation is based on the full value of the house (£1.5 million). The wife had a 50% interest in the property, which is valued for IHT purposes at £750,000.

Take another example. Assume that Patrick owns a set of six highly collectable figurines. Together, the figurine collection is worth £24,000 (this means that each individual figurine is worth £4,000). However, a single figurine on its own will only fetch £1,000. Assume that many years ago, Patrick gave one figurine to his wife as a gift. This means that the collection is technically broken: Patrick has five individual figurines (which are worth £5,000) and his wife has one figurine (worth £1,000). What does this mean when Patrick dies? The figurines are clearly related property, within the meaning of s 161, and since they are owned by two spouses, they have to be considered together (as a collection). Their collective value, as said, is £24,000. Patrick's IHT valuation is therefore £20,000 (five figurines at £4,000 each).

10.4.1.3 Quoted shares

Quoted shares are shares listed on a stock exchange, such as the London Stock Exchange. The Stock Exchange will list a high and a low daily price for the shares in that company. For example, the daily stock price for XZY Plc may be given as 115p/123p. The rule is to take one quarter of the difference and add it to the lower price. The difference is 8p, and a quarter of that is 2p. Add 2p to the lower price and the IHT valuation of the share is 117p. The valuation date is the day of death or the nearest trading day.

10.4.1.4 Deducting liabilities from the value of the estate

Once the whole estate has been valued, it is necessary to deduct any liabilities that the deceased might have had (s 162). An obvious liability is a mortgage on the house. Assuming that a house is valued at £200,000, but has a mortgage debt of £30,000 on it, the IHT valuation is £170,000. Other debts include credit card debts and any unpaid bills or tax liabilities. Reasonable funeral costs can also be deducted (s 172).

The estate will normally foot the bill for any legal or procedural fees (such as probate costs, solicitor fees, or the cost of hiring a professional valuer), but these cannot be deducted for IHT purposes.

10.4.2 Steps two and three: deduct any exemptions and reliefs from the value

Once the estate has been valued, the next two steps are to deduct any exemptions and reliefs from the value. It is only once the exemptions and reliefs are deducted that IHT can actually be calculated.

10.4.2.1 Deduct any exempt transfers

There are a number of exemptions from IHT. The value of these gifts must be deducted from the estate valuation.

For lifetime transfers only, there is an annual gift exemption of £3,000 and a wedding gift exemption of up to £5,000 (see more below).

For all transfers (whether lifetime gifts or transfers on death) further exemptions apply. Indeed, it is possible for entire estates to be exempt from IHT. Gifts to political parties (s 24 – which imposes certain criteria) and gifts to national purposes (s 25 – such as gifts to museums, the National Trust, the NHS or universities (set out in Sch 3)) are exempt from IHT. Individual gifts to charities are IHT exempt. If the entire estate is left to charity, no IHT is due since the whole estate is exempt. Another key exemption is a gift to a spouse or civil partner (s 18). Again, if the entire estate is left to a spouse, no IHT is due. Further, no IHT is due on the estate of a member of the armed forces who dies in active service (s 154).

By making lifetime gifts and other exempt gifts on your death, it is possible to ensure that no IHT is due, either by making the whole estate exempt or by bringing the taxable portion of the estate below the £325,000 threshold.

10.4.2.2 Deduct any applicable reliefs

Further, there are two key reliefs available, both for lifetime transfers and transfers on death. The first is called business property relief (BPR) (s 104) and the second is called agricultural property relief (APR) (s 116).

BPR applies to certain business property which the deceased has owned for at least two years. The relief is either 100% (ie no IHT is paid on this asset) or 50%. The full relief is available to business assets owned by a sole trader or to shares held in an unquoted company (that is, a company not listed on a stock exchange; Companies Act 2006, s 385). The half relief is available to shares in a quoted company, provided that the deceased had control of it (requiring 51% ownership), and to business assets (such as land or machines) owned by a quoted or unquoted company that the deceased controlled or by a partnership that the deceased was part of.

- Assume Patrick owned shares in an unquoted company. They were valued at £15,000. In 2018, he gave the shares to Claire. In 2021, Patrick died. This gift is a PET (see further below). Because Patrick died within seven years, IHT is due. Since the shares are in an unquoted company, 100% BPR is available. This means that no IHT is payable.

- Assume that Patrick runs a fish-and-chip shop with his friend Gary, which they operate as a partnership. They jointly own the freehold to the shop, which is valued at £100,000. This means that Patrick's share is £50,000. Patrick dies, leaving his share in the freehold to Claire. Since it is partnership property, 50% BPR is available. This means that IHT is due on £25,000.

APR applies to agricultural property, which is defined as farmland and buildings. The property must have been occupied by the deceased for at least two years and used for agriculture; or owned by the deceased for at least seven years and let out to someone for agricultural purposes for those seven years. Where the deceased owned the freehold or leasehold, 100% APR is available. If the deceased did not have the right to obtain possession within a year from a tenant (because the tenant has a long lease), 50% APR is available.

10.4.3 Step four: calculate the cumulative total by considering PETs and LCTs

The fourth step is to consider whether any PETs or LCTs have been made within seven years of the deceased's death.

10.4.3.1 Potentially exempt transfer

If a person makes a gift and dies within seven years, IHT is payable on that gift. However, there are some exemptions. The exemptions also apply to LCTs, which are discussed below.

Small gifts, valued at less that £250, are exempt (s 20).

There is an annual gift exemption of £3,000, which can be rolled forward for one year (only) if it is unused (s 19). Consider the following example:

- Patrick died in 2021.
- Assume that in 2018, he gifted £3,000 to Claire. This gift is IHT exempt because it falls within the annual exemption.
- Assume instead that in 2018, he gifted £5,000 to Claire. This gift is also IHT exempt, since Patrick can roll forward the £3,000 exemption for 2017 and use the £3,000 exemption for 2018. Indeed, he will have £1,000 of the 2018 exemption left, which he can roll forward to 2019.
- Assume instead that in 2018, he gifted £10,000 to Claire. He can use the 2017 exemption (£3,000) and the 2018 exemption (£3,000). This means that the remaining £4,000 of the gift is now subject to IHT, given that Patrick died within seven years of making the gift.

Money paid to another as 'normal expenditure' is exempt (s 21). The requirement is that the expenditure was normal, which is to say, something ongoing for a period of time. The expenditure must have been paid from the transferor's income, and the transferor must have had sufficient income left afterwards to maintain their own 'usual standard of living'.

- Assume that Patrick is a well-paid solicitor. He has a daughter, Chloe, who is at university. Using his monthly salary, he pays her £400 per month to help with her rent and other household bills. Having done so he can still maintain his own standard of living. The payments to Chloe are IHT exempt.

Gifts made in consideration of marriage are IHT exempt (s 22). Each parent (including a step-parent (s 22(2)) can make a gift of £5,000; other ancestors can make a gift of £2,500; and anyone else can make a gift of £1,000. It is possible to use the annual gift exemption together with the marriage exemption.

- Assume that in 2019, Chloe got married. Patrick, her father, gave her a gift of £10,000. Patrick died in 2021. This gift is IHT exempt.
  - Patrick can use the 2018 gift exemption (£3,000)
  - Patrick can use the 2019 gift exemption (£3,000)
  - Patrick can use the marriage exemption (£5,000)
- Assume that Patrick instead gave Chloe a gift of £20,000.
  - Patrick can use the 2018 gift exemption (£3,000)
  - Patrick can use the 2019 gift exemption (£3,000)
  - Patrick can use the marriage exemption (£5,000)
  - The remaining £9,000 is subject to IHT, given that Patrick died within seven years.

As with testamentary gifts, any lifetime gifts to charities are IHT exempt (s 23).

If the transferor survives for more than seven years, there is no IHT payable on the transfers. The seven-year cut-off point is there to ensure that people cannot avoid IHT by gifting away their entire estates just before dying. Bearing in mind the seven-year cut-off point, as well as the annual gift exemptions, people can undertake some tax planning in order to minimise their IHT liability.

If tax is payable, taper relief is available. It applies as follows. If the transferor dies between three and four years after making the transfer, only 80% of the IHT is payable. If the transferor dies between four to five years, only 60% of the IHT is payable; between five and six years, only 40%; and between six and seven years, only 20%. The operation of taper relief is shown in some of the examples later in the chapter.

10.4.3.2 Lifetime chargeable transfers

If the transfer is not a PET, it will be an LCT. LCTs operate on the same basis as PETs, to stop people avoiding IHT by transferring their property just before dying. One of the key things LCTs were designed to stop was the use of discretionary trusts. As such, since 2006, LCTs are any transfer into a trust, except into a disabled trust (where the beneficiary has a disability), or to a company.

The main difference between PETs and LCTs is that, for LCTs, IHT is payable immediately. If the LCT is valued between £0–£325,000, the IHT is taxed at 0%

(the so-called nil-rate band, or NRB). If the LCT is valued above £325,000, the portion above the NRB is taxed at 20%. This has to be paid immediately. However, if the transferor dies within seven years, the IHT has to be recalculated so that the full 40% IHT tax rate can be paid. Then, if the transferor has survived for more than three years but less than seven, taper relief is available. This means that between three and seven years, the tax payable will be gradually less than 40%. The concept of taper relief was outlined above.

LCT – example 1

Assume that Zara died in 2021. In 2016 (five-and-a-half years earlier) she paid £500,000 into a discretionary trust for the benefit of herself and other family members.

What IHT was paid by the trustees in 2016?

- Step 1: value: £500,000
- Step 2: exemptions: deduct any exemptions: annual gift exemption of £3,000 for 2016; annual gift exemption of £3,000 for 2015 (rolled forward); the total exemption is £6,000
- Step 3: reliefs: deduct any reliefs; there are none applicable
- Step 4: cumulative total: add together any previously paid LCTs and PETs; there are none applicable
- Step 5: calculate IHT: identify the IHT value: £494,000
- IHT is payable as follows:
  - NRB: £325,000 is taxed at 0%
  - The balance, £169,000, is taxed at 20%
  - The IHT liability is £33,800.

What IHT must the trustees pay in 2021, given that Zara died within seven years? The trustees must recalculate the IHT and then also account for the 2016 tax payment. This is where steps 6 and 7 come in.

- Step 1: value: £500,000
- Step 2: exemptions: (as above)
- Step 3: reliefs: (as above)
- Step 4: cumulative total: (as above)
- Step 5: calculate IHT: £494,000
- IHT is payable as follows:
  - NRB: £325,000 is taxed at 0%
  - The balance, £169,000, is taxed at 40%
  - The IHT liability is £67,600
- Step 6: taper relief: Zara died five-and-a-half years after the LCT was made, so taper relief applies. The trustees only have to pay 40% of the total IHT
- Applying taper relief, the IHT payable is £27,040 (40% of £67,600)
- Step 7: account for tax already paid: the trustees paid £33,800 in 2016, which is more than what is now required. This means that no more tax is actually payable in 2021. Sadly, the law does not allow for refunds.

LCT – example 2

Assume instead that Zara died in 2019, three-and-a-half years after making the LCT. What IHT is payable in 2017?

- Using the same steps above, we know the IHT liability is £67,600
- Step 6: taper relief: Zara died three-and-a-half years after the LCT was made, so taper relief applies. The trustees only have to pay 80% of the total IHT. Applying taper relief, the IHT payable is £53,600 (80% of £67,600)
- Step 7: account for tax already paid: the trustees paid £33,800 in 2016. That will be deducted from the IHT liability: £53,600 – £33,800 = £19,800. That is the additional IHT payable in 2019.

10.4.4 Step five: calculate IHT

At this point, the estate has been valued, exemptions and reliefs deducted, and PETs and LCTs identified. Now, IHT will be calculated. In fact, this has already been shown in the examples above, but this section will consider it in more detail.

IHT is levied at three main rates, set out in s 7, Sch 1 and Sch 1A.

- If the estate is valued between £0–£325,000, the IHT rate is 0%. This is known as the nil-rate band (NRB).
    - It is important to emphasise that this is not an exemption. IHT is actually levied, just at 0%.
- If the estate is valued at £325,001 and above, IHT is levied on the portion above the NRB at 40%.
- If at least 10% of the estate value is left to charity, the IHT is instead levied on the portion above the NRB at 36%.
    - Remember, the portion given to charity is IHT exempt, and if the whole estate is given to charity, then there is no IHT payable at all. The 36% rate applies to the remainder, if at least 10% of the total estate was given to charity.

In addition, if a person owns a house and leaves it to direct descendant (such as a parent leaving the family home to their child), up to an additional £175,000 is charged at 0% (for the 2021/22 tax year) (s 8D). This is known as the residence nil-rate band (RNRB). The RNRB only applies to people who died after April 2017 and only applies where the house is left to a direct descendant.

key terminology

Direct descendant: the RNRB only applies where the house is left to a direct descendant, which is defined as a child, grandchild, or other lineal descendant, as well as their spouse or civil partner. The definition of a child includes a stepchild, an adopted child, a child being fostered by the deceased, or someone the deceased acted for as a legal guardian.

A spouse or civil partner can inherit any unused NRB and RNRB (s 8A). If the deceased leaves everything to their surviving spouse, the estate is IHT exempt, as explained above. This means that the deceased has used none of their NRB or RNRB. The surviving spouse thus inherits it. The surviving spouse, when they die, is therefore entitled to a £650,000 NRB and (provided they leave their house to a direct descendant) a £350,000 RNRB, giving them a combined tax-free allowance of £1,000,000.

A few examples will be considered in order to better understand IHT.

IHT – example 1

Let us use Patrick as an example. Here is his estate. Assume he died in May 2021 (so the 2021/22 tax code applies).

Assets (assume these were solely owned by Patrick)	Value (on death)
A freehold estate	£350,000
Household contents	£25,000
Car	£18,000
Cash savings in Bank	£12,000
Premium Bonds	£35,000
Shares in PZA Ltd, an unquoted company	£30,000
Liabilities	**Value (on death)**
Mortgage on freehold estate	£20,000
Credit card debt	£3,000
Unpaid invoice for boiler repair	£1,000
Unpaid CGT for 2020/21 tax year	£6,000

Assume Patrick leaves his entire estate to his wife, Amanda

Step 1: value the estate

The first step is to value the estate. In short, this means adding up the assets and deducting the liabilities. The total value of Patrick's assets is £470,000. The value of his liabilities is £30,000. These have to be deducted. As such, for IHT purposes, Patrick's estate is valued at £440,000.

Step 2: deduct exemptions

Gifts to spouses are IHT exempt. Since Patrick leaves his entire estate to Amanda, there is no IHT payable.

There is no need to consider steps 3, 4 and 5 in this example, as no IHT is payable due to the spouse exemption. Amanda also inherits Patrick's full NRB and RNRB.

Assume instead that Patrick leaves his entire estate to his daughter, Chloe

Step 1: value the estate

The IHT value is £440,000 (as above).

Step 2: deduct exemptions

There are no applicable exemptions.

Step 3: deduct reliefs

Patrick owns £30,000 shares in PZA Ltd, an unquoted company. This entitles Patrick to business property relief. A 100% relief applies to shares in an unquoted company. As such, £30,000 has to be deducted. At this point, Patrick's estate is valued at £410,000 for IHT purposes.

Step 4: cumulation

Patrick has not made any PETs or LCTs.

Step 5: calculate IHT

The estate is valued at £410,000. The first £325,000 is taxed at 0% (the NRB). Since the estate consists of a house, which is left to a direct descendant, the RNRB applies. The remaining £85,000 of the estate falls within the RNRB and is taxed at 0%.

Patrick's wife, Amanda, inherits the unused portion of the RNRB (£90,000).

IHT – example 2

Let us assume that Patrick's estate is a bit different. Again assume he died in May 2021 (so the 2021/22 tax code applies).

Assets (assume the stated assets are jointly owned with his wife as joint tenants in law and equity)	Value (on death)
A freehold estate (as joint tenant with his wife Amanda)	£175,000
Household contents (as joint tenant with his wife Amanda)	£12,500
Car (as joint tenant with his wife Amanda)	£9,000
Cash savings in Bank	£12,000
Premium Bonds	£35,000
Shares in PZA Ltd, an unquoted company	£30,000
Liabilities	**Value (on death)**
Mortgage on freehold estate (joint liability with his wife Amanda)	£10,000
Credit card debt	£3,000
Unpaid invoice for boiler repair	£1,000
Unpaid CGT for 2020/21 tax year	£6,000

Assume that Patrick leaves his entire estate to his daughter, Chloe

Step 1: value the estate

As the table shows, Patrick owns the freehold, the household assets and the car, on a joint tenancy with his wife. As such, only half their value can be included in the calculation. Patrick's assets are worth £273,500. His liabilities are valued at £20,000, and these must be deducted. Patrick's estate is therefore IHT valued at £253,500.

Step 2: deduct exemptions

The property owned on joint tenancy passes to Amanda through the doctrine of survivorship – this goes to Amanda as the survivor, regardless of what it says in Patrick's will. The spousal exemption applies. As such, the freehold (£175,000), the household contents (£12,500) and the car (£9,000) have to be deducted. Patrick's estate is now valued at £57,000. No other exemptions apply.

Step 3: deduct reliefs

Again, business property relief at 100% applies for the unquoted shares. £30,000 must therefore be deducted. Patrick's estate is now valued at £27,000.

Step 4: cumulation

Patrick has not made any PETs or LCTs.

Step 5: calculate IHT

Patrick's estate is IHT valued at £27,000. This fits within the NRB and is taxed at 0%. Patrick's wife Amanda inherits the remaining £298,000 NRB and the full £175,000 RNRB.

IHT – example 3

Using the same estate as in Example 2 above (where the estate value on death was £27,000), assume that the following also took place. Five-and-a-half years ago, Patrick gifted £100,000 to his daughter, Chloe, on the occasion of her marriage. Three-and-a-half years ago, Patrick sold a lot of investments and paid £450,000 into a trust fund for his children. Patrick has now died.

IHT has to be calculated on these various chargeable transfers. The £100,000 marriage gift is a PET, and IHT is now due since Patrick did not survive for seven years. It came first in time, and has to be treated as such. However, the trust settlement was a LCT, and was taxable at the time. This means that you have to:

(a) look at the LCT (because it was paid at the time it was made);

(b) take account of the PET (and treat it as being first in time, since the PET was transferred before the LCT);

(c) revisit the LCT (recalculate it because of the PET);

(d) finally, look at the estate at the point of death.

This is where steps 6 and 7 come in, namely applying taper relief on the PET and LCT (if applicable) and accounting for any tax already paid on the LCT when it was set up.

LCT

The LCT was made three-and-a-half years ago. Because it was an LCT, IHT was payable immediately at 20%.

- Step 1: value
  - The LCT was worth £450,000
- Step 2: exemptions
  - Annual gift (four years ago): £3,000
  - Annual gift (three years ago): £3,000
  - IHT value: £444,000
- Step 3: reliefs
  - None apply
- Step 4: cumulation
  - Not applicable, as no gifts (other than the PET) were made in the previous seven years before death
- Step 5: IHT calculation on the LCT
  - £444,000 value
  - £325,000 (NRB) is taxed at 0%: £0
  - £119,000 is taxed at 20%: £23,800.

This means that three-and-a-half years ago, when the trust was set up, the trustees paid £23,800 in IHT.

PET

Patrick has now died. This means that the PET becomes chargeable. It is also first, chronologically, and has to be treated as such.

- Step 1: value
  - £100,000
- Step 2: exemptions
  - Annual gift (six years ago): £3,000
  - Annual gift (five years ago): £3,000
  - Marriage gift: £5,000
  - IHT value: £89,000
- Step 3: reliefs
  - None apply
- Step 4: cumulation
  - Not applicable (even though IHT was paid on the LCT, as above, the PET was chronologically first in time, and must be treated as such)
- Step 5: IHT calculation on the PET
  - £89,000
  - The full NRB applies to it

Note that taper relief is not applicable here, as no IHT is actually payable (the £89,000 fits within the NRB). If the value of the PET was higher, and the IHT due on the PET did exceed the NRB, taper relief would apply, and only 40% of the value would be payable as Patrick died five-and-a-half years after making the gift.

LCT revisited

Given that Patrick has died within seven years, full IHT (at 40%) is due on the LCT. Some tax was paid when the LCT was made, but it must now be reconsidered. The reconsideration must also take into account the PET, which was made before the LCT. This comes up in step 4. Further, as explained at **10.4.3** above, taper relief is available.

- Step 1: value
  - £450,000
- Step 2: exemptions
  - Two annual gifts
  - £444,000
- Step 3: reliefs
  - None apply
- Step 4: cumulation
  - £89,000 of the NRB has already been used by the PET
- Step 5: IHT calculation
  - £236,000 of the NBR remains and is taxed at 0%: £0
  - £208,000 is taxed at 40%: £83,200
- Step 6: taper relief
  - The LCT was made 3–4 years ago, so only 80% of the tax has to be paid
  - IHT payable is £66,560
- Step 7: account for tax paid when the trust was set up
  - £23,800 was paid by the trustees when the trust was set up (identified above)
  - This can be deducted from the £66,560
  - £42,760 is now due in IHT.

Patrick's estate

We are using Example 2 (above) setting out Patrick's estate on his death. Applying steps 1 to 5, it was established that Patrick's estate on his death was valued at £27,000. However, the PET and the LCT have now eaten up the entire NRB. This means that the £27,000 has to be taxed at 40%, which is £10,800. Note, the RNRB does not apply here since the house was not left to Chloe (Patrick jointly owned the house with his wife Amanda, so it passed to her through survivorship).

The total IHT liability is the £42,760 due for the LCT and the £10,800 due for the estate, which amounts to £53,560.

10.5 Paying IHT

When a person dies, it is their PR who has to pay the IHT. Accounting and paying IHT are amongst the very first things that have to be done. Importantly, the court will not issue a grant of representation to the PR until IHT has been paid.

In short, the grant is a court order proving that the PR has legal title to the estate and may dispose of estate assets. The exact rules for when a grant is required and how it is obtained are set out in the next chapter. A grant might not be necessary for small-value assets but will definitely be required for high-value assets, such as a house. Given that IHT is likely to run into the tens of thousands, a grant is very likely necessary for those estates that pass the £325,000 threshold. So, how is IHT actually paid if the PR is unable to access the estate assets?

The PR has to submit an IHT tax form to HMRC. There are different forms depending on whether IHT is actually due (eg if the estate is above or below the NRB/RNRB, or if the entire estate is exempt because it goes to a spouse or to charity). If IHT is due, HMRC will provide a tax reference. This can be used to access money held by the deceased in their bank account, any savings held with National Savings and Investments (such as Premium Bonds or ISAs run by NS&I) or any ownership of British government bonds. Otherwise, the PR will personally have to pay IHT and then claim it back from the estate. Many banks will provide a probate loan to allow the PR to pay IHT. This may seem surprising, but it is a practical way for HMRC to ensure that estates are properly valued and that IHT is actually paid.

Tax is normally due by 31 January in the following year. However, IHT works differently. Instead, IHT is due at the end of the sixth month after the deceased died. So, if Patrick died on 7 May 2021, the IHT is due by 30 November 2021. The PR can apply to pay the IHT by instalments, and HMRC can allow the PR to pay using up to 10 annual instalments. In Patrick's case, if the PR asks to pay in annual instalments, the first payment will be due on 30 November 2021, and the 10th and final payment will be due on 30 November 2031. This can be of particular importance if the main asset is a residential house, and the PR (or any other beneficiary) wants to keep living in it. Otherwise, it is likely that the house, as the most valuable item, will have to be sold in order to foot the IHT bill (or, more accurately, to reimburse the PR). However, interest is charged on the IHT due if it is paid in instalments, so it is important to consider carefully whether paying a lump sum or by instalments is the preferred method.

10.6 Further reading

Always check the latest tax rates on the gov.uk website. The relevant pages on income tax, capital gains tax and inheritance tax contain clear explanations of the rules and a range of further guidance documents.

summary

This chapter has outlined the key rules for income tax, capital gains tax and inheritance tax, using the 2021/22 tax code. Remember that the tax code changes on an annual basis (the tax year runs from 6 April each year). Always check the latest tax brackets and percentage points. It is extremely important for a PR to have an understanding of tax, especially IHT. It is only once IHT has been paid that the administration process can begin. Hopefully the IHT examples have also demonstrated that the NRB, the RNRB and the allowed exemptions and reliefs can ensure that IHT is not an overly onerous tax and that most estates will not be liable to pay IHT at all.

Administration I – The Grant

In **Chapter 9**, we looked at personal representatives (PRs) and how they are appointed. In **Chapter 10**, we saw that one of the first obligations of a PR is to account for inheritance tax (IHT). Once IHT has been accounted for (by submitting the correct tax forms and, if applicable, the payment), the PR can apply to the Probate Registry (a part of the Family Division) for formal permission to administer the estate. This is known as 'applying for a grant'.

This chapter considers the grant and the process for applying for it. This is the first of four chapters that look at the administration process and outline the duties that the PR is subject to. The remedies available for wrongful administration are considered later in **Chapter 16**.

This chapter addresses the following issues:

- What happens when a person dies?
- What estates are exempt from a grant?
- What is a grant of probate?
- What is a grant of simple administration, and what is a grant of administration with the will annexed?
- How can a grant be challenged and revoked?

11.1 Events following death

The first thing that must be considered is what actually happens when a person dies. Some of the tasks that follow death might not necessarily be undertaken by the PR, but rather by the deceased's family, relatives or friends.

When a person has died, the first thing that must be arranged is for the body to be examined by a doctor. The doctor must then issue a medical certificate, which will confirm the death and set out the cause of death.

Once a medical certificate has been issued by a doctor, the death has to be registered at a Register Office. The Register Offices are administered by local authorities, such as a city or county council. They form an important part of government administration by keeping formal records of births, deaths and marriages/civil partnerships. Most people are probably familiar with the Register Office as the place to register (and hold) civil marriages/partnerships, but, as said, they are also responsible for registering all births and deaths.

A death registration should ideally be made at the Register Office nearest to where the deceased died, though it can be made at any Register Office in England and Wales. The death should be registered within five days of death (see Births and Deaths Registration Act 1953, ss 16 and 17). News reports in the past few years have suggested that registrations are being delayed, for example because the medical certificate is not provided in time, or, due to budget cuts, because of delays caused by the short-staffing of Register Offices.

A number of people are entitled to register the death, also set out in ss 16 and 17 of the Births and Deaths Registration Act 1953. The death should be registered by a relative who was present at the time of death, or present during the deceased's final illness, or who lived nearby. It can alternatively be registered by anyone else present at the time of death (such as a hospital administrator), by another person who was residing with the deceased, or by the person arranging the funeral (but not by the actual funeral director). Therefore, it might not be the PR who is responsible for registering the death.

If the death was due to natural or explained causes, the death can be registered immediately using the medical certificate. If the death was unexplained, sudden, suspicious or due to a criminal act, the death will be referred to the coroner (the rules for this are beyond the scope of this textbook, but, generally, see the Coroners and Justice Act 2009). There may be a post-mortem examination of the body and there may also be a coronial inquest. The coroner has sole responsibility to order a post-mortem or an inquest. An inquest is, in essence, a trial of fact in the Coroner's Court, which aims to establish the cause of death. This is highly relevant as, for example, a finding of unlawful killing will trigger a police investigation. If an inquest is held, the death can only be registered once the coroner has completed the inquest. The inquest is likely to take many months, in particular if a post-mortem examination has to be performed.

When the death is registered with the Register Office, the Registrar will provide three key documents (the Registrar is the officer responsible for the Register Office and has the legal authority to register the birth, death or marriage, and to issue the relevant legal documents):

- The first is a certificate for burial or cremation, which is commonly referred to as the 'green form'. This is required for a burial or cremation to take place and must be handed over to the funeral director.
  - If the death cannot be registered due to a coroner's inquest taking place, the coroner may issue his own burial order to allow a burial or cremation once the post-mortem examination has taken place. This allows for a burial before the inquest is completed. Even though the body is buried or cremated, the death will not be registered until after the inquest.
- The Registrar will also issue a death certificate, which will be required for the administration process. Even if no grant is required (see more below), a death certificate will be required in order to access the deceased's assets, such as a

bank account. At the moment, death certificates have to be purchased and cost £4 in England and Wales. The PR may require one death certificate for each institution that the PR needs to access, for instance if the deceased had accounts with multiple banks.

- The Registrar will also issue a certificate of registration of death, known as BD8, which, if the deceased was in receipt of a state pension or state benefits, must be sent to the Department of Work and Pensions. The BD8 is free and comes with a pre-paid envelope.

The section below looks at small estates, where the probate process is relatively straightforward. The PR will be able to administer the estate using the death certificate and does not require a formal grant. Thereafter, the chapter will consider the position where the administration process can only begin after a grant has been obtained.

11.2 Estates exempt from a grant of probate or administration

Some estates do not require a grant of probate or administration. A typical example is an estate which was jointly owned and therefore passes in its entirety through survivorship to the surviving spouse. If the deceased had a personal bank account, a grant may still be needed in order to access that account.

Small estates might also be exempt from a grant (Administration of Estates (Small Payments) Act 1965). This is known as the small estates procedure. However, in practice this will turn on what processes are used by each relevant institution where the deceased had assets. This includes banks, building societies, insurance companies, pension funds and so on. The PR must therefore contact each relevant institution to ask whether or not they will release the funds without a grant. The institution will definitely require a copy of the death certificate, which was mentioned above. In general, a grant is required if the estate is worth more than £5,000, but some institutions may forgo a grant even for larger estates. For example, some banks surveyed by the author are willing to forgo a grant for bank accounts worth up to £50,000. This simplifies the probate process and makes it quicker and cheaper.

example

Dorothy has died intestate aged 80. She lived in a nursing home, and the fees were paid by Peter, her only child. At the date of death, Dorothy's estate consisted of the following:

- Cash in hand: £45
- Personal bank account: £1,740
- State pension arrears for the month of death: £145
- Cash in an ISA held with National Savings & Investments (NS&I): £3,780

No individual asset is worth more than £5,000. Dorothy's total estate is worth £5,710. It is unlikely that the bank or NS&I will require a grant. On producing the death certificate, both the bank and NS&I should release the funds to Peter. Peter will send the BD8 to the DWP, which will pay the state pension arrears for the month Dorothy died and then close her account.

The administration of Dorothy's estate should take no longer than a few months from the date the death was registered, depending on how efficiently the bank and NS&I process Peter's request to have the funds transferred to him.

11.3 Grant of probate or letters of administration

The chapter will now look at the position where a grant is required. A grant is, fundamentally, a court order authorising the PR to act.

11.3.1 Types of grant

There are three different types of PR, as discussed in **Chapter 9**:

(a) The first is an *executor*, who is validly appointed through a will.

(b) The second is an *administrator with the will annexed*, who is appointed by the court where the deceased left a will but did not validly appoint an executor.

(c) The third is an *administrator*, who is appointed by the court where the deceased died intestate.

An executor derives their authority to deal with the estate through the will. Therefore, they can lawfully take possession of the deceased's property immediately after death. As indicated above, they might not need a grant at all. However, if the deceased owned substantial assets, a grant is going to be necessary. Many asset holders (such as banks and building societies) will insist on the production of a grant in order to combat fraud. The executor will apply for a grant of probate.

Administrators derive their authority to act through their appointment by the court. Unless exempt, they cannot deal with the deceased's property until they have been authorised to do so by the court. As noted above, a grant might not be necessary for small estates. An administrator with the will annexed will apply for a grant of letters of administration with the will annexed. An administrator will apply for a grant of letters of administration, which is also referred to as simple administration.

key terminology

Executor: grant of probate

Administrator (with a valid will): grant of letters of administration with the will annexed

Administrator (without a valid will): grant of letters of administration

11.3.2 Applying for a grant

A grant is a formal legal document, issued by the Family Division of the High Court (Senior Courts Act 1981, ss 25, 61 and Sch 1, para 3(b)(iv)). Even though there is a difference between a grant of probate and a grant of letters of administration, this process is generally referred to as 'probate' and 'probate proceedings'.

If the grant of probate is sought by a private individual acting as a PR, it is generally applied for in one of the District Registries located throughout England and Wales. It can also be applied for online. If probate is sought by a solicitor or a probate practitioner, it must, since November 2020, be applied for online, through an online portal called MyHMCTS. The grant will be sealed by the Registrar, which means that the document is stamped with the court's seal and signed by the Registrar. The grant will include the name of the deceased and confirm whether the deceased left a valid will (any will is annexed to the grant). More is said about the application and the information that it must contain at **11.4.3** below.

11.3.3 Authority to make a grant

The court can issue a grant either on proof that the deceased died intestate or on the production of a valid will. To be a valid will, all of the formality requirements discussed in **Chapters 2** and **3** must be satisfied. The will must be produced to the court. As stated in the previous chapter, the court cannot issue a grant until IHT has been accounted for (and paid, if necessary) (Senior Courts Act 1981, s 109).

11.3.4 Common form and solemn form probate

There are two types of probate proceedings, and it is important to draw a distinction between them.

Non-contentious, or common form, probate refers to a grant where there is no dispute about the validity of the will or the entitlement of the PR seeking the grant (see the definition in the Senior Courts Act 1981, s 128). Most grants will be in the common form. If there are several people entitled in the same class to a grant of administration under either r 20 or r 22 of the Non-Contentious Probate Rules (NCPR) 1987, and there is a dispute over who should be appointed, this will be resolved by the Registrar, and it will still be classed as non-contentious. Common form probate is issued by the Family Division of the High Court (which, in practice, means the District Registries, as mentioned).

Contentious, or solemn form, probate refers to grants issued after a dispute about the validity of a will or whether a person is entitled at all to a grant under r 20 or r 22 (this can include, for example, claims for passing over someone with priority). Solemn form probate also applies to grants issued after a successful challenge to a previously issued common form grant; for example, if letters of administration were granted in common form and later a will was discovered, then the letters of administration must be revoked. A solemn form grant of probate will be issued to the executor or administrator with the will annexed. Solemn form probate disputes are heard by the Chancery Division of the High Court.

Anyone with an interest in the estate can challenge a common form grant (Civil Procedure Rules 1998, r 57.7(1)). This includes beneficiaries in an earlier will, who are challenging the validity of a later will. It includes anyone who would be entitled on intestacy if the will was found to be invalid. It includes a person who is entitled to bring a claim against the estate for financial support under the Inheritance (Provision for Family and Dependants) Act 1975 (see **Chapter 15**) (*Re Seagrave* [2007] EWHC 788 (Ch), [2007] 1 WLR 2002). It also includes a creditor of any of the above, but not a creditor of the deceased.

key case

Randall v Randall [2016] EWCA Civ 494, [2017] Ch 77.

Two people, Colin and Hilary, got married. For a while, they were Mr and Mrs Randall. They then got divorced. They agreed to a divorce settlement. It said that if Hilary were to inherit more than £100,000 from her mother, Sylvia, then Hilary would keep the first £100,000 and the surplus would be divided equally between Hilary and Colin. Of course, Sylvia promptly wrote a new will, which gave £100,000 to Hilary and the remainder of the estate (roughly £150,000) directly to Hilary's children.

When Sylvia died, Colin sought to challenge the will, arguing that it did not comply with the formality requirements in s 9 of the Wills Act 1837. The Court of Appeal found that Colin had an interest in Sylvia's estate. This was because Hilary was a beneficiary under the will but would also be entitled to the entire estate if Sylvia died intestate. As a creditor of Hilary, Colin had a right to ensure that Hilary got the most amount of money, so that she could pay Colin what he was owed under the divorce settlement. If Hilary took Sylvia's entire estate on intestacy (£250,000), Colin would be entitled to £75,000 (half of the value above the initial £100,000). The Court of Appeal noted that Colin's position was very different from a creditor of the deceased: they have no interest in who inherits, just that their debt is paid. A creditor of a beneficiary, however, has an interest in who inherits: they want their debtor to get as much as possible.

The judgment has been subject to criticism, as it significantly widens who has standing to issue contentious probate proceedings (see Mark Baxter, 'Standing in contentious probate claims after *Randall v Randall*' (2017) 23 Trusts & Trustees 152–61).

If a challenge is successful, the grant will be revoked and a new grant issued to the relevant party.

11.3.5 General and limited grants

The court has the power to issue either a general grant or a limited grant. Most grants issued will be general. This means that there are no restrictions imposed on the PR and they can act freely in administering the estate.

In some circumstances, a limited grant is issued instead (Senior Courts Act 1981, s 113). It will impose certain restrictions on the PR, and those restrictions are imposed at the court's discretion. A limited grant can be issued, for example, over only specific property or for only a specified time (*In the Goods of Baldwin* [1903] P 61). If a will makes specific gifts but does not include a residuary clause, the named beneficiary can become administrator with the will annexed for the property specifically mentioned, but the next of kin could obtain a grant to administer any residue, which would pass on intestacy (*In the Goods of Watson* (1858) 1 Sw & T 110, 164 ER 651). In the case of *In the Goods of Suarez* [1897] P 82, the deceased ran an import business and died intestate. His family lived in Bolivia. To keep the business running, a grant was issued to an accountant of the business, limited in time until a relative could apply for a general grant.

Another example of a limited grant is a grant of administration *de bonis non administratis* (usually just referred to as a grant *de bonis non*). The Latin name refers to property which has not yet been administered. This grant can be issued where an administrator has died without completing the administration process. As seen in **Chapter 9**, if an executor dies in office, their own executor becomes PR for both estates; this is known as a chain of representation. The grant *de bonis non* is required if the chain is broken or if the PR was an administrator (see **9.4**). This is because the law does not permit a chain for administrators. The grant *de bonis non* is also issued where an earlier grant has been revoked. In the case of *In the Goods of Galbraith* [1951] P 422, both executors lost mental capacity due to old age; their grant of probate was revoked and a grant *de bonis non* was issued to another relative willing to act. The grant *de bonis non* is necessarily limited to any property which remains unadministered.

A further example of a limited grant is a grant of administration *ad colligenda bona*. This is an interim grant made to a person for the purpose of holding and preserving specific assets until such time that a general grant can be issued. Remember, the general grant can only be issued once IHT has been accounted for, which can take several months. If the deceased owned assets that need preserving or administering immediately, the grant *ad colligenda bona* is required. For example, the deceased might have owned a business or a farm, meaning that someone needs immediate authority to keep the operation running. In the case of *In the Goods of Bolton* [1899] P 186, for instance, the deceased died intestate owning a newsagents in Battersea. His next of kin, an uncle, lived in Montevideo in Uruguay, and it would take several months to receive instructions from the uncle. The store needed selling immediately, because its goodwill would disappear if it closed down and customers went elsewhere. A grant *ad colligenda bona* was made to a friend of the deceased for the purpose of immediately selling the store. *Bolton* concerned the selling of the store and a friend holding the money until a general grant could be applied for; this can be distinguished from *Suarez* above, where a limited grant was issued for the purpose of actually running the business.

The grant *ad colligenda bona* must be made to someone impartial, whom all of the beneficiaries might trust (*Ghafoor v Cliff* [2006] EWHC 825 (Ch), [2006] 1 WLR 3020). The grant will only be made where it is actually necessary to collect in the assets. In the case of *Caudle v LD Law Ltd* [2008] EWHC 374 (QB), [2008] 1 WLR 1540, the claimant wanted to collect in some documents held by a law firm, relating to the financial affairs of the claimant's ex-wife, who had just died. He said he needed the documents to apply for a general grant of administration. The court said there was nothing that required the claimant to take immediate possession of those documents, and no grant *ad colligenda bona* was issued. Once a general grant had been obtained by the claimant, he would be allowed take control of the documents.

11.3.6 When property vests – liability for acts done before a grant is issued

Legal title to the deceased's assets will vest in an executor at the moment of death, since the executor's authority derives from the will (*Chetty v Chetty* [1916] 1 AC 603). It follows that an executor can immediately start dealing with the estate assets (such as take possession of them, collect in debts, and start making payments to creditors and then beneficiaries). The executor can also take legal action on behalf of the estate or continue ongoing legal actions. The grant of probate is a formality, which, as discussed above, is necessary in some, but not all, cases. As seen, it will definitely be needed for larger estates. The grant of probate is also necessary as proof of title in any court case.

Where the deceased dies intestate, or with a will that does not validly appoint an executor, legal title vests in the Public Trustee at the moment of death (Administration of Estates Act (AEA) 1925, s 9(1) and (2)). Legal title will only vest in the administrator once a grant of administration has been issued by the court. Under s 9(3), the Public Trustee does not have any duties imposed on them in terms of administering the estate, meaning that a grant *ad colligenda bona* or a limited grant can be applied for if required.

In the intervening period, the administrator cannot take possession of the assets, nor can they begin litigation on behalf of the estate. In the case of *Millburn-Snell v Evans* [2011] EWCA Civ 577, [2012] 1 WLR 41, the daughters of the deceased began a proprietary estoppel claim against Ms Evans, claiming that their father had a 50% beneficial interest in a property owned by Ms Evans. The claim was struck out because the daughters had commenced the action before obtaining a grant of administration. They also had to pay Ms Evans' legal costs, which is a clear warning to administrators to ensure that they have authority before they start acting. The daughters, of course, could reissue the claim once they had received the grant.

The grant of administration, however, relates back to the date of death (*Re Pryse* [1904] P 301). This means that the administrator can take legal action for anything done to the estate since the date of death. For instance, in the case of *Tharpe v*

Stallwood (1843) 5 M & Gr 760, 134 ER 766, the deceased's landlord seized the deceased's assets after she had died, claiming it was to recover outstanding rent. The administrator was allowed to sue for trespass once the grant of administration had been issued. This liability works both ways. In the case of *Youngmin v Heath* [1974] 1 WLR 135, the deceased had a periodic tenancy of two furnished rooms. The deceased died intestate. There was nothing in the tenancy agreement that said that the tenancy ended on the tenant's death. Two years later, a grant of administration was made and the administrator formally served notice to determine (end) the tenancy. The landlord claimed two years' worth of rent arrears. The court held that the administrator had to pay the arrears, using the estate's assets. If, instead, the administrator had taken possession of the rooms, and used them for his own personal purposes, then the administrator would be personally liable for the rent arrears.

11.4 Obtaining the grant

The person entitled to the grant (the executor or the administrator with priority) can apply for the grant once IHT has been accounted for (and paid, if necessary) and they are in receipt of the correct HMRC tax forms. Important changes have been introduced in recent years, with the aim of streamlining the probate process and to move it online. Since November 2020, probate applications by professionals must be made online, doing away with a cumbersome old paper-based application process. Probate applications by private individuals can be made online or by using a streamlined paper-based application form. These changes were underway before the Covid-19 pandemic, but the pandemic has further emphasised the need for court services to be provided online.

11.4.1 Caveats

Before turning to the probate application itself, it is convenient to start by looking at caveats. Under r 44 of the NCPR 1987, a person may lodge a caveat in the Family Division. The purpose of the caveat is to stop a grant being issued without the caveator receiving notice of this and being given the opportunity to object to a grant. For example, the caveator may wish to challenge the validity of a will and thus get a grant themselves under a previous will or through intestacy. The caveat is valid for six months but the caveator may apply to extend the duration of the caveat.

Where an applicant for a grant is faced with a caveat, the court will issue a warning to the caveator. There are two routes available, depending on what the caveat concerns.

The caveator can be asked to state their interest in the estate (perhaps they are executors under an earlier will or entitled on intestacy if the existing will is found to be invalid) and how it differs from the applicant's interest in the estate. Normally, this will result in a solemn form probate action, and the court will rule on the validity of a will or declare that a person died intestate. As noted in **Chapters 2** and **3**, common objections include arguing that the will is invalid because the testator lacked testamentary capacity, the will fails to comply with the formality requirements, or that the will was the product of undue influence.

Alternatively, the caveator's interest might not differ from the applicant's, but they are still objecting to the applicant getting probate (for example, the applicant and the caveator may have equal standing under r 20 or r 22). Here, the applicant will ask the court for directions, and the court will determine who is entitled to the grant.

No grant will be made until the court has made a determination, which can delay the administration proceedings. A caveat can be removed by the caveator at any point. It is of course also possible that a negotiated settlement can be reached between the caveator and anyone else entitled to a grant, which would allow the administration process to proceed unhindered subject to the terms of the settlement.

11.4.2   When can a grant be applied for?

Rule 6 of the NCPR 1987 states that a grant of probate or a grant of administration with the will annexed will not be issued within seven days of the deceased's death, and a grant of simple administration will not be granted within 14 days of the deceased's death. However, the Registrar or District Judge in the Probate Registry has discretion to issue a grant earlier. There is no time limit for applying for a grant, and sometimes a grant is not applied for until many years after the deceased's death. One of the reasons for a delay is that no one wants to seek a grant; the law cannot force someone to undertake the duties of a PR (*Chappell v Somers & Blake* [2003] EWHC 1644 (Ch), [2004] Ch 19). Again, no grant can be issued until IHT has been accounted for.

11.4.3   The probate application form

Important changes have been made to the probate application process in recent years, not least the introduction of an online application process, which must be used when probate is applied for by a professional, such as a solicitor acting for the PR (NCPR 1987, r 4). Probate can also be sought by a private individual who is intending to act as a PR. The entitlement to be an executor or administrator was explained in **Chapter 9**.

A solicitor or other probate practitioner may apply for probate, either because they are the named executor, or because they have been instructed to act for the PR. Given the complexities of administering an estate, the latter is very common. Since November 2020, if the grant is applied for by a professional, it must be applied for online through the online application portal on MyHMCTS, set out in r 4 of the NCPR 1987. The information sought via the online portal is the same as in the paper form that can still be used by a PR applying in person, and is explained below. As one would expect with a new online platform, there have been some practical challenges with the transition from the old system to the new portal, but hopefully these difficulties will quickly be resolved.

If a lay PR (that is, a PR who is not undertaking the role as a professional) is applying, they have a choice. They can apply via the online portal (NCPR 1987, r 5ZA) or apply using the Probate Application form (PA1), which can be posted to the probate office of HMCTS (HM Courts and Tribunals Service) (NCPR 1987, r 5).

There are two versions of the PA1 form. PA1A is used for an application for a grant of administration, where there is no will. PA1P is used for an application for a grant of probate or administration with the will annexed. Below is a quick overview of what information the forms ask for, but do have a look at the forms yourself on the www.gov.uk website.

The PA1A form, for a grant of simple administration, asks for the following information:

- Section A:
    ▶ Part 1: the personal information of the applicant or applicants who are seeking the grant of administration. As explained in **Chapter 9**, a maximum of four people can apply for a grant.
- Section B:
    ▶ Part 2: the personal information of the deceased. That includes their name, address, marital status, and whether they owned assets abroad.
    ▶ Part 3: information about the deceased's family and relatives. The form goes through the relatives who would be entitled on intestacy, as set out in s 46 of the Administration of Estates Act 1925 (see **Chapter 8**).
    ▶ Part 4: this part only applies if the applicant is applying as an attorney on behalf of the PR (if the PR does not have capacity per the Mental Capacity Act 2005). The attorney provides their details, explaining that they have authority to act on behalf of the PR.
    ▶ Part 5: this part only applies if the deceased was domiciled abroad, and the form asks for details of where the deceased lived and what property the deceased owned in the UK.
    ▶ Part 6: in this part the applicant will provide details relating to inheritance tax, explaining whether IHT was due, how much has been paid, and what IHT forms have been submitted to HMRC. If an IHT summary was submitted to HMRC online, there is no need to duplicate the information in the PA1 form.
- Legal statement: this replaces the oath/statement of truth (see **11.4.4** below). The applicant is asked to sign the form, thereby confirming the following things. First, the applicant confirms that they will comply with their legal duties (explained further in the following chapters). Secondly, the applicant agrees to provide information to the court if requested and to return the grant

to the court if requested (see **11.5** below). Thirdly, the applicant confirms that they understand that criminal liability for fraud applies if they deliberately have provided incorrect information.

The PA1P form, for a grant of probate or letters of administration with the will annexed, asks for the following information:

- Section A:
  - ▸ Part 1: the personal information of the applicant or applicants who are seeking the grant of probate or administration with the will annexed. As explained in **Chapter 9**, a maximum of four people can apply for a grant.
- Section B:
  - ▸ Part 2: the personal information of the deceased. That includes their name, address, marital status, and whether they owned assets abroad.
  - ▸ Part 3: details of the will and/or codicil that the testator has left, including the date on which it was made (if known). If one of the named executors is not applying for probate, the applicant must explain why not. As explained in **Chapter 9**, agreeing to be an executor is voluntary, and any named executor can renounce probate. This section helps to prove that the applicant is entitled to a grant.
  - ▸ Part 4: details of any family and relatives of the testator.
  - ▸ Part 5: this part only applies if the applicant is applying as an attorney on behalf of the PR (if the PR does not have capacity per the Mental Capacity Act 2005). The attorney provides their details, explaining that they have authority to act on behalf of the PR.
  - ▸ Part 6: this part only applies if the deceased was domiciled abroad, and the form asks for details of where the deceased lived and what property the deceased owned in the UK.
  - ▸ Part 7: in this part the applicant will provide details relating to inheritance tax, explaining whether IHT was due, how much has been paid, and what IHT forms have been submitted to HMRC. If an IHT summary was submitted to HMRC online, there is no need to duplicate the information in the PA1 form.
- Legal statement: this replaces the oath/statement of truth (see **11.4.4** below). The applicant is asked to sign the form, thereby confirming the following things. First, the applicant confirms that they will comply with their legal duties (explained further in the following chapters). Secondly, the applicant agrees to provide information to the court if requested and to return the grant to the court if requested (see **11.5** below). Thirdly, the applicant confirms that they understand that criminal liability for fraud applies if they deliberately have provided incorrect information.

The relevant PA1 form is then submitted to the probate office of HMCTS. The probate registrar will then issue the grant to the applicant or, if necessary, seek further information from the applicant before the grant is issued. If the PR wants multiple copies of the grant, perhaps to give to various banks and other institutions, the PR will have to pay for each additional copy. This can be indicated in the PA1 form.

As noted, if a professional applies using the online platform, they will be asked to provide the same information as in the PA1 forms. The grant will then be issued to them by HMCTS.

11.4.4 The old statement of truth (oath)

Historically, in addition to applying for the grant of probate, the PR had to sign an oath (an affidavit) in the presence of a commissioner for oaths. A commissioner for oaths is a legal office held by certain people; for instance, all solicitors are commissioners for oaths. The oath was sworn by the PR to indicate that they had provided true information in the probate application and that they would lawfully undertake their duties as PR. The oath was submitted to the probate registry alongside the probate application itself, together with the relevant IHT tax forms, and, if applicable, a copy of the will.

In November 2018, the oath was renamed a statement of truth. The exact content of the statement varied depending on the circumstances of each estate, but all statements followed the same basic structure. The statement of truth has now been incorporated into the PA1 form or the probate application through the online portal, where the applicant signs their name on the form to indicate that the information provided is correct, and is now referred to as the 'legal statement'. There is no requirement for a separate document signed before a commissioner for oaths, which clearly streamlines the probate application process.

The old oath and statement confirmed that the deceased had died, and it stated the name, date of birth and date of death of the deceased. The statement confirmed where the deceased was domiciled, which is to say, where the deceased had their primary residence. Ordinarily this will be England and Wales, but this confirmation is particularly important where the deceased owned property overseas.

If the deceased left a will, the statement confirmed that the PR believed that the will was genuine and set out the final testamentary wishes of the testator. If the deceased did not leave a will, the statement confirmed that the deceased died intestate.

The statement confirmed on what basis the PR claimed to be entitled to a grant. The PR may be the named executor in the will, or otherwise have priority under r 20 or r 22 of the NCPR 1987. If the PR applied for a grant of administration (simple or with the will annexed), they had to confirm that they had priority or explain how they had 'cleared off' anyone else with priority above them (see **Chapter 9**). They also had to confirm whether any beneficiary was a minor or obtained only a life interest. As discussed in **Chapter 9** (see **9.2.1.3**), in those circumstances the court will, if necessary, appoint a second PR to ensure there is a minimum of two PRs. As seen above, this information is now provided in the PA1 form or the online portal.

The statement confirmed whether or not the estate contained settled land, within the meaning of the Settled Land Act 1925. Since 1997, it is not possible to create settled land (Trusts of Land and Appointment of Trustees Act 1996), so this is very unlikely to be the case, but confirmation is required. The definition of settled land is outside the scope of this book. In short, it referred to a freehold estate that was held in strict succession within a family (usually it went to the oldest male heir), meaning that the beneficiaries had no right to convey the land and the oldest male heir was forced to accept it.

The statement then confirmed that the PR was willing to take on the duties of a PR. This is now asked for in the legal statement. There are three key duties, set out in s 25 of the AEA 1925 (see **12.4**).

Finally, the statement confirmed the value of the estate. The valuation will already have been made for IHT purposes, but it must be set out again in the statement. The statement confirmed whether or not IHT was due. Further, the estate value had to be stated because there is an administration fee payable to obtain the grant. This is discussed at **11.4.7** below. As seen, this information is broadly replicated in the PA1 form and the online application form on the online portal.

11.4.5 Additional documents

In some circumstances, the Probate Registry can ask for additional documents before it issues the grant. This is set out in r 8 of the NCPR 1987.

One problem that can arise is where a will cannot be found or has been accidentally damaged or destroyed. The court can ask for copies of the will, if available, to be submitted. Alternatively, an attesting witness or lawyer present during the execution can submit their own affidavit or witness statement, providing evidence as to the validity of the will and its contents (NCPR 1987, rr 14 and 16). As noted in **Chapter 6**, a lost will is presumed to have been revoked. The PR will need to rebut that presumption (*Sugden v Lord St Leonards* (1876) 1 PD 154). In *Sugden*, the court found that the lost will was not revoked but rather had been stolen. The court allowed oral testimony as to the contents of the will.

As noted in **Chapter 3**, if the will has an attestation clause, the court will presume that it was properly executed. Otherwise, the attesting witnesses, or anyone else present when the will was executed, can swear an affidavit or provide a witness statement stating that the will was properly executed, set out in r 12 of the NCPR 1987. The law generally presumes that the will was properly executed, which is a helpful presumption if the witnesses cannot be found. The greater the formalities, the stronger the presumption, which reinforces the benefit of executing the will together with a solicitor. In the case of *Re Webb* [1964] 1 WLR 509, a will was lost during the Blitz. However, the attesting witness could not remember the attestation. The court admitted a draft copy of the will into probate, saying that the attestation clause in the draft was sufficient to presume that the will itself had been properly attested, even though the witness could not fully recall the event.

The PR may also have to prove to the court that the testator knew and approved of the contents of the will (see **2.4**). This is particularly important if the testator was blind or illiterate. Here, the expected procedure is for the will to be read aloud to the testator before the testator signs the will. The PR may have to swear an affidavit that this process was followed.

The PR or any other person may be asked to swear an affidavit or provide a witness statement explaining alterations made to the will or any attempt to revoke the will. A friend or relative might have found the will in a poor condition, and may be asked to explain the circumstances in which the will was stored and found. Perhaps the will was damaged due to damp rather than by the testator trying to revoke it by destruction. The court must be satisfied as to the full validity of the will before they can issue a grant. This is known as an affidavit of plight and condition; see rr 15 and 16 of the NCPR 1987.

11.4.6 Removing words from the will

The court has the right to remove words or phrases from the will in certain circumstances, and the PR may make an application to that effect. The words are removed from the official probate copy of the will, and the estate will be administered without reference to those words or phrases. Parts of a will or codicil might have been inserted at a time when the testator did not have capacity or as a result of undue influence. Alternatively, alterations might have been made but were not been properly attested. The court can also remove words from the probate copy if the words do not affect the testamentary dispositions but are nonetheless defamatory or offensive. In the case of *Re White (Deceased)* [1914] P 153, a husband disinherited his wife, adding defamatory comments about her in his will. The court removed those words. The operative clause left his entire estate to his brother, and this was the only clause needed in the probate copy.

11.4.7 Fees

There are various fees associated with the grant. The government position is that these fees are levied to help pay for the court service. The main fee is the so-called probate fee, which must be paid in order to obtain the grant.

Where the estate is valued below £5,000, there is no fee payable. Where the estate is valued above £5,000, there are two possible flat fees to be paid, as set out in the Non-Contentious Probate Fees Order 2004 (SI 2004/3120), Sch 1, para 1 (as amended). If the PR applies in person, the fee is £215. If a solicitor applies on behalf of the PR, the fee is £155.

There is also a fee of £3 to lodge a caveat. A number of additional fees apply for various tasks, such as seeking to inspect a will or lodging affidavits.

11.5 Revoking a grant

The court has the right to revoke a grant after it has been issued. It can either be done with the consent of the person who has the grant or after trial if the revocation is opposed by the grant-holder. There are a variety of reasons why a grant may be revoked.

In the first instance, it might transpire that the grant was made to the wrong person. An obvious example is where a grant of administration is issued but a valid will is later discovered. The grant of administration will be revoked and the court will issue a grant of probate over the will.

In the case of *Nicholls v Hudson* [2006] EWHC 3006 (Ch), a testator was married to his third wife, whom his daughter did not get along with. He wrote a will, which included his daughter as a beneficiary, and gave a copy of the will to the daughter. When the testator died, the wife took out a grant of simple administration, claiming that she could not find a will and that, because it was lost, the presumption was that the will had been revoked. The daughter sought to have the grant revoked, claiming that the will had been lost by accident, which meant that it was still valid. The court revoked the grant of administration and admitted the daughter's copy of the will into probate. A similar outcome was found in the case of *Rowe v Clarke* [2005] EWHC 3068 (Ch), which was discussed in **Chapter 6** (see **6.2.3**). A grant of administration was revoked and the court admitted a copy of a lost will into probate. The presumption that the will was revoked because it was lost was rebutted because the testator had been a careless person.

A grant of probate can be revoked if the will is found to be invalid in a later probate action. For instance, in the case of *Paynter v Hinch* [2013] EWHC 13 (Ch), the named executor of a 1996 will argued that a 2004 will was invalid on the grounds that the testator did not know and approve of the contents of the 2004 will. This claimed failed; the 2004 will was found to be valid. However, had the claim been successful, the grant of probate for the 2004 will would have been revoked and a new grant issued to the executor of the 1996 will. The case of *Williams v Evans* [1911] P 175 states that an executor, who begins to doubt the validity of a will, can challenge the will and have their own grant revoked if the will is found to be invalid.

Other cases are more unusual. In the case of *In the Goods of Napier* (1809) 1 Phill 83, 161 ER 921, news had returned to England saying that a Mr Charles Napier had died at the Battle of Corunna, Spain, during the Napoleonic Wars. A grant of probate was issued to his executor. However, Mr Napier had not died. On his return to England, he personally attended court to ask for the grant of probate to be revoked. In the case of *In the Estate of Evon* (1963) 107 SJ 893, the deceased's sister pretended to be his widow and obtained a grant of administration. The grant was revoked when the actual widow learned of the sister's fraud.

The grant can also be revoked by changing circumstances. In the case of *In the Estate of Thomas* [1912] P 177, an administrator emigrated to New Zealand before finishing the administration process, taking the grant with him. The court revoked the grant and issued a grant *de bonis non* over the assets left unadministered. Similarly, in the case of *In the Goods of Loveday* [1900] P 154, a grant of administration was issued to the widow of the deceased. However, before she completed the administration, she disappeared (there was no proof to this effect, but it was assumed that she had herself died). The grant was revoked and a grant *de bonis non* was issued to one of the deceased's children, who could complete the administration. The same occurred in the case of *In the Goods of Covell* (1889) 15 PD 8, where the administrator was missing and presumed to have committed suicide.

The grant is also revoked if the PR loses mental capacity during the administration process (*In the Goods of Galbraith* [1951] P 422). If there are multiple PRs, the grant is revoked and a new grant issued to the PRs who still have capacity. Otherwise, a grant *de bonis non* is issued to whoever has priority under r 20 or r 22 of the NCPR 1987 (these rules were set out in **Chapter 9**).

11.5.1 The legal position of third parties where a grant is revoked

Once a grant is issued, the PR will start administering the estate. This will include collecting in the estate assets, calling in loans, selling estate assets to pay off debts or to reimburse the PR for any IHT payment, and finally beginning to distribute the assets to the beneficiaries. However, what happens if the PR's grant is later revoked?

If the estate asset has been sold to a third party, they are protected by s 37 of the AEA 1925. The Act provides a broad definition of a conveyance in s 55, but it requires a written document. The third party must purchase the estate asset in good faith (genuinely believing the PR to have authority) and for consideration. Section 37 does not apply to oral contracts, but in this situation the third party is protected by the rule laid down in the case of *Hewson v Shelley* [1914] 2 Ch 13. Again, the third party must have purchased the item in good faith and for consideration. Further, s 204(1) of the Law of Property Act 1925 also states that a purchaser's title is not affected by the later revocation of any court order, such as a grant. Thus, if the grant is revoked, neither the new PR nor the beneficiaries can reclaim the property from the third party.

If the PR called in a debt, the debt is discharged, even if the grant is later revoked (AEA 1925, s 27(2)). Neither the new PR nor the beneficiaries can pursue the debtor for the debt. This is particularly relevant if the original PR negotiated a payment plan or accepted a lower sum in return for a quick payment.

The PR can validly exercise their office until such a time as they learn that someone is contemplating a probate claim (s 27(1)). If the PR keeps acting after they learn about a potential challenge, they may be liable to personally reimburse the estate for any payment that they make (*Guardian Trust & Executors Company of New Zealand Ltd v Public Trustee of New Zealand* [1942] AC 115, PC). Thus, if a will leaves a pecuniary gift of £5,000 to X, a friend of the deceased, the PR cannot make that payment if they know that someone is planning to challenge the validity of the will. If the will is found to be invalid, X, as a friend, would not be entitled on intestacy. If the PR anyway pays the £5,000 to X, and the will is later found to be invalid, meaning the grant of probate is revoked, the PR will have to pay £5,000 into the estate as compensation.

However, if the PR makes a payment to a beneficiary, the new PR (or other beneficiaries) can bring a claim to recover that property. This is because the beneficiary is a volunteer and not a good faith purchaser (therefore, they cannot rely on s 205 of the Law of Property Act 1925; s 37 of the AEA 1925; or the rule in *Hewson v Shelley*). Claims to recover property wrongfully paid out (eg to a will beneficiary where the will is later found to be invalid) will be considered in **Chapter 16**.

11.6 Further reading

The gov.uk website provides a range of information, including a step-by-step guide to follow when a person has died: www.gov.uk/when-someone-dies.

summary

This chapter has explained the grant and when a PR needs to obtain a grant. There are three types of grant: probate, administration with the will annexed, and simple administration. A PR of a small estate might be exempt from having to obtain a grant, but this will generally depend on the assets of the deceased and their value. The chapter has explained the process a PR must go through in order to apply for a grant. Finally, the chapter has explored the reasons why a grant might be revoked and the consequences that follow if a grant is revoked.

12 Administration II – Calling in and Managing the Estate

We discussed who can be a PR and how they can be appointed in **Chapter 9**. The previous **Chapter 11** showed what PRs have to do to obtain the grant. As seen, a grant will be needed for many, but not all, estates. Thus, everything that has been covered so far has really concerned the PR and their appointment to their office.

This chapter moves beyond the appointment phase and begins to consider the duties that a PR is subject to. This chapter looks at the PR's first duty, namely to ensure that they have legal title to all of the property contained in the estate and then to call in and realise that property.

The chapter considers the following issues:

- How does a PR obtain legal title to the estate?
- What property is not subject to administration?
- How does a PR realise the estate?
- What responsibilities does the PR have in managing the estate?

12.1 Obtaining legal title

12.1.1 The estate devolves on the PR

When a person dies, their estate ultimately devolves on their PR.

key terminology

Devolve: the passing of legal title to property from one person to another, such as from the deceased to their PR.

However, there is a difference between an estate where there is a validly appointed executor and an estate where the deceased died intestate or without validly appointing an executor. In a testate estate with a validly appointed executor, the legal title passes automatically to that executor. The grant of probate, discussed in the previous chapter, may be required as proof of that legal title – this is an important distinction: the grant is not how legal title is obtained; it is merely proof of the legal title that the executor obtained automatically. However, if a person dies intestate, or leaves a will but no executor, the legal title instead devolves on the Public Trustee (Administration of Estates Act (AEA) 1925, s 9). Once a grant of administration (whether simple or with the will annexed) is issued by the court, legal title devolves from the Public Trustee to the administrator.

The estate devolves automatically on the PR, following the process set out above (AEA 1925, s 1). No further legal documentation or proof of transfer of title is required.

12.1.2 Property that does not devolve on the PR

However, there is some property that does not devolve on the PR. It is important to take note of this, as the PR cannot lawfully deal with any property that has not devolved on them. Doing so would amount to trespass and would open the PR up to liability for wrongful interference with that property.

Perhaps the most common form of property that does not devolve on a PR is property which the deceased co-owned as a joint tenant. A joint tenancy includes the right of survivorship, which says that the surviving joint tenant retains full legal and beneficial interest in the property. This has been discussed in the intestacy chapter (see **8.3.1.3**) and in the inheritance tax chapter (see **10.4.1.1**). The last surviving joint tenant takes full legal title, and that is devolved on their PR when they die.

A similar position arises if the deceased died whilst being a trustee and was appointed alongside other trustees. The trustees will collectively hold legal title on a joint tenancy. If the deceased was a sole trustee, legal title to the trust fund devolves on the PR, who can either administer the trust or appoint a new trustee (Trustee Act 1925, s 36) (the right of a PR to appoint a replacement trustee will be considered in more detail in an Equity & Trusts textbook).

Another type of property which does not devolve is where the deceased only had a life interest in property under a trust. That interest automatically ends when the life tenant dies, and the beneficial interest in the trust now passes to the so-called 'remainderman'. The deceased might also have had a pension policy; the policy holder usually indicates that they want the pension to be held on trust for another when they die, so the pension policy would not devolve on the PR.

12.1.3 Other rights and entitlements that devolve on the PR

The PR does not only take legal title to the estate assets. Other rights and entitlements also devolve onto the PR. One such right is the right for the PR to enforce contracts to which the deceased was a party. This can include calling in debts owed to the deceased, which is discussed further in the next chapter. The reverse is also true: a third party can enforce contracts against the estate. The PR is also entitled to bring and defend tort claims. This is set out in s 1 of the Law Reform (Miscellaneous Provisions) Act 1934.

A key case is *Beswick v Beswick* [1968] AC 58. A husband owned a coal business. He transferred the entire business to his nephew. The transfer came with a condition, which the nephew agreed to. The nephew was to pay the husband a weekly sum of money for the rest of his life and thereafter, if he was survived by his wife, to pay a weekly sum to the widow for the rest of her life. The husband died. The nephew made one weekly payment to the wife but then stopped the payments. The wife, as administrator of her husband's estate, was entitled to enforce the agreement and obtained an order for specific performance. The House of Lords conversely held that she was not allowed to enforce the contract in her personal capacity (since she was not a party to it), though this position might now have been altered by the Contracts (Rights of Third Parties) Act 1999.

In the case of *Wentworth v Cock* (1839) 10 Ad & El 42, 113 ER 17, the deceased had ordered goods, to be delivered monthly for a period of 18 months. The deceased died during the contract period. When the next monthly delivery arrived, the PRs refused to accept delivery and also refused to pay. The suppliers successfully sued the PRs, with the court saying that the contract was enforceable for its full duration, notwithstanding that the deceased had died. This is a very important principle in the modern world, as many people purchase goods on credit (for example, they might buy a TV or a mobile phone on a 12-month repayment plan). These contracts are binding and the PR must carry them out. The key proviso is that the PR is only obliged to pay if there is money in the estate. The next chapter will consider the situation where the deceased died insolvent (ie without enough funds to pay all debts).

All tort claims can be continued by the PR except a claim for defamation. For example, in the case of *Raggett v Kings College Hospital NHS Foundation Trust* [2016] EWHC 1604 (QB), Mr Raggett's executors successfully brought a medical negligence claim against the defendant. The PR likewise will have to defend any tort claims brought against the estate by third parties.

12.2 Collecting in the estate

12.2.1 Collecting in assets

The first thing that the PR should do is to take control of the estate and collect in all of the assets. This can include taking physical control of property, such as a house or a car. It can also include identifying and accessing intangible property, such as bank accounts or other forms of investments (including savings accounts, ISAs, funds or shareholdings).

The estate assets must be looked after with reasonable care. Section 19 of the Trustee Act 1925 allows PRs to insure property, and to pay the insurance premiums out of the estate. This can include paying for home insurance for the deceased's house or for car insurance for the deceased's car. When insuring the estate assets, the PR is subject to the statutory duty of care set out in s 1 of the Trustee Act 2000, which says that they must act with reasonable care and skill. The PR is not liable for accidental damage or loss to the estate assets, but if insurable property (such as a home or car) was not insured, the PR may have fallen foul of their statutory duty of care. The PR is also not liable for estate assets which are stolen (subject to insurance) (*Jones v Lewis* (1751) 2 Ves Sen 240, 28 ER 155).

Despite the general duty to take control of the estate property, the law has said that a PR is not under any specific duty to take control of assets that are specifically gifted to a beneficiary. The PR can give their assent for the item to vest directly in the beneficiary (rather than for legal title to vest first in the PR and then be transferred to the beneficiary). Assents are discussed at **14.2**. An assent cannot be given if the property is needed to pay off the estate's debts, as discussed further in the next chapter. In the case of *Re Fitzpatrick* [1952] Ch 86, a testator left valuable chattels, including jewellery and furniture, to a beneficiary. These chattels were physically located in Monaco. The court held that it was the beneficiary's financial obligation to take control of the chattels, insure them, and ship them back to England. The costs of doing so could not be borne by the estate. In the case of *Coutts & Co v Banks* [2002] EWHC 2460 (Ch), a beneficiary who was entitled to various chattels claimed that one chattel had been stolen. The court held that it was the beneficiary's responsibility to bring a claim to recover the property, not the executor's. Again, the cost of such legal action could not be borne by the estate.

12.2.2 Calling in debts

The PR must then ensure that all debts owed to the estate are accounted for and that payment for these debts is received. However, this is not necessary if the debt is secured by a mortgage. If the estate has the benefit of a mortgage charge, there is no need for the PR to enforce the charge, since repayment is secured and thus, generally, guaranteed. The PR will have to enforce the charge if the money is needed to pay funeral costs or other estate debts.

In *Re Chapman* [1896] 2 Ch 763, Lindley LJ said, at 773:

> Under such a will as this, the duty of the executors was simply to call in the testator's unsecured debts, and to convert into money so much of his personal estate as was necessary to enable them to pay his funeral and testamentary expenses, and his debts and pecuniary legacies, and to hand over to the trustees whatever personal estate was not wanted for those purposes. No doubt, speaking generally, it is the duty of executors to get in debts due to their testator; but it was no part of the duty of the executors as such to realize mortgage securities of their testator not wanted for the above-mentioned purposes.

Unsecured debts should be called in within the so-called executor's year, but, generally speaking, the debts should be called in as soon as practically possible. The money called in from debtors might be needed to reimburse the PR for funeral costs, probate costs or an IHT payment. It might also be needed to quickly pay off the deceased's own debts, which might be generating interest. Unsecured debts owed to the deceased could include rent payments on properties let out by the deceased as a landlord (*Tebbs v Carpenter* (1816) 1 Madd 290, 56 ER 107).

When it comes to calling in debts, the PR has wide powers under s 15 of the Trustee Act 1925 in deciding how the debt is to be satisfied. The PR may choose to accept a different repayment plan, to accept one payment in lieu of another (for example, to accept goods instead of money), to accept a lower repayment value or to forgive the debt in its entirety. If the PR is exercising their powers under s 15, they are bound by the statutory duty of care imposed by s 1 of the Trustee Act 2000, which commands them to act with reasonable care and skill.

12.3 Realising the estate

In short, realising the estate means disposing of its assets in order to raise money. Money may be required, first of all, to pay off debts and to reimburse to PR for funeral costs, probate costs and IHT. Secondly, it is common for wills to state that the PR has the power to sell the estate and hold the proceeds on trust for the residuary beneficiaries (after specific legacies have been paid). The sample will in **Chapter 4** included such a residuary clause, and you might want to quickly revisit it at this point.

The PR has the power to sell the estate assets. Where a person dies intestate, the administrator has the power to sell the estate assets under s 33 of the AEA 1925. A more general power to sell testate and intestate estates derives from the common law and is now captured in s 39 of the AEA 1925. The statute gives the PR all the powers of an absolute legal owner, which includes the right to sell the property, or to mortgage or lease the property, in order to raise money. As already discussed in the previous chapter (see **11.5**), a purchaser of an estate asset is protected (AEA 1925, s 36), even if the PR's grant is later revoked. Estate creditors or beneficiaries cannot seek to reclaim property from a purchaser. The purchaser is not protected if the transaction is done in bad faith (*Scott v Tyler* (1788) Dick 712, 21 ER 448). An example given in that case is if the PR and the purchaser fraudulently agree that the purchaser can buy the estate asset for minimal value. Whilst the PR has broad discretion in realising the estate, they have to obtain a fair price for the estate assets (see **16.4.4.3**).

All property devolves on the PR (with the exceptions discussed above). This includes a freehold estate, a leasehold estate, business assets if the deceased was a sole trader, and trust property if the deceased was a sole trustee.

If the deceased was carrying out a business as a sole trader, the PR is generally not allowed to carry on that business (*Kirkman v Booth* (1848) 11 Beav 273, 50 ER 821). If the deceased wants the PR to carry on the business, authority to do so must be clearly stated in the will. If the deceased was a partner in a general partnership, the PR should call in the deceased's partnership assets. However, the PR can carry out business activities that are necessary to properly realise the business assets

(*Marshall v Broadhurst* (1831) 1 Cr & J 403, 148 ER 1480). For instance, they may complete a contract to supply goods, in order to collect the money owed under the contract. Equally, they can carry out day-to-day business activities in order to sell the business as a going concern (*Dowse v Gorton* [1891] AC 190). For example, if the deceased owned a corner shop, it will be more valuable to sell it as a business rather than just the building. The PR can therefore carry on the business until a buyer for the shop is found. When the PR is carrying on the business, they are entitled to be indemnified out of the estate for any costs. However, if the PR signs a new contract, the PR is personally liable for it, even though the PR may claim an indemnity from the estate. This is important since there is always a risk that the estate is not solvent enough to indemnify the PR.

If the deceased had a lease, the lease devolves on the PR. The PR is liable to pay rent and other leasehold costs out of the estate until the PR can assign the lease onwards (*Wollaston v Hakewill* (1841) 3 M & G 297, 133 ER 1157). The PR's liability is limited to the value of the estate. If the PR takes possession of the leasehold property, by physically entering it, the PR becomes personally liable for the rent and other proprietary covenants (*Mayor, Aldermen, and Burgesses of Stratford-upon-Avon v Parker* [1914] 2 KB 562). The PR is entitled to be indemnified out of the estate for their liability as PR (liability for rent and covenants when the PR has not taken possession) (Trustee Act 1925, s 26). If the PR takes on personal liability by taking physical possession, they are also entitled to be indemnified out of the estate (*Re Owers* [1941] Ch 389). In both cases, the PR can set aside estate assets as an indemnity fund. The indemnity fund will be distributed to the beneficiaries once the PR's liability comes to an end, usually when the leasehold is assigned to a third party (which, of course, can be one of the beneficiaries) (*Re Lewis* [1939] Ch 232).

12.4 Managing the estate

On their appointment, the PR becomes subject to s 25 of the Administration of Estates Act 1925. It sets out the following:

25 Duty of personal representatives

The personal representative of a deceased person shall be under a duty to—

(a) collect and get in the real and personal estate of the deceased and administer it according to law;

(b) when required to do so by the court, exhibit on oath in the court a full inventory of the estate and when so required render an account of the administration of the estate to the court;

(c) when required to do so by the High Court, deliver up the grant of probate or administration to that court.

This section will consider subsections (a) and (b). The requirement in (c), to return the grant of probate to the court if necessary, was discussed in **Chapter 11**.

12.4.1 Obtaining legal title and administering the estate assets

The requirement to obtain legal title to the estate assets has been covered already in this chapter. Once the PR has legal title to the estate assets, the PR has to look after those assets *in specie*.

Have a think about what the PR might have to do when they take control of the following types of property:

- a house
- a car
- a valuable painting
- an investment portfolio of shares and funds
- a savings account.

House: If the deceased left a house or a flat, there are numerous things the PR may need to do. The first may be to take physical possession and verify whether anyone else is in occupation (such as a spouse, partner, child, or a tenant) and what rights to the property they might have. The PR needs to ensure that the estate continues to pay council tax on the house, if applicable. If there is a mortgage, the estate must continue to make the mortgage payments, and the PR will need to discuss with the mortgage provider what the next steps should be (normally, the mortgage must be paid off by the estate, which may necessitate selling the house). If the house needs to be sold to satisfy a debt (such as a mortgage), the PR takes charge of that process, and may use estate assets to instruct an estate agent and a conveyancing solicitor. The PR may need to use estate assets to pay for home insurance on the property, which would be useful in case something happened to the property (such as flood or fire damage). Mortgage providers often insist on home insurance, so it will be a very common expense. If the PR has to use their personal money to pay for any of these expenses, they can later use estate assets to reimburse themselves. The process for paying the estate's debts is discussed further in **Chapter 13**.

Car: If the deceased left a car, the PR will need to take physical possession of it. The car may need to be stored and maintained (such as receiving an MOT). Car insurance must be paid on the car if it is to be used. Again, the costs come out of the estate, or the PR can reimburse themselves from the estate if they use their personal funds to pay for any of the above.

Valuable painting: The deceased may leave valuable chattels behind, such as a painting, other artwork, or perhaps a piano or other expensive instruments. Each estate will be different. Chattels of this nature must be stored properly and may require insurance.

Investment portfolio of shares and funds: The PR will need to monitor the investment portfolio to ensure that the estate does not suffer unnecessary losses. The PR is not liable for changes to the market (such as a market crash), but the PR will have to oversee the investment and consider whether or not it is advisable to sell the shares or funds. If the PR is asked to hold the investments on trust for a beneficiary in the long term, the duty of care under s 1 of the Trustee Act 2000 applies (meaning they must act with reasonable care and skill in managing the investment).

Savings account: If the deceased left money in a savings account, there is not much the PR must do, other than take control of the account. There is no major risk in leaving the savings account for a few months whilst the administration process unfolds.

This is obviously an overview of the type of management tasks that the PR may need to undertake. It is important to emphasise that the precise tasks will, of course, vary from estate to estate, as they depend on what kind of property the deceased left behind.

12.4.2 Duty to inventory the estate

Section 25(b) imposes an obligation to inventory the estate and, if needed, to exhibit that inventory before the court.

When the PR first takes control of the estate, they have to draw up a full inventory. That is a list of all assets and their financial value. This is needed for IHT purposes, as explained at **10.4.1**. As will be explained in **Chapter 13**, the PR must also account for all debts owed to the estate and all debts owed by the estate. In *Ali v Taj* [2020] EWHC 213 (Fam), the court explained that the 'inventory should ordinarily contain a true and perfect description and valuation of all the estate, real and personal, in possession and in action, to which the representative is entitled'.

It is vital that the PR completes a full inventory. As noted, a valuation of the estate is required to complete the IHT forms. Furthermore, the beneficiaries of the estate are entitled to ask the PR to present the inventory to court. This is to ensure that no estate assets are missing; that no assets are misappropriated by the PR or by someone else; or that no assets are valued too high or low by the PR (as that could affect the IHT burden, how effectively the estate debts are paid off or how much money is available for distribution to the beneficiaries at the end of the administration process).

The inventory, fundamentally, may end up as a piece of paper listing all estate assets one-by-one and stating their financial value. As explained at **10.4.1**, HMRC guidance says that for items that are believed to be worth less than £250,000, the PR can make a best guess as to the item's market value. For items believed to be worth more than £250,000, a professional valuation should be made. Of course, for some assets, such as money in a bank account, the true financial value must be stated exactly.

To hold the PR to account, anyone with an interest in the estate (that is, anyone inheriting under a will or who would be entitled on intestacy) can apply to court to ask for the inventory to be exhibited to court (*Myddleton v Rushout* (1797) 1 Phil

Ecc 244, 161 ER 973). The PR can be asked to exhibit the inventory at any time whilst the estate is being administered.

Whilst the beneficiaries are always entitled to ask, the court has discretion whether or not to actually order the PR to provide the inventory to court. It would certainly help the applicant to provide a reason why they are seeking the inventory to be exhibited. There is generally no defence for the PR to say that exhibiting the inventory would be practically difficult. Historical examples include cases concerning formal paperwork (such as title deeds) being located abroad and therefore relatively inaccessible to anyone in England (*Taylor v Rundell* (1841) Cr & Ph 104, 41 ER 429). Today, as the world is increasingly digital, such practical difficulties should be fewer. Nonetheless, the PR cannot avoid providing an inventory simply because of practical difficulties in putting together all the paperwork. That is because completing the inventory is a key duty that the PR accepts when agreeing to the role. However, the court can refuse to order an inventory if there is no good reason to do so. For example, in *Scurrah v Scurrah* (1841) 2 Curt 919, 163 ER 630, the court declined to order an inventory where 18 years had passed since the deceased had died and it appeared that the administration had long since been completed. The inventory would have served no function.

12.4.3 Duty to account

Under s 25(b), the PR also has a duty to account for their dealings with the estate and, if required, must provide all relevant evidence to the court. This duty follows on from the duty to provide an inventory. The inventory is a list of the estate assets, including its debts (owed to the estate and owed by the estate). The account is a record of all dealings done by the PR with the estate assets. In the Singapore case of *Lim v Lim* [2020] SGHC 49, the court observed:

> [T]rustees and executors are under a duty to keep accounts of the trusts, to be constantly ready with the accounts, and to allow the beneficiaries to inspect them as requested. Beneficiaries are entitled, within proper bounds, to be furnished with an account of the funds in the trust/estate, and this duty is not contingent on any allegation or establishment of breach of fiduciary duty.

Any of the beneficiaries of an estate are entitled to ask the PR to provide an account. Equally, if a beneficiary is inheriting the estate of X, and X's estate is entitled to inherit from the estate of Y, then X's beneficiary may be able to obtain an account from Y's PR (on the basis that their entitlement to inherit from X is dependent on X inheriting from Y, and that Y's estate therefore must be properly administered) (*Howes v Howes* [2021] EWHC 591 (Ch)).

Having to provide an inventory and account is not automatic, but the court will generally make such an order, especially if the beneficiaries can provide an explanation as to why they seek it (*Ali v Taj* [2020] EWHC 213 (Fam)). However, the beneficiaries do not have to allege or prove any actual wrongdoing, as explained in *Lim v Lim*. There are any number of reasons why the beneficiaries may seek an inventory and an account; these reasons can include any delays in the administration of the estate or concerns that property may be missing. The beneficiaries can ask for an account at any point in the administration process. As with the inventory, the court can refuse to order an account if there is no valid reason to provide one.

What might the account show? For example, the inventory might show that the estate includes a freehold estate subject to a mortgage. To raise cash to pay off the mortgage, the PR may need to sell the house. The account would include an explanation as to why the house was sold (to pay off the mortgage), proof of the sale (such as the contract of sale signed by the PR and the buyer), and bank records showing the proceeds of sale coming into the estate's bank account and thereafter being used to pay off the mortgage. The bank should also provide a receipt as proof that the mortgage has been paid off. To use another example, the house might be sold to raise cash to reimburse the PR for any inheritance tax that has been paid on the estate (see **10.5**). Again, bank statements may prove the various transactions. If the PR personally paid the IHT, the PR should provide a written receipt once they have been reimbursed by the estate. If the PR took out a personal loan to fund the IHT, bank statements may be used to prove that the IHT loan was repaid.

Equally, if the PR uses estate funds to pay for insurance on the house, or insurance on a car or another chattel, a written confirmation of the insurance will be provided by the insurance company (which must be retained by the PR and presented to the court as part of the account), and bank records may be used as evidence to show that the insurance premium payments have been made. The duty to account can also include the PR having to provide the estate's bank account statements and being asked to explain each payment in and out of the bank account.

The inventory and the account are the first steps in a process of holding the PR responsible for their actions. If the inventory or the account were to reveal that some wrongdoing has occurred, remedies may follow. For example, the inventory may show that items have not been properly valued. The account may show that the PR has transferred estate assets to someone who is not entitled to the property. As for what remedies may apply, see **16.4**.

The duty to account for their dealings remains even if the PR is removed from their position. The court can still ask them to account for any dealings with the estate assets that they undertook before their removal (*Taylor v Newton* (1715) 1 Lee 15, 161 ER 7; *In the Estate of Thomas, Deceased* [1956] 1 WLR 1516). This highlights the importance of keeping proper records and having them at hand even after the PR has been removed.

The duty to account can be a rather onerous one, especially in a larger estate where there have been many dealings with the estate assets, sometimes potentially over several years. However, it is a fundamental part of the duties placed on a PR (in *Ali v Taj* [2020] EWHC 213 (Fam) it was described as a 'cardinal duty'), and any practical inconvenience cannot be used as an excuse to avoid having to account. This shows that being a PR is a major undertaking and that no one should lightly agree to be a PR.

Once they have received the grant, the PR's first duty is to take control of the estate assets. Executors have an automatic right to do so under the will (a grant is a formality, as explained in the previous chapter); administrators only get this right through the grant. The duty includes taking physical control of land and chattels, accessing intangible property, and calling in debts owed to the deceased. The PR must also identify if the deceased was a sole trustee over a trust fund or was a sole trader or partner in a partnership. Once the PR has control over the estate assets, they have to manage the estate assets in accordance with their legal duties. They may be required to provide an inventory of the estate and account for their dealings with the estate assets to court. Next, they must identify if any property was designated as a specific gift in the will. All other estate assets can then be sold, if needed, to cover the estate's debts (including funeral costs, probate costs, IHT and other contractual debts owed by the deceased). **Chapter 13** will outline how the debts are to be paid off and **Chapter 14** will consider how the remaining assets are distributed to the beneficiaries.

Administration III – Paying Debts

The previous chapter showed that the first duty a PR has, once appointed, is to collect in the estate assets and to call in any debts owed to the estate. This chapter follows on from that, by looking at the PR's next duty. Once they have called in the estate, and have control over the estate assets, the PR must pay off all of the deceased's debts.

The chapter covers the following issues:

- What is the PR's duty to pay off debts?
- What is the difference between a solvent estate and an insolvent estate?
- How does the duty to pay off debts differ between the two?

13.1 Debts

Many, if not most, people will die with debts still to be paid off. There is a lack of hard data in the UK. In 2016, the credit agency Experian reported that 73% of Americans die with debts. It would not be a surprise if the UK figures were similar. These statistics presumably do not include everyday debts, such as a monthly phone bill, which almost every person will have when they die.

At the same time, it has been suggested that many people believe that their debts die with them. It is really important to emphasise that this is not the case. The estate is liable for all of the deceased's debts. Equally important is the fact that no one can 'inherit' someone else's debt. The debt must be paid out of the estate. If there are insufficient funds to pay off all debts, those debts must be written off. The beneficiary is therefore in a fairly safe position: they can never be asked to pay off the deceased's debts, but likewise, if the deceased had a lot of debts, there might be nothing left for the beneficiary to inherit after the debts have been paid off.

Common debts include a mortgage and credit cards. Goods, such as a car, computer or TV, might have been purchased on credit (for example, with a 12-month repayment plan). If the deceased rented a property, rent must be paid until the PR determines (ends) the lease. It is important not to forget the small, day-to-day debts which must be paid, such as council tax and utility bills (electricity, gas and water). It is important to remember that people do not die 'neatly' at the end of the tax year or end of the month when the bills fall due. With these small debts in mind, it is unlikely that too many estates will be overburdened, and it should be relatively straightforward for the PR to pay them off. However, there are repeated warnings about rising levels of private debt, so the difficulties a PR faces should not be underestimated.

13.2 Solvent and insolvent estates

For the purpose of administration, it is important to distinguish between a solvent estate and an insolvent estate. The rules on how debts are paid off differ between the two. A solvent estate is an estate where there are sufficient assets to pay off all the debts. An insolvent estate is an estate where there are insufficient assets to pay off all the debts. In a solvent estate, the beneficiaries will be able to inherit the balance, once the debts have been paid. In an insolvent estate, some debts will not be paid off (since there are insufficient funds) and consequently there will be no assets to distribute to the beneficiaries. Whether an estate is solvent or insolvent is a question of fact and depends purely on a financial balance between available assets and existing debts (*Re Pink* [1927] 1 Ch 237). If necessary, the court can order an inquiry into whether the estate is solvent or insolvent (*George Lee & Sons (Builders) Ltd v Olink* [1972] 1 WLR 214). This can be particularly useful if the deceased had a lot of money owed to them, which has to be called in before the deceased's own debts can be paid off.

13.3 Assets

All of the deceased's real and personal property are assets which can be used to pay off debts (Administration of Estates Act (AEA) 1925, s 32(1)). Section 32(1) states that the deceased's property includes trust property which the deceased is entitled to appoint to a third party. A trust may allow a primary beneficiary to appoint alternate beneficiaries, who will benefit when the primary beneficiary dies. If the primary beneficiary makes such an appointment, the trust fund is available to the PR to use to pay off the primary beneficiary's debts (*Re Phillips* [1931] 1 Ch 347). It is not clear how common such powers of appointment are.

Assets also include property which comes into the PR's hands after the date of death, such as interest on savings, income from investments, rental income, or debts owed to the deceased that the PR has called in (*Re Tong* [1931] 1 Ch 202).

Assets also include property which the deceased has given away in specific circumstances. One is where the deceased has made a gift *donatio mortis causa* (see **3.4.2**). Such a gift is colloquially referred to as a deathbed gift: a donor, in contemplation of their impending death, makes a gift of property to a donee by handing over the asset or title to the asset (see *King v Dubrey* [2015] EWCA Civ 581, [2016] Ch 221). The PR can, if necessary, reclaim that property and use it to pay off the deceased's debts. The deceased might also have transferred property away with the express intention of hiding it from their creditors. For example, a debtor may gift the legal title of their house to their child, in an attempt to stop creditors claiming the house. Such a transaction is fraudulent and can be set aside

(Insolvency Act 1986, ss 423–425). If it is set aside, by a court order, it becomes an asset the PR can use to pay off the debts.

Generally speaking, property that does not devolve on the PR cannot be used to pay off debts. Such property was discussed in the previous chapter (see **12.1.2**). However, property that the deceased co-owned on a joint tenancy, which passes on survivorship to the surviving joint tenant, can be used if the deceased died insolvent; this is explained further below.

Remember from **12.4.2** that the PR has a duty to provide a full inventory of the estate. That includes identifying all assets, as well as what debts are owed to the estate and what debts are owed by the estate. This inventory is vital to understand what assets are available to be used to pay off existing debts but also to know what debts the PR can collect from other parties.

13.4 The PR's duty to pay debts

The PR's fundamental duty is to pay all lawful debts with 'due diligence', using whatever estate assets are available (*Re Tankard* [1942] Ch 69). There is no obligation to pay debts where the estate has run out of assets. The PR is liable to the estate if the debts are not paid with due diligence. For example, the debt may carry interest, which would not have arisen if the debt had been properly paid off (*Re Stevens* [1898] 1 Ch 162). Alternatively, the PR might have distributed the estate assets to the beneficiaries before paying off all the debts, which would allow a creditor to claim against the PR.

What is meant by due diligence is fact specific. It is normally expected that the debts are paid off within the so-called executor's year, but there may be reasons why it takes more than a year to pay off a debt. There may be justifiable delays in paying IHT, which means there is a delay in obtaining probate. Even if the PR obtains probate, it might take longer than expected to realise the estate assets to raise the necessary cash.

The liability to pay off debts with due diligence begins once the PR has accepted their role. There is no claim against a PR for a delay in seeking probate (*Re Stevens* (above) and *Chappell v Somers & Blake* [2003] EWHC 1644 (Ch), [2004] Ch 19). The position is different when the PR appoints a legal adviser to assist in seeking probate; the legal adviser can be liable for losses caused by their delay (*Chappell*). The legal adviser's liability will be discussed in more detail in **Chapter 16**.

The PR has to pay off all the deceased's debts and is personally liable if they fail to do so. This is true even if the PR did not know about a particular debt. The PR is therefore under a particular duty to make proper enquiries to find out whether the deceased had any debts. There are two key routes available to PRs to protect themselves from liability for unknown debts.

The first route is to advertise for creditors, using s 27(1) of the Trustee Act 1925. Section 27 allows the PR to advertise their intention to distribute an estate, and to ask all creditors to come forward within a specified timeframe. This must be at least two months. The advert must be placed in the *London Gazette*, appropriate newspapers in the area where the deceased lived, and any other appropriate fora. For example, if the deceased lived abroad, it will be necessary to advertise in newspapers in that country (*Re Achillopoulos* [1928] Ch 433). Ultimately, this is fact specific (*Re Bracken* (1889) 43 Ch D 1). It is not immediately clear how s 27 is meant to work in the modern world, where fewer and fewer people actually read physical newspapers, and hardly anyone knows what the *London Gazette* is. No doubt, soon, the method for advertising for creditors will need reform.

Section 27(2) further imposes an obligation on the PR to make all proper enquiries that they are otherwise 'advised to make', which is a rather broad phrasing. For example, if the deceased owned a freehold or leasehold title, the PR must search the land register to ascertain whether there is a mortgage charge or any other security on the property. They can also check the bankruptcy register to confirm that the deceased was not bankrupt on death. Again, these checks are fact specific.

The PR is protected from liability if they distribute the estate after the s 27 notice period has expired. The PR must still pay off all debts that they are aware of, even if that creditor has not responded specifically to the s 27 notice (for example, a mortgage charge or a credit card debt that the PR identified when taking control of the estate).

In addition to s 27, the PR can apply to court for a court order, allowing them to distribute the estate. In the case of *Re Gess* [1942] Ch 37, a Polish man died intestate in England. It was impossible to advertise for creditors in Poland, given the ongoing Nazi occupation during World War II. The court allowed the administrator to distribute the estate. This order is referred to as a *Benjamin* order, from the case of *Re Benjamin* [1902] 1 Ch 723.

Where a PR has distributed the estate, s 27 or a court order will protect them. A creditor who later emerges with a lawful claim cannot bring an action against the PR, but the creditor can try to bring an action against the beneficiary who has received the estate asset, which will be looked at in **Chapter 16**.

In addition to having a duty to pay debts, the PR is also under a duty to ensure that the estate does not pay debts that it does not legally have to (*Midgley v Midgley* [1893] 3 Ch 282). For example, the PR is entitled to rely on the Limitation Act 1980 as a defence against old debts. That said, the PR is entitled to pay old debts if they so choose without being liable to the estate, unless there is a court order specifying that the debt is statute-barred. It is therefore advisable for a creditor to demand payment from the estate, even if the repayment date was more than six years prior. However, if the PR refuses to pay, the creditor cannot bring a legal action in court, since the claim is statute-barred. As seen at **12.2.2**, whenever the PR acts in regards to paying debts, exercising their powers under s 15 of the Trustee Act 1925, they are bound by s 1 of the Trustee Act 2000, which imposes a duty to act with reasonable care and skill. It is arguable that if the PR volunteers to pay a debt which is statute-barred, they have not acted with reasonable care and skill. The principles from *Midgley v Midgley* have not been tested following the Trustee Act 2000, so it remains to see how the court would decide this issue.

As seen at **12.4.3**, the PR must keep proper records of any payments made out of the estate (such as paying off debts) and of any payments made to the estate (when collecting debts owed to the estate). If necessary, they must provide an account to the court for their dealings with the estate assets.

13.5 Administrative debts

The first things that will be paid are the various administrative costs. These include funeral costs and the costs of probate.

13.5.1 Funeral costs

The PR has a duty to properly dispose of the deceased's body, whether by burial or cremation. This duty rests on the PR, though it is perfectly acceptable for another person to make the funeral arrangements. A body cannot be owned, but the PR has the legal obligation to take possession of the body in order to dispose of it. As a consequence, the law has long held that a person cannot give legally binding directions as to their own funeral (*Williams v Williams* (1882) 20 Ch D 659). If the deceased, through their will or any other instrument, gives directions that they want to be buried in one way or another, the PR may certainly consider the requests, but they are not legally bound to follow them. The PR's sole obligation is to lawfully dispose of the body.

The person who organises the funeral, whether the PR or some other person, is responsible under the contract to pay the funeral director. The funeral director's legal recourse for non-payment is to sue the organiser for breach of contract (*Newcombe v Beloe* (1865-69) LR 1 P & D 314). The organiser is, however, entitled to be reimbursed from the estate. Reimbursement, of course, is dependent on there actually being funds in the estate. However, the organiser is entitled to be reimbursed before the estate assets are used to pay off any other debts (*Re Walter (Deceased)* [1929] 1 Ch 647).

The person organising the funeral can only be reimbursed for reasonable funeral costs. Fundamentally, this includes the cost of disposing the body, paying for a suitable memorial service, and providing a headstone or other marker. However, what is reasonable depends on who the deceased was and the size of the estate (*Edwards v Edwards* (1834) 2 Cr & M 612, 149 ER 905). The funeral of a celebrity, for example, can reasonably cost a lot of money, since more people, including strangers, may want to attend to pay their respects. In all instances, the organiser should also consider any religious affiliation of the deceased, and whether that religion requires special services or ceremonies. If the estate is insolvent, the organiser must take extra care that the funeral does not cost too much, since this would impact on the other creditors. Even if the estate is solvent, the organiser must take care that the funeral costs remain reasonable and do not inadvertently turn the estate insolvent. The organiser must also consider whether the deceased made any special requests. Although such requests are not legally binding, they can help determine whether the costs were reasonable. For example, in the case of *Stag v Punter* (1744) 3 Atk 119, 26 ER 872, the deceased wanted to be buried 30 miles from his home, which of course incurred additional transportation costs.

With the rise in funeral costs in recent years, special funeral insurance is being offered, which is designed to provide a lump sum payment towards the funeral costs. The PR will have to check whether the deceased had funeral insurance. If so, that money should be used, and then there is no need to use estate assets for the funeral.

The court can make an order under its inherent jurisdiction to dispose of the body, if the PR fails to do so in a proper or timely manner (*Hartshorne v Gardner* [2008] EWHC 3675 (Ch), [2008] 2 FLR 1681 and *Re K (A Child) (Disposal of Body: Court's Power to Authorise)* [2017] EWHC 1083 (Fam), [2017] 4 WLR 112).

13.5.2 Administration costs

The PR is entitled to use the estate assets to pay any administration costs, or to reimburse themselves for any payment they have made, and this also has priority over other debts. There is no statutory definition of administration costs, but it relates to the administrative expenses a PR has to pay.

The first thing to note is that administration costs include inheritance tax. The PR is entitled to reimbursement for any IHT payment that they have made, either using their personal funds or by mortgaging their own property. How IHT is paid was discussed in **Chapter 10**.

Administration costs include the cost of obtaining probate (*Re Clemow* [1900] 2 Ch 182). If the PR instructs a solicitor to apply for probate, the PR can pay the legal fees and the probate fee out of the estate (*Sharp v Lush* (1879) 10 Ch D 468). The cost of probate was discussed at **11.4.7**.

Other administration costs include those associated with keeping the property or advertising for creditors. As seen in the previous chapter, the PR is entitled to insure estate property, and this is a type of administration cost. Administration costs also include paying inheritance tax in other jurisdictions, in order to claim title to property located in those jurisdictions (*Re Sebba* [1959] Ch 166). However, as seen in the previous chapter, the PR does not have to take possession of property which was specifically gifted to a beneficiary, and there is no administration cost applicable in, for example, transporting such goods back to the UK (*Re Fitzpatrick*

[1952] Ch 86). Such costs must be borne by the relevant beneficiary (*Re Grosvenor* [1916] 2 Ch 375).

What administration costs are applicable will vary depending on the nature of the estate. Simply by way of illustration, a few example costs can be mentioned, taken from the Singapore case of *Lim v Lim* [2020] SGHC 49. One of the executors applied to be reimbursed out of her mother's estate for the following items that the executor had paid for with her personal funds during the administration process:

(a) mortgage payments on the mother's house (allowed on the facts);

(b) service charges on the mother's house (allowed on the facts);

(c) property tax on the mother's house (allowed on the facts);

(d) TV licence (allowed on the facts);

(e) home insurance (allowed on the facts);

(f) miscellaneous:

  (i) For example, the executor claimed reimbursement of a taxi fare, having travelled with a debt enforcer to collect a debt owed to the estate. This would have been allowed if the executor had provided a receipt for the taxi fare. Without such evidence, the claim was dismissed.

  (ii) The executor claimed reimbursement for the cost of photocopying various documents that she said were needed for the administration of the estate. This would also have been allowed if the executor had been able to explain why the photocopying was done and why it was necessary to do so. Without such an explanation, the claim was dismissed.

This is merely an illustration of some costs that can arise during the administration process. As outlined at **12.4.1**, the PR must maintain the estate assets before they are distributed to the beneficiaries. Costs associated with looking after the estate assets can include, as in *Lim v Lim*, making mortgage payments and paying the service charges on the property, as well as paying applicable taxes and paying for insurance.

13.6 Payment of debts in solvent estates

Where the estate is solvent, s 34(3) – which refers to Pt II of Sch 1 – of the AEA 1925 sets out an order in which property is to be used to pay off the debts. The PR must start with property which falls in para 1, if any, and only if that is insufficient would the PR go on to property in para 2. Only if the property in para 2 is insufficient would the PR then go on to property in para 3, and so on. This order must be used, unless the will very clearly specifies otherwise.

(1) Property undisposed of by a will, subject to a fund set aside to pay pecuniary gifts

The first property that the PR must call upon to pay off debts is any property which passes outside the will on a partial intestacy. However, out of this property, the PR can first set aside the value required to pay any specific pecuniary gifts (ie gifts of money – see **14.3.3**).

(2) Any property gifted in the residue, subject to a fund set aside to pay pecuniary gifts

If there is no property falling outside of the will on a partial intestacy, the second fund that the PR should call upon is the residue of the estate. Again, the PR can set aside the value required to pay specific pecuniary gifts, if any. For most estates where a valid will is left by the testator, the debts will be paid out of the residue.

(3) Property specifically given for the payment of debts

(4) Property charged for the payment of debts

The testator has the right to specify (at (3) above) that specific property is to be used to settle debts. Furthermore (at (4)) property that is charged (such as with a mortgage) should be used. It is perhaps surprising that these come third and fourth on the list. Despite the wording of the statute, it is possible for testators to vary the statutory order, by explicitly stating so in the will. A clause can state that the debts should be paid using specific property, such as a specified bank account. Whether the statutory order has been varied (so the specified property is used instead of the residue) or whether the property simply falls in (3) or (4) (meaning that the PR starts paying debts from the property identified in (1) and (2)) is a matter of construction. Alongside the rules for paying debts in insolvent estates (see below), this is an example that shows that the AEA 1925 is not the most well-drafted of statutes and would benefit from clarification.

In the case of *Re Meldrum's WT* [1952] Ch 208, the testator, in cl 4(q) of his will, gifted to his daughter a number of things, including '… all moneys standing to the credit of my current account with Lloyds Bank … and the residue of my deposit account at Lloyds Bank Dartmouth after all legacies debts funeral and other expenses have been liquidated but excluding death duties and testamentary expenses'. Later in the will there was a gift of the residue. The court held that the testator's main debts were to be paid from the Lloyds Bank account, as directed by cl 4(q). As the clause states, any inheritance tax and administration costs were not to be paid out of the Lloyds Bank account, and they were accordingly paid from the residue. In the earlier case of *Re James* [1947] Ch 256, a testator gifted certain freehold land and money in a bank account on trust, subject to the payment of debts and testamentary expenses, and later provided a general residue clause. The court determined that all debts were to be paid from the real property and money mentioned in the clause, and that it had varied the statutory payment order.

(5) The pecuniary legacy fund

If a fund has been set aside under paras 1 and 2, it will now be used to pay off debts.

(6) Property specifically gifted

Paragraph 6 refers to property that has been specifically gifted in the will. The testator may, for example, gift 'my shares in ABC Ltd to Y'. This is an example of a specific gift. All specific gifts will be used 'ratably according to value'. Thus, if the testator leaves 'my shares in ABC Ltd to Y and my shares in DEF Ltd to Z', the debts will be paid off by taking the same percentage value from both the ABC shares and the DEF shares.

For example, assume that the ABC shares are worth £100,000 and the DEF shares are worth £10,000. The total value therefore is £110,000. Assume that the testator dies with £11,000 in debt, which must be paid from the shares. The debt is 10% of the total value. Thus, 10% will be taken from the ABC shares (£10,000) and 10% will be taken from the DEF shares (£1,000).

(7) Property appointed under the will under a general power

As mentioned above, the testator may have the right to appoint new beneficiaries to a trust fund under a general power of appointment. If the testator is entitled to make that appointment through their will, the trust fund will be used to pay off the testator's debts. If there are several appointments, each trust fund will be used 'ratably according to value'.

13.6.1 Property subject to a charge

If the deceased died with some of their property subject to a charge, the charged property will be used to pay off the charge (AEA 1925, s 35(1)). This is the key practical variation of the statutory order under s 34(3).

The most common form of charge is a mortgage charge, which will typically apply to the testator's home. In such an instance, the home may have to be sold in order to pay off the mortgage. To avoid selling the home, the PR can use other estate assets to pay off the mortgage, but the PR will then have to use different assets to compensate the beneficiaries who might have lost money.

Let us take an example. Assume that Patrick has a freehold property worth £100,000, subject to a £10,000 mortgage charge. Patrick leaves the house to his partner, Ashley. Patrick also has £15,000 in a bank account, which he has gifted to his friend, Natasha. Applying s 35(1), the house will bear the burden of paying off the debt, and may have to be sold to do so. Alternatively, the PR can use £10,000 from the bank account to make the payment, but then the estate will owe Natasha £10,000. This method might be preferable, in order to keep the house in the family, or to quickly discharge the mortgage (to save on interest payments). The PR must then ensure that Natasha is paid £10,000, for instance by taking out a different loan on the house. In practice, Ashley may personally agree to pay Natasha the £10,000.

The testator can vary s 35(1) through the will. For instance, Patrick may gift 'my freehold property to Ashley, free of mortgage' and state that 'the mortgage is to be paid from my bank account'. In this case, the PR must use £10,000 from the bank account to pay off the mortgage. Natasha will be entitled to whatever is left, which in this case would be the remaining £5,000.

13.6.2 Marshalling

The PR can ultimately use any property in the estate to pay off the debts. It might be necessary to use property inconsistently with the statutory order, to quickly pay off debts (perhaps to avoid penalties or interest). If that is done, the beneficiaries are entitled to marshalling. This is a process which ensures that when the estate is finally distributed, it is distributed according to the statutory order (*Re Cohen (Deceased)* [1960] Ch 179).

Assume that Patrick leaves the residue (consisting of a freehold title and his car) to Ashley, his shares in ABC Ltd to Ali, and his book collection to Zara. Patrick dies with £12,000 in debt. The residue should be used to pay the debt. However, the shares in ABC Ltd are quickly sold, and the proceeds are used to pay off the debt to save on interest. Ali can now demand that £12,000 from the residue is given to her instead, for example by requiring the sale of the car or even the freehold title. The PR must ensure that the estate is distributed correctly. This means that the PR cannot transfer the residue to Ashley until Ali has been given the £12,000. Otherwise, the PR may face liability (*Re Matthews' WT* [1961] 1 WLR 1415).

13.7 Payment of debts in insolvent estates

Where the estate is insolvent, the order of payment works differently. The order of payment is set out in the Administration of Insolvent Estates of Deceased Persons Order 1986 (the '1986 Order'). Unlike in solvent estates, the order of payment for insolvent estates cannot be changed.

The PR must follow the order of payment for insolvent estates where the PR knows that the estate is insolvent. It is also prudent to follow this order of payment where the PR suspects that the estate might be insolvent, even if this is not known for certain. It is a case of better safe than sorry. If the deceased died bankrupt, the trustee in bankruptcy continues to administer the estate until the debts have been cleared or the estate assets exhausted; the trustee in bankruptcy will also follow this order of payment.

13.7.1 Insolvency administration order

If a person dies with an insolvent estate, the normal course of action is for the PR to administer the estate using the 1986 Order. A PR or a creditor can apply to the bankruptcy court (part of the Chancery Division) for an insolvency administration order, meaning that the estate will be administered by a trustee in bankruptcy. The application is made in the same way as if the deceased was alive (see ss 264–271 of the Insolvency Act 1986). To make an application, the debt owed to the applicant creditor must be at least £5,000. The benefit of having an insolvency administration order is that it allows the PR to rely on certain provisions of the Insolvency Act 1986.

For example, s 339 (which is subject to ss 341–342) allows the PR to apply for a court order to set aside any transaction that the deceased entered into at an 'undervalue'. For example, the deceased might have sold his car very cheaply to his friend in order to hide it from his creditors. If the transaction is set aside, the car is once more part of the estate and can be used to settle the deceased's debts.

Further, if the deceased was a joint tenant (for example, the family home was owned on a joint tenancy with a spouse or partner), s 421A allows the PR to apply for a court order. The court order, if granted, would require the survivor (who took the family home on survivorship) to pay to the estate the value lost to the estate (normally, in a co-owned family home, the value lost is half the value of the house). When the court is exercising its discretion whether to make an order, s 421A(3) says that the interest of creditors normally outweighs the interest of the surviving joint tenant. In order to pay the value lost, the survivor may be required to sell the property. The court will order a sale of the property, even if there are children living there, if that is necessary to satisfy the debts. Only in very exceptional circumstances will the court not order a sale; see the comments made in *Re Citro* [1991] Ch 142 and *Barca v Mears* [2004] EWHC 2170 (Ch), [2005] 2 FLR 1. In *Re Citro*, Nourse LJ famously remarked that consequences such as having to move houses, having to find new schools for children, and so forth, were simply 'the melancholy consequences of debt and improvidence with which every civilised society has been familiar'. In *Barca*, the child in question had special education needs, but even that was not sufficient to stop a sale. Even if the court does not order an immediate sale, it will often merely postpone the sale until any children have grown up. At that point, the property can be sold to satisfy the debt (*Re Holliday* [1981] Ch 405).

13.7.2 Order of payment in an insolvent estate

The 1986 Order provides how the debts are to be paid off. All debts can be proven against the estate, including future and contingent debts (Insolvency Act 1986, s 382). Debts include the capital and any unpaid interest accrued up unto the date of death. If the debt is a future or contingent debt, its value must be estimated (Insolvency Act 1986, s 322). The value of the debt and interest has to be ascertained with reference to the date of death (*Lockston Group Inc v Wood* [2015] EWHC 2962 (Ch), [2016] 1 WLR 2091).

In *Lockston*, a Russian oligarch living in Britain died insolvent, with debts of more than £40 million. Part of the debt was owed in Russian roubles, and a creditor applied to have the value assessed on the date the insolvency administration order was issued. The court held that the correct date was the date of death – this made a difference given the currency fluctuations between pound sterling and the rouble.

13.7.3 Funeral costs and administration expenses

The first debts to be paid off are the funeral costs and administration expenses, such as the cost of probate or a bankruptcy petition. The funeral costs come first in line, provided that they are reasonable (*Re Walter (Deceased)* [1929] 1 Ch 647). What is meant by reasonableness was discussed above.

13.7.4 Secured debts

Once funeral costs and administration expenses have been paid, the next debts to be paid off are secured debts. These are debts where the creditor has a proprietary security in assets owned by the debtor. The most common example is if a bank has a mortgage charge over the debtor's house. The creditor does not have to prove their debt to the PR or trustee in bankruptcy but can simple enforce the charge (Insolvency Act 1986, s 285(4)). This will be the normal course of action where the asset has sufficient value to discharge the secured debt. If the asset has insufficient value, the secured creditor can sell the asset and then prove the balance against the PR or trustee in bankruptcy, but to this extent of the debt the creditor becomes an unsecured creditor. Any surplus from the sale of the secured property goes back to the estate.

The fact that secured creditors are paid first is a key reason why creditors often try to claim an implied trust over property when the debtor becomes bankrupt or insolvent; see *Barclays Bank Ltd v Quistclose Investments Ltd* [1970] AC 567 and related case law. The so-called *Quistclose* trust will be discussed in greater depth in any Equity & Trusts textbook (see generally, Richard Hedlund and Amber Lavinia Rhodes, 'Loan or Commercial Trust? The Continuing Mischief of the *Quistclose* Trust' [2017] Conv 254–68).

13.7.5 Specially preferred debts

The third category consists of specially preferred debts. They include money the deceased had which belonged to a friendly society (Friendly Societies Act 1974, s 59). They also include any expenses the deceased owed as part of an insolvency administration, if the deceased incurred costs during a voluntary arrangement (Insolvency Act 1986, ss 264(1)(c) and 276). Specially preferred debts are unlikely to arise in most estates.

13.7.6 Preferential debts

The fourth category consists of preferential debts. If there is more than one preferential debt, they rank equally, except Category 8. The debts abate equally if there are insufficient assets to pay all debts. There are seven categories of preferential debts, though due to changes in the law, they are now oddly numbered. They are set out in Sch 6 of the Insolvency Act 1986. Categories 4, 5, 6, 6A and 7 are ordinary preferential debts and are paid first; Categories 8 and 9 are secondary preferential debts and are paid after the ordinary preferential debts have been paid (Insolvency Act 1986, ss 328(1B) and 386):

- Category 4: Money owed to an occupational pension scheme;
- Category 5: Money owed as remuneration to employees – only money payable for the four months before the deceased died are preferential debts, and there is a current limit of £800 for each employee (Insolvency Proceedings (Monetary Limits) Order 1986 (SI 1986/1996), art 4);
- Category 6: Levies owed for coal and steel production under the ECSC Treaty – it remains to be seen how this category is affected by Brexit;
- Category 6A: Debts owed to the Financial Services Compensation Scheme;
- Category 7: Debt owed to a deposit covered by the Financial Services Compensation Scheme;
- Category 8: Debts owed to other deposits, specified by paras 15BA and 15BB in Sch 6;
- Category 9: Certain debts to HMRC. They are any unpaid VAT and any income tax deductions made by an employer on behalf of an employee. Employers generally deduct income tax, national insurance contributions and student loan repayments from their employee's pay cheque and pay that to HMRC on the employee's behalf. Any such deductions are covered by Category 9 insofar as the deduction has been made from the employee's pay cheque but not yet paid to HMRC. These are set out in para 15D, which came into force on 1 December 2020.

Categories 4 and 5 are likely to be the more commonly applicable, but, even so, preferential debts will probably not affect many estates. Unpaid taxes used to be, in general, a preferential debt until they were removed by the Enterprise Act 2002. As seen, IHT is an administration expense and can be paid first. In general, unpaid tax is now an ordinary debt. VAT and certain income tax deductions were added as a secondary preferential debt from 1 December 2020.

13.7.7 Ordinary debts

The fifth category is likely to be the largest category for any estate. Ordinary debts will cover all other contractual or legal debts of the deceased. This will include credit card debts, debts for assets bought on credit, as well as any personal and business loans. The ordinary debts rank equally and must abate equally if there are insufficient assets (Insolvency Act 1986, s 328(3). If there are insufficient assets, as stated above, an ordinary creditor may try to argue that they are, in fact, a secured creditor, with reference to an implied trust.

13.7.8 Interest on preferential and ordinary debts

The sixth category is the interest due on the preferential and ordinary debts that has arisen since the death of the deceased. The interest on all debts ranks equally, regardless of whether the debt itself was preferential or ordinary. The interest rate is the higher of either the interest rate stated for the debt or the interest rate set out in s 17 of the Judgments Act 1938, which is currently 8%; see s 328(4) and (5) of the Insolvency Act 1986.

13.7.9 Deferred debts

The seventh and final category consists of deferred debts. These are debts owed by the deceased to a spouse or civil partner (Insolvency Act 1986, s 329). For example, a husband might have lent money to his wife for her to start a business. This is a deferred debt if it has not been repaid when the husband dies.

13.7.10 Duty to follow the statutory order of payment

The PR or trustee in bankruptcy has a legal duty to pay the debts in the order provided (AEA 1925, s 25). The PR incurs personal liability if they pay a lower-ranked debt before a higher-ranked debt, if it transpires thereafter that there are insufficient assets in the estate to satisfy the higher-ranked debt. The PR is not liable if they paid the lower-ranked debt in good faith, without notice of the higher-ranked debt and having made proper enquiries (such as under s 27 of the Trustee Act 1925, discussed above); see also *Harman v Harman* (1685) 2 Show KB 492, 89 ER 1060 and *Re Fludyer* [1898] 2 Ch 562. The PR is also not liable if they, in good faith, did not believe the estate to be insolvent and paid debts using the order for solvent estates (Administration of Estates Act 1971, s 10(2)). This applies only if the PR genuinely did not believe the estate to be insolvent. It highlights the need for the PR to do a timely valuation of the estate (which should anyway be done for inheritance tax purposes) and advertise for creditors. As stated at the start of this section, if there is any doubt, the PR should play it safe and follow the insolvent estates repayment process.

summary

The duty to pay debts can be quite onerous on PRs, depending on the size of the estate and the amount of debt owed by the deceased. This chapter has demonstrated the two orders of payment, one for a solvent estate and the other for an insolvent estate. It is the PR's obligation to check whether the estate is one or the other, and then to pay the debts using the correct order. If the PR fails to do so, they may be personally liable for the deceased's debts, which can be significant. As seen in **Chapter 12**, the PR must keep proper records when dealing with the debts, as they may be required to account to court for these dealings.

Once the debts have been paid off, the PR can move on to distribute the estate to the beneficiaries.

Administration IV – Distribution

After the PR has been appointed and has accounted for inheritance tax, obtained the grant, called in the estate assets and paid off all debts, the PR can finally distribute the estate to the beneficiaries. Distribution is the final duty that a PR has to undertake.

This chapter covers the following issues:

- When can the PR distribute the estate?
- What rights do the beneficiaries have in the estate prior to distribution?
- How does the PR distribute specific gifts?
- How does the PR distribute pecuniary gifts?
- How does the PR distribute the residue?
- When does a PR transition from being a PR to being a testamentary trustee?

14.1 Distribution

When the PR has called in the estate assets, identified the debts, and paid off all the debts in the correct order, the PR can finally distribute the estate assets to the intended beneficiaries. The distribution process will depend entirely on whether the estate is testate or intestate. The distribution of an intestate estate follows the process set out in **Chapter 8**. The distribution of a testate estate will depend on what types of gifts were included in the will. This will be discussed further below.

The PR is not under any legal obligation to distribute the estate until one year after the deceased's death (Administration of Estates Act (AEA) 1925, s 44). This is the so-called 'executor's year', which was deemed by Parliament to be a reasonable period to complete administration of most estates. Until the expiry of the executor's year, the beneficiaries have no right to call on the estate to be distributed to them. Of course, if the debts have all been paid off earlier than that, the PR is entitled to begin distributing the estate, but this is at the PR's discretion. Equally, if the PR has made 'reasonable arrangements' to pay debts, the PR should not refuse to transfer other property (not needed for the payment of debts) to the relevant beneficiaries (AEA 1925, s 36(1)). However, if the administration takes longer than one year, the PR can justifiably delay distribution. This all depends on the circumstances of each case. In *Re John (Deceased)* [2018] EWHC 21 (Ch), which concerned the rather sizeable estate of the Eighth Earl of Bathurst, the judge agreed that a PR 'must act diligently, timeously and reasonably in the fulfilment of his/her duty', and if there is an unreasonable delay, the PR may be required to justify their actions to the court.

Where a person dies, their estate devolves in its entirety to the PR, with some exceptions, such as property held on a joint tenancy, as discussed in **Chapter 12** (see **12.1.2**). The law is very clear on the fact that beneficiaries have no proprietary interest (whether legal or equitable) in the estate (*Re Hayes WT* [1971] 1 WLR 758). Their only right is to ensure that the PR properly administers the estate.

14.2 Assents

When the PR is ready to distribute the property, the PR will make an assent.

key terminology

Assent: the act of a PR by which estate property is transferred to the beneficiary, and the beneficiary obtains legal title to that property (*Re King's WT* [1964] Ch 542).

Where the estate asset is personal property, the PR's assent can be in writing, it can be made orally, or it can be implied from conduct (*Barnard v Pumfrett* (1841) 5 My & C 63, 41 ER 295). Prudence suggests that the assent should always be in writing. As seen at **12.4.3**, the PR has a duty to account, and written assents are good evidence to provide to the court if the PR is asked to account for their dealings with the estate assets.

Where the estate asset is real property, the PR's assent must be in writing, signed by the PR, and it must specify the beneficiary (AEA 1925, s 36(4)). If the PR is selling the land, for example to raise money to pay off debts, a written statement by the PR that no prior assent has been given is sufficient protection for the third-party purchaser (s 36(6)). Section 36 does not protect purchasers if they know they are not entitled to purchase the property from the estate (*Re Duce* [1937] Ch 642). For example, the purchaser might know that an assent has already been given to someone else. Alternatively, an investigation of the title may reveal that the house was owned on a joint tenancy (and is therefore not part of the estate) or that it might be encumbered by some third-party interest, such as a mortgage or an overriding interest of a person in actual occupation (*Williams & Glyn's Bank Ltd v Boland* [1981] AC 487).

The assent must be read together with the will, and the assent cannot give a larger or smaller interest in the property than envisaged by the will. In *Thompson v Bee* [2009] EWCA Civ 1212, [2010] Ch 412, a testator left land subject to an identified right of way, which at the time of death was only used for agricultural purposes, to the defendants. The testator left the land on which the right of way was located to the claimant. The defendants later tried to build residential homes along the property. The claimant sought an injunction, stopping the houses from being built, arguing that the right of way was necessarily limited to agricultural use and could not be used to access the new homes. The Court of Appeal read the assent together with the will, from which it was clear that the right of way was not limited to agricultural use, but was simply a right of way. As such, an injunction to stop the houses from being built was refused. The outcome would have been different if the will had stipulated that the right of way was limited to agricultural use.

14.3   Types of gifts

A will can include several different types of gifts. It is important to distinguish between these different types, since the rules of distribution vary between them. Examples of different types of gifts were included in the sample will in **Chapter 4**, which you might want to revisit at this point.

The first distinction that must be drawn is between legacies and devises. A legacy, which can also be called a bequest, is a gift of personal property. This includes tangible property, such as the testator's car, jewellery, or shares in a company. It is a slight quirk in property law, but leaseholds have traditionally been treated as personal property, though that might have changed with s 1 of the Law of Property Act 1925. A devise is a gift of real property. Typically, this will mean the testator's freehold title.

Assume that Patrick is writing his will. He wishes to give his gold wristwatch to his son Ronald. As a chattel, this is a legacy (or bequest). Patrick's will should formally read: 'I bequeath my gold wristwatch to my son Ronald.' Patrick also wishes to leave his freehold property to his daughter Sandra. Patrick's will should formally read: 'I devise my freehold property, 10 Smith Street, London, to my daughter Sandra.' However, in the past few decades there has been a deliberate effort to declutter the law of the old, technical terminology. This is particularly relevant in succession law, since many wills are home-made by testators who do not have legal training. Today, therefore, it is perfectly acceptable – indeed normal – to simply write 'I gift' in relation to both personal and real property.

The second distinction that must be drawn is between three classes of gifts. Testamentary gifts can be specific, general or demonstrative. A legacy can fall into any of the three classes. A devise will most likely be specific.

14.3.1   Specific gifts

Specific gifts are gifts of particular and identified property. Examples of specific legacies include the testator's car, jewellery, or shares in a company. A devise, a gift of real property, will most likely be specific. The item must be identified and it must be possible to segregate it from the testator's other assets.

Once the PR is satisfied that a specific asset is not needed to pay off debts, the PR can assent and transfer the asset to the intended beneficiary. The beneficiary will also be entitled to any income or profit made on the property from the date of death, such a rental income on a house or dividend payments on shares. There are two main reasons why a beneficiary will not receive the specific asset. The first is if the PR needs to sell it to pay off debts. The other is if the property has adeemed.

Ademption occurs where the testator has, prior to their death, disposed of the specific property. The testator might have sold the property or given it away as a lifetime gift. The disappointed beneficiary has no claim against the estate. Ademption was discussed at **6.5.5**.

For this reason, it may be preferable to leave a general gift. This will not adeem merely because a specific asset has been sold.

14.3.2 General gifts

A general gift is a gift of value rather than a gift of particular property. A common example of a general legacy is a pecuniary gift (see more below), which is simply a gift of money. Assume that Patrick is writing his will and wants to leave some money to his friend Alan. The will may simply state 'I leave £10,000 to my friend Alan.' It does not specify where the £10,000 should come from and the PR will have to raise the money using the rules outlined below.

Alternatively, Patrick may write in his will, 'I leave 10,000 shares in Egerton Ltd to my friend Alan.' If Patrick owns 10,000 shares in Egerton Ltd and writes in the will, 'I leave my 10,000 shares', the gift is specific. If it simply says, 'I leave 10,000 shares', the gift is general. If Patrick has shares in the company, they can be used to satisfy the general legacy; if Patrick does not actually own shares in the company, the PR will have to buy 10,000 shares and then transfer them to Alan (*Bothamley v Sherson* (1875) LR 20 Eq 304). The gift would fail if it was impossible to carry it out, for instance if Egerton Ltd had closed down before the testator died.

It is possible for a devise to be general as well. Patrick can say in his will, 'I leave a house in Gloucester to my friend Alan.' If Patrick does not actually own such a house (which would make the devise specific), the PR would have to purchase a house in Gloucester and transfer it to Alan.

The beneficiary is also entitled to interest on the value of the gift, from the date of the testator's death to the date of distribution. The interest rate is currently set at 4%. The PR will have to take that into account when distributing the value of the gift.

Because a general legacy will not adeem, the courts prefer to interpret gifts as general rather than specific (*Re Rose* [1949] Ch 78). Many judgments concerning gifts of shares, where the testator owned exactly the number of shares gifted in companies specifically named in the will, have declared these gifts to be general (*Re Willcocks* [1921] 2 Ch 327; *Re O'Connor's WT* [1948] Ch 628). One of the key things that will lean the court in favour of finding a gift to be specific is the use of the possessive pronoun: a will reading 'I leave my shares' is more likely to be a specific gift. Ultimately, it is a question of construction whether a gift is specific or general (*Re Nottage (No 2)* [1895] 2 Ch 657). Following the introduction of s 21 of the Administration of Justice Act 1982 (see **5.2.7**), wills must today be interpreted based on the testator's intention rather than strict rules of language. Even so, given the risk of ademption, the courts will probably still prefer to find gifts to be general rather than specific.

14.3.3 Pecuniary gifts

The will may leave a gift of money to a beneficiary. This is known as a pecuniary gift. Regrettable uncertainty has arisen in the law concerning pecuniary gifts. The question is what estate assets are meant to be used to pay the gift. This is a practical question of fundamental importance to PRs. However, the legal uncertainty has arisen because this point was not fully addressed in the AEA 1925 (indeed, various sections in the Act seem to contradict each other on this point). The resulting case law has also been contradictory and it is not possible to reconcile the authorities. It is vital, therefore, if a testator wishes to leave a pecuniary gift, that the will specifies clearly what asset is meant to be used to pay that gift.

Before the AEA 1925, the law on this point was well established. In the case of *Robertson v Broadbent* (1883) 8 App Cas 812, the House of Lords confirmed the general rule. Pecuniary gifts were to be paid using any personal property that had not been specifically gifted. If this fund was insufficient, the pecuniary gifts had to abate proportionately. This rule was confirmed by the House of Lords in the case of *Higgins v Dawson* [1902] AC 1. Here, a testator left pecuniary gifts and then left specific personal property to three beneficiaries, subject to the payment of debts. The testator later obtained further personal property, which was not mentioned in the will, and the will did not contain a general residuary clause. This new personal property therefore passed on partial intestacy. There was no instruction on how the pecuniary gifts were to be paid. The House of Lords confirmed that only the undisposed-of personal property could be used to pay the pecuniary gifts, despite the fact that this property was insufficient.

However, the testator could, in the will, state a contrary intention. The testator could instruct the PR to pay the pecuniary gifts using other personal property or even the real estate. Equally, if the will gave the real and personal estate together to one beneficiary, the testator was presumed to have intended both to be used for the pecuniary gift (*Greville v Browne* (1859) 7 HLC 689, 11 ER 275). The personal property is applied first, and the real property is applied if it is needed (*Re Boards* [1895] 1 Ch 499).

The AEA 1925, as mentioned, did not provide an outright answer to how pecuniary gifts are to be paid. This is a very unfortunate omission.

Where a person dies intestate, s 33(1) states that the PR takes the intestate estate on trust and has a power to sell it, in order to pay debts and distribute the residue to the next of kin (or to the Crown on *bona vacantia*). Section 33(2) goes on to say that the PR should use the money from the sale to pay all debts. It also states that the PR should set aside a fund to pay pecuniary gifts. Section 33(2) therefore clearly applies to a testator who dies partially intestate. The PR should use the property passing on partial intestacy to pay any pecuniary gifts contained in the will. The section makes no distinction between real and personal property, so the pre-1926 rules are clearly altered where a partial intestacy arises (*Re Worthington* [1933] Ch 771 and *Re Berrey's WT* [1959] 1 WLR 30). So far, so good.

However, s 33(2) does not make it clear what happens if the undisposed-of property (passing on partial intestacy) is insufficient to pay the pecuniary gifts. Since it imposes a trust, s 33 cannot apply where the will itself imposes a trust, such as asking the PR to hold the residue on trust (see s 33(7)). It also does not apply where a testator dies fully testate. The previous chapter discussed the payment of debts in solvent estates, which is governed by s 34(3) (and Pt II of Sch 1) of the AEA 1925. Section 34(3) does not mention pecuniary legacies, merely debts. Part II of Sch 1, however, does mention pecuniary gifts. Paragraph 1 says that undisposed-of property should be used to pay off debts first, subject to a fund set aside to pay pecuniary gifts (this seems to replicate s 33(2)). Paragraph 2 says that the residue should be used next, again subject to a pecuniary gift fund. Paragraph 5 says that the pecuniary gift fund should be used to pay off debts should all the preceding property be insufficient. This seems to suggest that s 34(3) also applies to pecuniary gifts, and that the order set out in Pt II of Sch 1 should be used to this effect. However, since s 34(3) does not mention pecuniary gifts, it is not clear that it can be used in that way.

If s 34(3) cannot be used, the obvious solution would be to keep using the pre-1926 rules. This is what most of the case law says. *Re Thompson* [1936] Ch 676 held that the old law still applies. The testator gave the mixed residue (both personal and real) to two hospitals. The court said that pecuniary gifts should be paid from the personal residuary property first and from the real residuary property if needed secondly. In the case of *Re Rowe* [1941] Ch 343, the testator left his real property and the residue of his personal property to two beneficiaries. The testator also made various pecuniary gifts. Since the residue was not mixed (the residuary clause only mentioned personal property), only the personalty could be used to pay the pecuniary gifts, despite being insufficient (applying *Robertson v Broadbent* and not applying the exception in *Greville v Browne*). In the case of *Re Anstead* [1943] Ch 161, the court confirmed that a pecuniary gift fund must be set aside out of the residue (applying para 2 of Pt II of Sch 1), and that this pecuniary fund should in the first place come from the personal estate and only come from the real property if needed.

In the case of *Re Beaumont's WT* [1950] Ch 462, the testator left various pecuniary gifts and then left the mixed residue on trust for four people. One of the four residuary beneficiaries predeceased the testator, meaning that the quarter portion of the residue failed and passed on partial intestacy. Despite para 1 of Pt II of Sch 1 (retain a pecuniary fund out of property undisposed of by the will), the court held that the whole personal residue should bear the burden of the pecuniary gifts, rather than using just the lapsed share. This view was affirmed in the case of *Re Taylor's Estate* [1969] 2 Ch 245. These cases clearly state that s 34(3) and Pt II of Sch 1 only concern what property is to be used to pay debts, and have nothing to do with pecuniary gifts.

However, in the case of *Re Worthington*, the Court of Appeal suggested that s 34(3) did apply to pecuniary gifts. The comments, however, are obiter since *Re Worthington* concerned s 33(2). In the case of *Re Martin* [1955] Ch 698, the testator died with his real property falling outside the will. The court applied para 1 of Pt II of Sch 1 to hold that the undisposed-of property was liable to pay the pecuniary gift. The court distinguished *Re Beaumont*, saying that that case concerned the lapse of a mixed residuary fund and that the present case concerned the partial intestacy of specific real property. *Re Beaumont* also concerned a trust for sale (where one-quarter interest lapsed) which the present case did not involve. It is not clear how persuasive that distinction is. It is also not clear why *Re Martin* was decided based on s 34(3) rather than s 33(2), which seems more applicable. In the case of *Re Midgley* [1955] Ch 576, the testator left the residue on trust for sale to six people, but by a codicil removed one of the six beneficiaries. That one-sixth interest therefore lapsed. The court held that the lapsed share was to be used to pay the pecuniary gifts, applying para 1. The court did not fully explain how it distinguished *Re Beaumont*, but, at the same time, *Re Beaumont* did not fully explain why para 1 did not apply.

The legal position is clearly unsatisfactory. When writing a will, the testator should specify what assets should be used to pay any pecuniary gifts. Otherwise, on balance, the courts seem to follow the pre-1926 rules, which go first to undisposed-of personalty; otherwise to personalty in the residue; or, where the residue is mixed, to the residue as a whole, but starting with the personalty.

The table below demonstrates how the courts have moved back and forth between different rules.

From personality	vs	From personalty and realty
	1859	*Greville v Brown* Exception to the general rule when the residue is gifted together – use the whole residue but start with personalty – only use the realty if the personalty is insufficient
Robertson v Broadbent The House of Lords confirms the general rule – pecuniary gifts to be paid from not specifically gifted personalty	1883	

From personality	vs	From personalty and realty
Higgins v Dawson The House of Lords reaffirms the general rule	1902	
	1925	Administration of Estates Act 1925 s 33(2) – where a person dies partially intestate, the property passing outside the will should be used for pecuniary gifts – does not clarify what happens if this is insufficient s 34(3) – this section outlines the payment of debts for testate estates, but does not mention pecuniary gifts – Sch 1, however, says that a pecuniary gift fund should be set aside before any undisposed-of property and the residue are used to pay debts
	1933	*Re Worthington* Applying s 33(2) – where a person dies partially intestate, any property falling outside the will can be used for paying pecuniary legacies
	1936	*Re Thompson* Applies the pre-AEA 1925 rule in *Greville v Brown* – the residue was mixed so the whole residue could be used for pecuniary gifts, starting with the personality
Re Rowe The residue only included personalty – only the residue could be used for the pecuniary gifts, even though it was insufficient	1941	
	1943	*Re Anstead* Applying s 34(3) and Sch 1 – a pecuniary gift fund must be set aside from the residue, starting with the personality but using realty if necessary

From personality	vs	From personalty and realty
Re Beaumont's WT Whole personal residue will be used for pecuniary legacies, not the lapsed mixed share – applies the pre-AEA 1925 rules and says s 34(3) is just about debts	1950	
	1955	*Re Martin* Applying s 34(3) and Sch 1, undisposed-of realty was used to pay pecuniary gifts
	1955	*Re Midgley* Applying s 34(3) and Sch 1, a lapsed mixed share of residue was used to pay the pecuniary gifts – distinguished *Re Beaumont*
Re Taylor's Estate The personal residue will be used for pecuniary legacies – applies the pre-AEA 1925 rules and says s 34(3) is just about debts	1969	

The law now most likely stands with *Re Taylor's Estate*, namely that s 34(3) only concerns paying debts and that pecuniary legacies are to be paid from the personal residue. If the residue is mixed, the exception in *Greville v Brown* continues to apply, meaning that the real residue can be used if the personal residue is insufficient.

14.3.4 Demonstrative legacies

A demonstrative legacy stands in between a specific and a general legacy. A demonstrative legacy will specify the primary source from which the legacy is to be paid (*Walford v Walford* [1912] 1 Ch 219). Patrick, writing his will, may write: 'I give £10,000 to my friend Alan, to be paid out of my Egerton Bank account.' If the Egerton Bank account was insufficient to satisfy the legacy, the PR would have to find the money in the general estate (*Hodges v Grant* (1867) LR 4 Eq 140). This is the key distinction from a specific legacy, which would adeem if the identified fund was insufficient. A gift stating 'I give the £10,000 in my Egerton Bank account to my friend Alan' is specific, and it would adeem if Patrick has transferred money out of the account. As with general gifts, a beneficiary of a demonstrative gift is also entitled to 4% interest on the value, from the date of the testator's death to the date of distribution.

14.3.5 Ademption and abatement

A specific gift adeems if the property is no longer a part of the estate when the testator dies. Any gift can abate if it is needed for the payment of debts. As seen in **Chapter 13**, the PR must use the general property first before using property that has been specifically gifted. Thus, if there is property missing, perhaps because the testator sold it during their lifetime, the beneficiary will try to argue that the gift was general and therefore has not adeemed. If the estate has a large number of debts, the beneficiary will try to argue that the gift was specific, so that the property is used last (and hopefully not used at all) for the payment of those debts. A demonstrative legacy is ideally placed here, since it is treated as a specific legacy for the purpose of the priority of debt payment, but if the specific property is insufficient, the PR can use any other property to ensure that the demonstrative legacy is paid in full. If it cannot be paid in full, it will abate ratably with the other specific legacies.

14.3.6 Residue

A gift of residue encompasses any property which has not been given away as a specific, general or demonstrative legacy or devise. It is common for a residuary clause to include both personal and real property.

14.4 When does the PR become a testamentary trustee?

As noted earlier, the beneficiaries under a will do not have any beneficial interest in the property until the administration has been completed. Whilst the PR is still calling in assets, paying off debts, and even paying specific gifts, the PR is still acting in that role. The administration of the estate is still ongoing. However, once all of this is done, the PR generally takes the residue and holds it on trust for the residuary beneficiaries. It is at this point that the PR becomes a testamentary trustee, and fully subject to the duties, powers and obligations of a trustee; see *Davies v Sharples* [2006] EWHC 362 (Ch) and *Green v Gaul* [2006] EWCA Civ 1124, [2007] 1 WLR 591. At this point, the administration process is completed, and all that is left is the testamentary trust. This is perhaps a minor distinction in many instances, but it becomes relevant if there is a claim against the PR or testamentary trustee for breach of duty. As will be discussed in **Chapter 16**, different remedies and defences are available, depending on whether the claim is made against a PR or against a testamentary trustee.

This chapter has set out the final duties of a PR, namely to distribute the estate assets to the beneficiaries. This is done by making an assent of the property and then transferring legal title. Whilst the PR can make an assent at any time, once they are satisfied that the property is not needed to pay off debts, the PR is given one year from the date of death before the beneficiaries can legitimately enquire about the property. As long as the PR is paying off debts with due diligence, the beneficiaries cannot make any claim to the property, even if more than one year has passed.

The chapter then discussed the difference between legacies and devises, and the difference between specific, general and demonstrative gifts. These differences are of major importance when it comes to ademption and abatement, as well as when it comes to determining what estate assets are to be used to satisfy the gifts. The rules on funding pecuniary gifts remain unclear but, on balance, seem unaffected by the AEA 1925.

15 The Family Provision Rule

chapter

It was noted in **Chapter 1** that English law recognises the doctrine of testamentary freedom. A testator is free to choose whom they want to benefit in their will and, conversely, whom they want to exclude. However, testamentary freedom is no longer absolute. This chapter looks at the so-called family provision rule, which limits testamentary freedom for people who die in England and Wales. The family provision rule was first introduced by the Inheritance (Family Provision) Act 1938 and is now governed by the Inheritance (Provision for Family and Dependants) Act 1975. In this chapter, the 1975 Act will simply be referred to as the Inheritance Act. In short, the Inheritance Act allows certain relatives and family members to apply for financial support from an estate, in situations where the applicant has not received reasonable financial support, either through the will or on intestacy.

This chapter addresses the following issues:

- What is testamentary freedom?
- Why was the family provision rule introduced?
- Who can make a claim for financial support under the Inheritance Act?
- How do the courts decide on whether or not to allow an applicant to obtain financial support from the estate?
- What property orders can the court issue to give the applicant financial support from the estate?

15.1 Testamentary freedom

From the 17th century through to 1938, English law allowed for complete testamentary freedom. Private ownership of property was taken very seriously. Philosophers such as John Locke, Jeremy Bentham and JS Mill, together with jurists like William Blackstone, saw private ownership as a natural right, which the government could not curtail. The role of property law was limited to regulating ownership, such as setting out rules on how property could be bought and sold.

Testamentary freedom was a key part of this philosophical view of property. Such freedom means that a testator can choose to leave their property to whomever they want. A testator is not forced to benefit their family or relatives. This means that a testator can choose to leave nothing to their children, for example. Testamentary freedom was taken seriously in England and, as evidenced by recent tabloid headlines concerning some Inheritance Act cases (see more below), it is still taken seriously today. Nonetheless, the law has always recognised that a testator should give serious consideration whether or not to exclude their children. In *Banks v Goodfellow* (1869-70) LR 5 QB 549, the court said that a 'moral responsibility of no ordinary importance' applies when a testator is exercising their testamentary freedom. Spouses, children, and other relatives, ought to be at the forefront of the testator's mind. This is evidenced by the mental capacity test set out in *Banks* (see **2.2.2**).

The testamentary freedom that exists in English law can be contrasted with the forced heirship rules that apply in civil law jurisdictions, such as France and Spain. The rules differ from country to country, but, in short, if the testator leaves a spouse, children or parents, the testator must leave part of their estate to those family members. These people are known as the forced heirs. The testator is afforded very little discretion (most civil law countries allow the testator to disinherit the forced heirs in extreme circumstances, such as where a child is violent towards a parent). In many US states, a homestead allowance applies instead, allowing a surviving spouse or children to take certain household assets (such as furniture, appliances and a reasonably priced family car) outside of the will.

By the turn of the 20th century, common law jurisdictions began moving away from complete testamentary freedom. Instead, a family provision rule was introduced. This allows close family members, who might have been excluded from a will or who might not be entitled on intestacy, to ask for reasonable financial support from the estate. It is for the court to decide whether or not to make an award to them. This means that testamentary freedom remains the starting point, but testators know that if they exclude a family member, such as their child, that person retains the right to go to court and ask for a payment out of the estate. The family provision rule began in New Zealand and Australia. It was finally introduced into English law in 1938.

The arguments in favour of the family provision rule focus on the obligations that family members have to each other. In the 19th and early 20th centuries, the husband would ordinarily be the breadwinner in the family, and he would have a legal obligation to maintain his wife and children (at least until the sons became adults and the daughters got married). It was argued that it was anachronistic that the husband could forgo these legal obligations simply by dying. Although family dynamics have changed considerably since then, the argument is still valid. Spouses and parents have legal obligations to each other. Divorced partners may continue to have legal obligations to each other, through a divorce or dissolution of a civil partnership agreement. At the same time (and equally important today in the post-World War II welfare state), there is a recognition that if a spouse or children are suffering financially, it is better that they are maintained out of the family member's estate, rather than by taxpayer-funded welfare. The courts, however, have held that reducing the welfare burden is not a factor they should consider – see *Wellesley v Earl Cowley* [2019] EWHC 11 (Ch).

A further argument in favour of the family provision rule is the outdated nature of the intestacy rules. As seen in **Chapter 8**, certain family members that are common in modern families, such as unmarried cohabitants and stepchildren, are not included within the intestacy rules. Whilst that might be an argument to reform the law on intestacy, in the short term at least, there is comfort in knowing that such family members might have the right to apply under the Inheritance Act.

A final argument in favour is that a will, although reflecting the testator's testamentary intention at the time the will was executed, might not reflect the testator's new intentions when he or she dies. A good example of this is the case of *Ubbi v Ubbi* [2018] EWHC 1396 (Ch). Here, the testator began an extramarital affair, which produced two children. He did not write a new will to benefit those children. The children successfully made an application under the Inheritance Act to get financial support from the testator's estate, which otherwise would have gone in its entirety to the widow. The award made to the children might reflect what the testator would have included in a new will, had he made one.

The arguments against the family provision rule remain focused on the philosophical ideas of private ownership and the notion that a testator should be free to choose whom they want to benefit. Even though most testators, before the Inheritance Act, did benefit their own family, the argument is that the testator is far better placed than the court to decide which family members most deserve to inherit. There are many reasons why a testator may choose to exclude a child from their will, for example, and the court should not be allowed to second-guess the testator's choice. A further, technical argument is that the Inheritance Act is too vague and gives too much discretion to the court. This was reiterated by the Supreme Court decision in *Ilott v The Blue Cross* [2017] UKSC 17, [2017] 2 WLR 979, where Lady Hale decried that the Inheritance Act 'gives [judges] virtually no help' in deciding applications. This judgment is considered in more detail later in the chapter.

15.2 The Inheritance Act

Regardless of the many arguments for and against testamentary freedom, the Inheritance Act is now an established part of English succession law. The following sections look at the key provisions in the Inheritance Act:

- The deceased must be domiciled in England and Wales.
- Who can make an Inheritance Act application?
- What court should the application be made in?
- What is meant by reasonable financial provision?
- How do the courts determine whether or not to grant the application?
- What time limits apply for making an application?
- What orders can the court make?
- What property is available for an order?

15.2.1 The deceased's domicile

Section 1 of the Inheritance Act makes it clear that an application can only be made against an estate of a person who died domiciled in England and Wales. Domicile is a technical legal term. In short, it refers to the jurisdiction where a person has their permanent home. They must also intend to live there permanently. These principles were set out in *Henwood v Barlow Clowes International Ltd* [2008] EWCA Civ 577. It follows that if a person born in England is living abroad for a long period of time, for example because they are working abroad, but always intend to move back to England at a later date, for example when they leave their job, they remain domiciled in England. Every person will have a domicile of origin (ordinarily where they are born) but can obtain a domicile by choice, if they move to another country and intend to settle there permanently. Every application under the Inheritance Act must show that the deceased died domiciled in England and Wales, either as a domicile of origin or as a domicile of choice.

In the case of *Proles v Kohli* [2018] EWHC 767 (Ch), the deceased was an Indian national who had moved to England, where he lived and worked for the 15 or so years before his death. He frequently travelled back to visit India. Indeed, he spent the last weeks of his life in India, where he died. The judgment concerned only the preliminary point of whether the deceased had died domiciled in England. On the facts, the court found that he had, since his ongoing intention was to live and work in England. That he often visited India and indeed died there did not change his domicile. An appeal was dismissed, reported at [2019] EWHC 193 (Ch).

15.2.2 Who can make an Inheritance Act application?

Section 1 of the Inheritance Act then sets out who is entitled to make an application for financial support from the estate:

- s 1(1)(a) – a surviving spouse or civil partner of the deceased;
- s 1(1)(b) – a former spouse or civil partner of the deceased, who has not remarried or formed a new civil partnership;
- s 1(1)(c) – any child of the deceased. Both a minor and an adult child can make an application;
- s 1(1)(d) – any person the deceased treated as their child. There must be some familial connection between the applicant and the deceased, such as through a marriage or civil partnership the deceased was party to. The most obvious example in this category is if the deceased was the applicant's step-parent, ie married to one of the applicant's parents;
- s 1(1)(e) – any person who was being, wholly or partly, maintained by the deceased immediately prior to the deceased's death. Section 1(3) provides further clarification, saying that an applicant was being maintained 'only if the deceased was making a substantial contribution in money or money's worth towards the reasonable needs of that person'. The key test is that the deceased

was making a 'substantial' contribution towards the applicant's financial needs. What is a substantial contribution will of course differ from person to person.

Two further classes of applicant were added by an amendment in 1996, and they apply only to estates where the deceased died on or after 1 January 1996:

- s 1(1A) – any person who lived in the deceased's household as their spouse for at least two years prior to the deceased's death;
- s 1(1B) – any person who lived in the deceased's household as their civil partner for at least two years prior to the deceased's death.

These new additions are important as they allow unmarried cohabitants to make an application, provided that they had been living with the deceased for at least two years. The provisions are particularly relevant if the deceased died intestate, because the cohabitant would not receive anything under the intestacy rules.

The right to make an application is personal and cannot be passed on to anyone else. In the case of *Roberts v Fresco* [2017] EWHC 283 (Ch), [2017] Ch 433, a wife died leaving a sizeable estate of some £16 million. In her will, she gave her husband only a pecuniary legacy of £150,000 and the income generated from £75,000. The husband was entitled to bring a claim under the Inheritance Act. However, he died a few months later, without having brought a claim (it is not known whether that was something which he was contemplating). He left his estate (which was comparatively small, at £320,000) to his child and grandchild from an earlier relationship. They attempted to bring an Inheritance Act claim on their father's behalf, but this was dismissed by the court. The right to bring a claim therefore dies with the potential applicant.

15.2.3 What court should the application be made in?

In which court the application is lodged will depend on a range of factors, not least the financial value claimed, but also on the inherent complexities of that particular claim. In general, claims for less than £100,000 ought to be heard in the County Court, though if the case is more complex, it can be heard in the High Court even if the value of the claim is lower. There are procedural rules in place for County Court judges to transfer a claim to the High Court, and for High Court judges to transfer a claim to the County Court. Such procedural matters are dealt with during case management hearings.

If the claim is brought before the High Court, the application can be lodged in either the Family Division or the Chancery Division, at the applicant's discretion (Civil Procedure Rules 1998, r 57.15). As will be noted upon below, there may be some benefits to choosing one Division over the other. The different merits of bringing a claim in either Division were explored in a 2003 article by Fiona Cownie and Anthony Bradney, 'Divided justice, different voices: inheritance and family provision' (2003) 23(4) Legal Studies 566–86.

15.2.4 What is meant by reasonable financial provision?

An applicant must show that they are not receiving reasonable financial provision from the estate. This might be because they have been excluded from a will or, if they are included in the will, because the will does not give them enough. This might also be because they are not entitled to inherit anything on intestacy, if the deceased died intestate. What is meant by reasonable financial provision is very vague and is divided into two classes.

15.2.4.1 Surviving spouse or civil partner

The first class is for a surviving spouse or civil partner. They must show that the estate does not provide them with 'such financial provision as it would be reasonable in all the circumstances of the case for a [spouse or civil partner] to receive, whether or not that provision is required for his or her maintenance' (s 1(2)(a) and (aa) – for spouses and civil partners respectively). What is reasonable therefore depends on the circumstances. As will be seen below, any other applicant can apply only for maintenance support, but a surviving spouse or civil partner is not limited to that. They can therefore apply for any reasonable financial support. There is no specific test for this; it depends entirely on the circumstances. However, a helpful yardstick would be to say that the surviving spouse or civil partner is entitled to continue with the same standard of living as they were accustomed to before the deceased died; see *Woolridge v Woolridge* [2016] Fam Law 451 (discussed further below).

15.2.4.2 Any other applicant

The second class is for any other applicant. They must show that the estate does not provide them with 'such financial provision as it would be reasonable in all the circumstances of the case for the applicant to receive for his maintenance' (s 1(2)(b)). What is reasonable again depends on the circumstances. Here, however, reasonable provision is also limited to maintenance support. If the applicant receives enough to support themselves, they are not able to bring an Inheritance Act claim.

Perhaps the most deserving applicant is a cohabitant who, as seen in the intestacy chapter, is not entitled to inherit anything if the deceased died intestate. It was suggested there that the intestacy rules might be in need of reform. The cohabitant can, under s 1(1A) or (1B), make an application if they meet the requirements. However, their award would still be limited to maintenance, since they are not a surviving spouse or civil partner. This suggests that the Inheritance Act might also be in need of updating, regardless of whether or not the intestacy rules change.

The courts have struggled to provide a clear definition of reasonable financial provision for maintenance. The definition must strike a balance between flexibility, so it can apply to an indefinite variety of personal circumstances, and certainty, so that judges can definitively state whether or not an applicant is entitled to bring a claim.

The key definition in English law comes from the case of *Re Coventry* [1980] Ch 461, where Goff LJ said that 'it does not mean just enough to enable a person to get by; on the other hand, it does not mean anything which may be regarded as reasonably desirable for his general benefit or welfare'. In the earlier Canadian case of *Re Duranceau* [1952] 3 DLR 714, the court posited this question: 'Is the provision sufficient to enable the dependant to live neither luxuriously nor miserably, but decently and comfortably according to his or her station in life?' The test aims to strike a balance between the bare minimum and improving the applicant's lifestyle. What is reasonable depends on the applicant's personal circumstances and their existing financial situation.

More recently, in *Ilott v The Blue Cross* [2017] UKSC 17, Lord Hughes said that 'section 1(2) shows that it cannot extend to any or every thing which it would be desirable for the claimant to have. It must import provision to meet the everyday expenses of living.' The applicant cannot ask for more financial support than what they need to continue their existing lifestyle. Financial support must also be limited to what they need for 'everyday expenses', such as rent, mortgage payments, utilities, food, and other day-to-day necessities. It is not possible to provide a clearer definition, since each case turns on its own facts.

The tests set out in s 1(2) are used for two purposes. The first is to determine whether the applicant is entitled to bring a claim. The second is to guide the courts in determining what order to make if they find that the applicant is entitled to financial support from the estate.

What is reasonable financial provision is dependent on the facts. The court will take into account the lifestyle that the applicant had prior to the deceased's death. What is reasonable for a very wealthy family is clearly different from what is reasonable for a family on a low income or on state benefits. It is for the applicant to prove that lifestyle. In the case of *Woolridge v Woolridge* [2016] Fam Law 451, a claim was dismissed because the applicant was 'endeavouring to establish a lifestyle that she would like to enjoy rather than one she did in fact enjoy'. The maintenance provision is not designed to improve the applicant's lifestyle.

15.2.5 How do the courts determine whether to make an award?

Section 3 of the Inheritance Act sets out a list of factors that the court will consider when determining (a) whether the applicant has received reasonable financial provision from the estate, and, if the answer is no, (b) whether an award should be made. It is important to emphasise that the applicant must be successful on both grounds. It is not sufficient just to show that the applicant is not receiving reasonable financial provision. Even if the applicant is receiving nothing from the estate (perhaps because they were deliberately excluded from the will), the court can still refuse to make an award.

The s 3 factors are outlined below. They will be considered in more detail later in the chapter:

- s 3(1)(a) – the applicant's financial resources and needs, both currently and in the reasonably foreseeable future;
- s 3(1)(b) – the financial resources and needs, both currently and in the reasonably foreseeable future, of any other potential applicant;
- s 3(1)(c) – the financial resources and needs, both currently and in the reasonably foreseeable future, of the beneficiaries (either under the will or those who would take on intestacy);
- s 3(1)(d) – any obligations and responsibilities that the deceased had towards the applicant and the beneficiaries;
- s 3(1)(e) – the size and nature of the estate;
- s 3(1)(f) – whether the applicant or the beneficiaries have any physical or mental disability;
- s 3(1)(g) – any other matter, such as the conduct of the applicant or the beneficiaries.

The first thing that comes out of s 3(1) is a financial balancing act. The court has to consider the financial situation of the applicant, the will beneficiary, and any other potential applicant (bearing in mind, for example, that multiple children may apply against the parent's estate). The Supreme Court in *Ilott v The Blue Cross* [2017] UKSC 17, [2017] 2 WLR 979 confirmed that the will beneficiary does not have to justify their entitlement, but the court may be more inclined to make an award if the will beneficiary has considerable financial resources. This is especially true if the applicant is living in more depressed financial circumstances.

Perhaps the most important factor is s 3(1)(g) – any other matters. This includes the applicant's conduct. A good example of this can be seen in the case of *Wright v Waters* [2014] EWHC 3614 (Ch). A daughter was disinherited by her mother. When her mother died, the daughter made an application. This application was rejected. One of the reasons why the application was rejected (which is also why she was disinherited in the first place) was that the daughter had sent her mother a letter, in which she wished her mother dead. Thus, even though the applicant had a disability (s 3(1)(f)) and lived in depressed financial circumstances (s 3(1)(a)), her conduct made it inappropriate to give her an award.

Some further guidance is provided in s 3(2) and (2A). The court is asked to consider the age of the applicant, and the duration of any marriage, civil partnership or cohabitation. The court will also consider whether the applicant had made any contribution to the welfare of the deceased or the deceased's family (such as paying for care or medical treatment). If the applicant is a surviving spouse or civil partner, the court will consider what kind of financial award the applicant might have received on a divorce or dissolution of a civil partnership, and the court can use this as guidance for determining the size of any Inheritance

Act award. Given that these are questions commonly determined by Family Division judges, it may be sensible for a surviving spouse or civil partner to bring their claim before the Family Division, rather than the Chancery Division.

Section 3(3) provides some further guidance where the applicant is a child. The court will consider how the child is being trained or educated or how the applicant might be trained or education. This clearly suggests that the guidance is relevant only to minors (or perhaps those at university age) and does not apply to an adult child. If the applicant is someone the deceased treated as a child (such as a stepchild), the court will consider the duration of the relationship, how much the deceased was contributing towards the applicant's maintenance and education, and whether other people have a legal obligation towards the applicant's maintenance (such as the biological parent).

Section 3(4) provides some further guidance where the applicant was someone who was being maintained by the deceased. Again, the court will look at the duration of the relationship and the extent to which the deceased maintained the applicant. For instance, was the applicant's living solely based on the deceased's financial contributions or can the applicant get by without that financial support?

Section 3(5) says that the court can consider all the facts that are known at the date of the hearing. This is important as it allows the court to consider what has occurred after the death of the deceased.

Section 3(6) clarifies how the court should assess the financial resources and needs of the applicant. The court should consider what earnings the applicant has or what their earning capacity is in the foreseeable future. The court will also take into account the financial obligations of the applicant. For example, the applicant might have their own children, for whom they need to provide financially.

Even though subsections (2)–(6) provide some guidance, the reality remains that s 3 is vague and leaves a lot to the discretion of the judge. As mentioned above, Lady Hale in *Ilott* argued that the s 3 factors do not give the court much guidance. Each case must be decided on its own facts. The risk with that approach is that cases become unpredictable and turn too much on the views of an individual judge.

It also leads to the risk of baseless claims being made by applicants who might 'try their luck' in court. For example, in *Shapton v Seviour* (2020, unreported), the court noted that the application was 'absolutely hopeless' and did not stand a chance of succeeding. These claims are obviously problematic, both in delaying the administration of the estate and causing distress to the beneficiaries, but also in clogging up court time and resources. In terms of the former, PRs may feel pressured to settle Inheritance Act claims out of court, in order to bring the administration process to an end more quickly, but cases like *Shapton* show that PRs should not settle too easily and should be prepared to defend a claim in court.

15.2.6 Time limits for making an application

Section 4 states that an application can be made at any time after the deceased's death but no later than six months after the grant has been issued. The court has discretion, however, to allow a claim to be brought at a later date.

Section 4 does not give any guidance to the court on what factors to take into account when deciding whether or not to permit an application out of time. As the court has mentioned many times, the section gives the court 'unfettered discretion', but the discretion must still be exercised within certain limits, as have been defined by case law (see *Begum v Ahmed* [2019] EWCA Civ 1794).

The court emphasised in the case of *Re Salmon (Deceased)* [1981] Ch 167 that it was the applicant who had to convince the court to allow a late application. In *Re Salmon*, a claim was brought some six months late. The court refused permission to allow the claim, saying that the delay was the applicant's own fault. In fact, it had been the applicant's solicitors' fault, and the court suggested she could bring professional negligence proceedings against her lawyers. The court said that all the facts must be considered, to see why there had been a delay. It is relevant to consider whether the applicant has given notice to the PR that they are considering an application (if notice has been given, it should not matter too much if the formal court documents are filed out of time). It is also relevant to consider whether the applicant had begun negotiations with the PR with the view of finding a settlement. In *Cowan v Foreman* [2019] EWCA Civ 1336, [2020] Fam 129, the Court of Appeal recommended the use of 'without prejudice' negotiations, and suggested that the court will likely allow a late claim if the delay was due to good faith negotiations between the applicant and the PR.

The court must consider whether the PR has already begun distributing the estate. Once the six-month deadline has passed, they can begin distribution without attracting any personal liability, but if the estate has been distributed, the assets can be recalled if needed for an applicant (s 20). The court may be less likely to allow a late claim if the estate has already been distributed, especially if the beneficiaries have already started using the gifts, such as making new purchases. Finally, the court will consider whether the applicant can pursue anyone else, such as, in *Re Salmon*, the applicant's own solicitors.

These factors were confirmed by the Court of Appeal in *Berger v Berger* [2013] EWCA Civ 1305. In *Cowan v Foreman*, the Court of Appeal further reiterated these factors and said that the court could allow late claims if the applicant is able to put forward a 'substantive claim' (one that has some basis of succeeding) and the court is satisfied that a late claim should be allowed, using the factors above. In *Begum v Ahmed*, the Court of Appeal emphasised that a key feature of the time limit is to not cause 'unnecessary delays' in the administration of the estate, and considering what impact the late claim will have on the administration will feature heavily in the judge's decision.

In the case of *Sargeant v Sargeant* [2018] EWHC 8 (Ch), the applicant was the surviving wife. The deceased had left almost all his assets on a discretionary trust. The discretionary beneficiaries were his surviving wife, their daughter, and further descendants. Some 10 years after the deceased's death, the applicant was struggling financially and tried to make an Inheritance Act application, to get estate assets out of the discretionary trust and into her name absolutely. The court refused permission to bring the claim, saying there was no good explanation why the claim had been brought so late. The applicant had been informed of the discretionary trust when the deceased died and would have understood its implications from the start.

Conversely, in the case of *Stock v Brown* [1994] 1 FLR 840, a surviving wife was allowed to bring a claim some six years out of date. She had been left a life interest in income under a trust when her husband died, but following the economic crash in the early 1990s, that income was insufficient for the applicant to survive on. Key factors included the fact that the applicant had not received legal advice as to the effect of the trust and that the economic crash was well beyond her own control.

15.2.7 What orders can the court make?

If the applicant has standing (s 1), has brought the claim within time (s 4), and has convinced the court that (a) they have not received reasonable financial provision from the estate and (b) they should get an award (s 3), the court will make an award. This section will first cover interim orders, which the court can make whilst the parties are waiting for a trial (s 5), and secondly the final orders the court can make after a trial, if the applicant is successful (s 2).

15.2.7.1 Interim orders

Interim orders under s 5 are limited to an applicant who is in 'immediate need of financial assistance' and thus cannot wait for a hearing to determine a final award. The court can grant a lump sum payment or order periodic payments to be made to the applicant. In making its decision, the court will have recourse to the factors listed in s 3, which were discussed above.

In *Weisz v Weisz* [2019] EWHC 3101 (Fam), the court granted an interim order to the applicant that included a monthly lump sum payment for living costs. The applicant asked for around £8,500 pcm, but the court disallowed some of the proposed needs as not being immediate and therefore granted £5,200 pcm. The court rejected an application for £20,000 to pay off an existing loan, as there was no evidence that the creditor was about to enforce the loan, meaning that it was not an immediate need (though it could be taken into account in the final hearing). The court did make an award for the applicant's legal fees, covering the period from the start of the claim and up to the final hearing, which was assessed at around £55,500. This serves as a reminder that the estate can be asked to shoulder the burden of covering the legal fees for Inheritance Act applications. The applicant's legal team were, of course, under a duty to return to the estate any money that they did not actually need between the interim hearing and the final hearing (such as if the case was settled prior to trial). The authority to make an interim award to cover legal fees was accepted (but rejected on the facts) in the earlier case of *Smith v Smith* [2011] EWHC 2133 (Ch).

In the case of *T v T* [2019] EWHC 214 (Fam), Lieven J referred to interim orders as 'draconian'. The concern, of course, is that an interim order is made but then the applicant's claim is dismissed at the trial. Normally, the applicant would then have to repay the interim award to the estate. However, if the interim award has been spent, such as on legal fees, such repayment is unlikely. The judge therefore suggested a rather cautious approach to interim orders, accepting, of course, that the court has full discretion to consider each claim on its facts. The claimant has the burden of proof in showing that they are in need of immediate financial assistance and that there is some merit in their claim for support under the Inheritance Act, ie they have an arguable case. On the facts of *T v T*, the application for an interim order was denied, partly because the applicant had not provided evidence that she had an immediate financial need for the money she was seeking. The court was thus wary of pre-determining the outcome of the eventual trial.

15.2.7.2   Final orders

Final orders are governed by s 2, which sets out the different kinds of awards that the court can make.

The court has wide discretion as to the orders it can make. These are listed in s 2(1). The most common orders include the award of a lump sum cash payment, the making of periodic cash payments, and the transfer of specific property. The court can vary an existing ante-nuptial agreement. The court can order property already distributed to be delivered up to the applicant by the beneficiaries, but, as seen above, this will only occur if the application is made late, and the court will only allow such applications in more extreme circumstances.

The court can also order property to be settled on trust for the applicant, with the applicant perhaps getting only a life interest, and on the applicant's death the property reverting to the originally intended beneficiary. The Supreme Court in *Ilott* emphasised that (unless the applicant is a surviving spouse or civil partner), the aim of the award is limited to maintenance. As such, it might be inappropriate to transfer specific property, especially if the property is valuable. Nonetheless, each case will turn on its own facts.

In the case of *Re Wynford Hodge* [2018] EWHC 688 (Ch), the court ordered that a freehold property, together with a sizeable cash award for its renovation, be transferred to the applicant. This was deemed appropriate because the applicant was 79 years old and in ill health. The house had been purchased for the applicant and the deceased to live in together as husband and wife. In the earlier cases of

Webster v Webster [2008] EWHC 31 (Ch), [2009] 1 FLR 1240 and *Negus v Bahouse* [2007] EWHC 2628 (Ch), [2008] 1 FLR 381, the court also ordered the transfer of a freehold estate, in order to provide a clean break between the applicant and the deceased's other relatives. In all these cases there had been a breakdown of relations between the applicant (an unmarried cohabitee) and the deceased's family. A clean break is therefore appropriate.

The court can also make an order allowing the applicant to purchase estate property (usually the house they lived in) from the estate at fair market value. This order was made, for example, in the case of *Lewis v Warner* [2017] EWCA Civ 2182, [2018] 2 WLR 1205. However, the court emphasised that this kind of order would be 'unusual'.

In *Re H* [2020] EWHC 1134 (Fam), [2020] 2 FLR 561, the Court also granted a financial award to cover the 'success uplift' in a Conditional Fee Agreement (CFA) that the applicant had entered into with her lawyers. In this case, the applicant's lawyers would be paid nothing if the claim failed but would get an uplift of 72% of the fee if the claim was successful. If the applicant had to pay this success uplift herself, that would potentially eat away at everything she had otherwise been awarded, making victory rather Pyrrhic. For example, an applicant may be awarded £100,000 for their Inheritance Act claim, and then have to pay their lawyers a success uplift of £80,000 (even if the basic legal fee is covered by the estate). It is a timely reminder that litigation can be very costly.

In *Re H*, the judge agreed on the facts to 'mitigate' the 'potential unfairness' to the applicant by awarding an additional sum to help cover that success uplift. This is a controversial decision. First, a success uplift cannot be included in a costs order (Courts and Legal Services Act 1990, s 58A(6)), so on principle it is wrong to include them in a substantive award. Secondly, and more generally, costs orders are separate from the substantive award, and they should not be conflated. It is not the defendant's fault if the applicant has entered into a CFA, and the defendant should not be disadvantaged by that (ie by having the estate used to cover the success uplift). The High Court in *Re Clarke* [2019] EWHC 1193 (Ch) refused to include a success uplift for those reasons. The judge in *Re H* included the success uplift for 'case specific reasons', which were not fully explained or justified, saying that paying for the success uplift was a genuine financial need that the applicant had to cover. Still, the decision remains controversial. It has been argued that a Court of Appeal decision is needed to settle the contradiction between the two High Court judgments (Francis Ng, 'Succession: success fees under the Inheritance Act' [2020] PCB 172–81).

15.2.8   What property is available for an order?

Section 2 states that the orders can be made out of the 'net estate'. This is given a fairly wide definition in the Inheritance Act, set out in ss 8 and 25(1).

The net estate is assessed once funeral costs, administration expenses, IHT and other debts and liabilities have been settled. The net estate includes all property which the deceased had the right to dispose of through their will. This includes property they legally owned or property in which they had an absolute beneficial interest under a trust. Property that passes under *donatio mortis causa* is also treated as being part of the net estate.

The net estate does not include money which would automatically pass to a nominated person, such as a pension fund payout or a life insurance payout (*Re Cairnes* (1983) 4 FLR 225). However, whether or not such money forms part of the estate or goes directly to the nominee may depend on the terms, and this should not be treated as an automatic rule. On the other hand, money that passes under a statutory nomination forms part of the estate. This included, for example, a death-in-service payout under the NHS Pension Scheme Regulations (*Goenka v Goenka* [2014] EWHC 2966 (Ch), [2016] Ch 267). Since the definition of the net estate is property which the deceased had the right to dispose of on death, it is arguable that property subject to a mutual will cannot be used for Inheritance Act purposes, though this has not been adjudicated upon (Law Com 231, [12.23]).

Section 9 states that the court has discretion to decide whether the deceased's interest in a joint tenancy should be severed and then treated as part of the net estate. In the case of *Hanbury v Hanbury* [1999] 2 FLR 255, a joint tenancy over various investments and bank accounts was severed in order to make an award for the applicant, a child of the deceased who had a mental disability that would require long-term care. The court will assess what share in the equitable interest the deceased would have obtained had the deceased severed the joint tenancy (*Dingmar v Dingmar* [2006] EWCA Civ 942, [2007] Ch 109). In a co-owned family home or investment, the share is likely to be 50%. Section 9(1A) says that the financial value should be assessed as if the severance had occurred just before the deceased's death, unless the court orders otherwise. This is important if the financial value of the asset significantly changes after the deceased's death.

15.3 Inheritance Act process

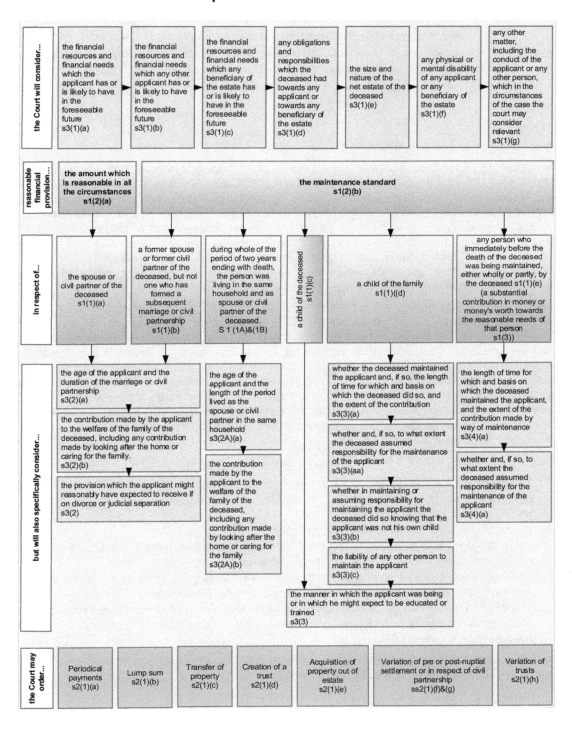

the Court will consider...

the financial resources and financial needs which the applicant has or is likely to have in the foreseeable future s3(1)(a)

the financial resources and financial needs which any other applicant has or is likely to have in the foreseeable future s3(1)(b)

the financial resources and financial needs which any beneficiary of the estate has or is likely to have in the foreseeable future s3(1)(c)

any obligations and responsibilities which the deceased had towards any applicant or towards any beneficiary of the estate s3(1)(d)

the size and nature of the net estate of the deceased s3(1)(e)

any physical or mental disability of any applicant or any beneficiary of the estate s3(1)(f)

any other matter, including the conduct of the applicant or any other person, which in the circumstances of the case the court may consider relevant s3(1)(g)

reasonable financial provision...

the amount which is reasonable in all the circumstances s1(2)(a)

the maintenance standard s1(2)(b)

In respect of...

the spouse or civil partner of the deceased s1(1)(a)

a former spouse or former civil partner of the deceased, but not one who has formed a subsequent marriage or civil partnership s1(1)(b)

during whole of the period of two years ending with death, the person was living in the same household and as spouse or civil partner of the deceased. S 1 (1A)&(1B)

a child of the deceased s1(1)(c)

a child of the family s1(1)((d)

any person who immediately before the death of the deceased was being maintained, either wholly or partly, by the deceased s1(1)(e) (a substantial contribution in money or money's worth towards the reasonable needs of that person s1(3))

but will also specifically consider...

the age of the applicant and the duration of the marriage or civil partnership s3(2)(a)

the contribution made by the applicant to the welfare of the family of the deceased, including any contribution made by looking after the home or caring for the family. s3(2)(b)

the provision which the applicant might reasonably have expected to receive if on divorce or judicial separation s3(2)

the age of the applicant and the length of the period lived as the spouse or civil partner in the same household s3(2A)(a)

the contribution made by the applicant to the welfare of the family of the deceased, including any contribution made by looking after the home or caring for the family s3(2A)(b)

whether the deceased maintained the applicant and, if so, the length of time for which and basis on which the deceased did so, and the extent of the contribution s3(3)(a)

whether and, if so, to what extent the deceased assumed responsibility for the maintenance of the applicant s3(3)(aa)

whether in maintaining or assuming responsibility for maintaining the applicant the deceased did so knowing that the applicant was not his own child s3(3)(b)

the liability of any other person to maintain the applicant s3(3)(c)

the length of time for which and basis on which the deceased maintained the applicant, and the extent of the contribution made by way of maintenance s3(4)(a)

whether and, if so, to what extent the deceased assumed responsibility for the maintenance of the applicant s3(4)(a)

the manner in which the applicant was being or in which he might expect to be educated or trained s3(3)

the Court may order...

Periodical payments s2(1)(a)

Lump sum s2(1)(b)

Transfer of property s2(1)(c)

Creation of a trust s2(1)(d)

Acquisition of property out of estate s2(1)(e)

Variation of pre or post-nuptial settlement or in respect of civil partnership ss2(1)(f)&(g)

Variation of trusts s2(1)(h)

15.4 Inheritance Act case law

This section will consider three Inheritance Act cases, in order to illustrate how the courts exercise their discretion whether or not to make an award. Each case is decided on its own facts, but looking at the case law is the only way to understand how the court exercises its discretion. This is especially important given the inherent vagueness of the Inheritance Act.

key case

Re Land (Deceased) [2006] EWHC 2069 (Ch), [2007] 1 WLR 1009

The judge aptly described this as a 'tragic story'. It concerned an overbearing mother and her only child, a son who had an unspecified developmental disorder. The son was accustomed to doing what his mother told him. She was described as 'domineering' and a person 'who shunned any type of "officialdom" including doctors'. When the mother got older, she asked her son to give up his job and come home to care for her. He did so, but the care he provided was wholly substandard. Over roughly two years, the mother developed bed sores and infections. When the son finally called for help, the mother had become unconscious. She died in hospital two days later. The son was charged with gross negligence manslaughter, in essence for his failure to call for help earlier. He was sentenced to four years' imprisonment.

The son was the sole beneficiary in the mother's will. However, where a beneficiary (whether under a will or on intestacy) is convicted of killing the deceased, they forfeit their inheritance under the Forfeiture Act 1982 (see **6.5.9**). This is an important principle of public policy, which ensures that no one can 'speed up' their inheritance through murder. In this case, the mother's estate was to be distributed to remoter relatives on intestacy. The estate was small, consisting primarily of the freehold house in which she and her son lived. However, the Forfeiture Act 1982 allows a beneficiary to ask the court for relief from the rule, but this application must be made within three months of the beneficiary's conviction (s 2(3)). In this case, the son missed the deadline. Section 3 then allows the beneficiary (if the beneficiary is one of the recognised applicants) to make an application under the Inheritance Act. This is what the son did.

The judge considered the s 3 factors and found that the son was entitled to an order:

- The applicant had no money and low employment prospects, both because of his inability to properly read and write as well as the criminal conviction. This would mean that he would become reliant on state benefits.
- His main maintenance need was accommodation.
- None of the remoter relatives (entitled on intestacy) had opposed the application and they had not provided evidence as to their own financial needs.
- The applicant was the sole child of the deceased (though it transpired that he had been adopted) and he had lived with and cared for his mother his whole life.
- The estate was very small, consisting mainly of the freehold property and some cash savings.
- The claimant's conduct had in essence been faithful to his mother, even though it had clearly been negligent towards the end.

The applicant was given the freehold title and a pecuniary gift of £1,000. The remainder of the mother's money passed on intestacy.

key case

Woolridge v Woolridge [2016] Fam Law 451

The deceased was a wealthy businessman. Whilst on a trip in Northern Ireland, he was in a helicopter crash and died. He left behind a widow, who was the Inheritance Act applicant, a son they had together, and an adult son from an earlier relationship. The deceased left a will, which gave the widow the matrimonial home (free of mortgage and at trial valued at some £4 million) and some £700,000 from various insurance policies. Broadly put, the deceased then gave his business interests to his two sons in equal shares. The widow brought a claim under the Inheritance Act, as a surviving spouse, arguing that the provisions of the will did not provide her with the lifestyle that she claimed the deceased had intended for her.

The court emphasised that when it comes to a surviving spouse, the maintenance cap does not apply. The court has to assess the lifestyle that the applicant and the deceased enjoyed prior to the deceased's death. The applicant claimed that she needed £372,000 per annum to maintain that lifestyle. However, this was taken with a pinch of salt, since the figure had gone up in each of her four witness statements. The judge concluded at [71] that the applicant was 'endeavouring to establish a lifestyle that she would like to enjoy rather than one she did in fact enjoy'. Her claim was dismissed.

The particular fact that spoke against the applicant was her own financial resources. She had sold her own business a few years earlier for around £1 million. She had made a successful Fatal Accidents Act claim against the helicopter operator, from which she received nearly £2 million (with a few hundred thousand pounds going to each son). The applicant's total assets, including what she had inherited under the will, were assessed at some £10 million. In addition, the court was keen not to disturb the estate so as to preserve the deceased's business assets and ensure that both sons were financially protected. The judge's conclusion that the applicant 'has enough' is somewhat of an understatement.

key case

Ilott v The Blue Cross [2017] UKSC 17, [2017] 2 WLR 979

This is the first Inheritance Act case to come before the Supreme Court. The applicant was the adult daughter of the deceased, her mother. At the age of 17, the applicant had eloped to start a relationship with a man whom the mother strongly disapproved of. Nonetheless, the relationship was successful. The applicant married and had five children of her own. The applicant did at times try to rebuild the relationship with her mother, but each attempt at reconciliation was rebuffed by the deceased. Ultimately, their estrangement lasted for some 26 years before the deceased died.

The deceased left her entire estate, which was valued at some £486,000, to various charities. She also attached a letter to her will, instructing her executor to resist any Inheritance Act claim that the daughter might bring. The daughter did make an application. This was on the basis that she (and her family) were living in depressed financial circumstances and that the will did not make reasonable financial provision for her (indeed, she was excluded altogether).

At first instance, the judge found in favour of the applicant. Her financial circumstances, and her financial obligations in looking after her children, were favourably compared to the financial needs of the charities (who were the chosen will beneficiaries). The applicant's conduct was also relevant, as she had made some attempts at reconciliation. It was not the applicant's fault that the deceased had rebuffed those attempts. The award made was a lump sum payment of £50,000.

The applicant appealed to the Court of Appeal. One of the arguments on which she was successful was that the trial judge had misunderstood the impact that £50,000 would have on her means-tested welfare benefits. The argument, accepted by the Court of Appeal, was that the award would, in the long term, make the applicant worse off. The Court of Appeal made a new award, giving the applicant some £143,000 to purchase her Housing Association home and a further lump sum payment of £20,000. The Court of Appeal seemed, in particular, to emphasise the fact that the charities did not need the money, and also appeared to criticise the deceased for rebuffing the attempts at reconciliation.

The significant award made by the Court of Appeal caused a public outcry, with many tabloid newspapers strongly criticising the judges. The charities successfully appealed to the Supreme Court. The Supreme Court was very critical of the Court of Appeal judgment. In their Lordships' view, the trial judge had actually made a proper assessment of the impact the £50,000 would have on the applicant's welfare entitlement. The Supreme Court also emphasised the reality of testamentary freedom. The deceased was free to disinherit her daughter and to rebuff attempts at reconciliation. The deceased had freely chosen those charities and they, as beneficiaries, did not have to justify whether or not they needed or deserved the money (though under s 3(1)(c) their financial situation is a relevant consideration). It was for the applicant to show that she needed the money. On the particular facts, the Supreme Court agreed that the Court of Appeal award was too generous to count as a contribution to the applicant's maintenance. This can be contrasted with cases where surviving spouses or cohabitants have been awarded the family home. Those facts are very different, as the house was meant to be a shared family home, and their applications are not limited to maintenance. The Supreme Court formally restored the trial judge's award of £50,000 (although in reality the charities and the applicant had settled for an undisclosed sum).

15.5 Further reading

Brook, Juliet, 'Testamentary Freedom – Myth or Reality?' [2018] Conv 19–30.

Coleman, Clarissa, Noel, Christopher and Winter, Natasha, 'Woolridge v Woolridge: Claims for Further Financial Provision in "Luxurious Lifestyle" Cases' [2016] Private Client Business 122–27.

Croucher, Rosalind, 'How Free is Free? Testamentary Freedom and the Battle between "Family" and "Property"' (2012) 37 Australian Journal of Legal Philosophy 9–27.

Hedlund, Richard, 'The Earl's Daughter – Lessons from the Inheritance Act' [2019] Conv 291–300.

Hedlund, Richard, 'The End to Testamentary Freedom' (2021) 41(1) Legal Studies 55–72.

summary

During the 20th century, common law jurisdictions, like England and Wales, moved away from absolute testamentary freedom. The family provision rule was introduced, in England and Wales through the Inheritance Act, which allows close family members to make an application for financial support out of the estate. The Inheritance Act is controversial, since testamentary freedom is ingrained in English legal culture (evidenced by the tabloid press reaction to the Court of Appeal decision in *Ilott*). Nonetheless, although surviving spouses and civil partners can claim for whatever is reasonable, all other applicants are limited to claiming maintenance support. The premise of the Inheritance Act is the moral (if not legal) obligations that family members have towards each other and, where relevant, a desire to keep people off welfare benefits. Even where families are estranged, it might be preferable to help them from out of the estate, rather than through benefits. However, the applicant has to convince the court that they are deserving of an award, using the s 3 criteria as a guide. There are many reasons why an application can be rejected, and success is by no means assured.

16 Remedies

This chapter looks at a range of claims and remedies available in succession law, both for those entitled to challenge the validity of a will and for any beneficiary of the estate. The chapter consists of three parts. First, the chapter will consider claims that are available against solicitors and will-drafters if they negligently prepare a will. Secondly, the chapter will consider non-contentious probate proceedings. Thirdly, the chapter will consider contentious probate, looking both at challenges against a will as well as what claims can be brought against a PR for wrongful administration of the estate.

The chapter addresses the following issues:

- What duties do solicitors and will-drafters have to their clients when drafting a will?
- What are non-contentious and contentious probate and who can bring contentious probate proceedings?
- What orders can the court make in contentious probate proceedings?
- What is a devastavit?
- What remedies are available against a PR for wrongful administration?

16.1 Duties of solicitors and will-drafters

Solicitors and will-drafters owe various duties to their client when agreeing to draft a will on the client's behalf. Liability may lie in negligence if the solicitor does not carry out their job properly. Solicitors also have a duty to provide information to the court.

This section will start by looking at a claim for negligence. It is an established principle in tort law that where a person undertakes to perform a professional service for another, and that service is relied upon by the other party, a duty of care is owed and the service provider must act with reasonable care and skill (*Henderson v Merrett Syndicates Ltd (No 1)* [1995] 2 AC 145). This principle applies to solicitors who are instructed by a client to draft a will. The solicitor must exercise such reasonable care and skill as one would expect from a reasonably competent solicitor. This duty of care applies also to anyone else, not being a solicitor, who drafts wills in a professional capacity (*Esterhuizen v Allied Dunbar Assurance plc* [1998] 2 FLR 668).

The duty of care arises in a variety of circumstances. Key duties include:

- a duty of care to ensure that the will is drafted in a reasonable time after the solicitor receives instructions;
- a duty of care to ensure that the will actually reflects the client's instructions;
- a duty of care to ensure that the client is properly advised on how to execute the will.

The main theoretical problem with such cases is that, ordinarily, a duty of care is owed between the solicitor and the client. However, it is not the client (the testator) who suffers any loss. It is the disappointed beneficiary. This point was resolved by the House of Lords in the case of *White v Jones* [1995] 2 AC 207.

16.1.1 Duty to act within a reasonable time

In *White v Jones*, the client made a will, in which his two daughters were excluded. There was then a family reconciliation and the client wanted to make a new will. He instructed his solicitors to this effect, stating that in the new will the daughters were to receive £9,000 each. The solicitors did not proceed with any haste. Two months after giving the instructions, the client died. Since no new will had been executed, the old will, in which the daughters were excluded, still had effect. The daughters sued for professional negligence. The House of Lords confirmed that the solicitor's duty of care extended to specific beneficiaries. The duty had been breached because of the delay in preparing the will. In this case, the daughters could claim £9,000 each in compensatory damages from the solicitors.

16.1.2 Duty to ensure the will reflects the client's instructions

The next duty of care owed by the solicitor is to ensure that the will gives effect to the client's testamentary intentions. If the will does not reflect those intentions, there is a loss to the intended beneficiaries. They are entitled to bring a negligence claim against the solicitor in order to obtain compensation for the loss.

In the case of *Carr-Glynn v Frearsons* [1999] Ch 326, the testator owned a property on a joint tenancy with her nephew. As joint tenants, it follows that when the testator died, the nephew would take the property through the doctrine of survivorship. The testator, however, wanted to sever the joint tenancy and give her new half-share to her niece. A will was drafted by the solicitor, leaving the half-share interest in the property to the niece. However, there was never any actual act of severance. The Court of Appeal allowed the niece's claim in negligence against the solicitors, who, by failing to properly ensure that there was a valid severance, had failed to carry out the testator's instructions.

In the case of *Shah v Forsters LLP* [2017] EWHC 2433 (Ch), [2018] PNLR 8, a testator owned two houses on a joint tenancy with her husband. She wanted to leave her severed interest to various charities. However, the will prepared by the solicitors did not sever her interest, and when she died the husband took both houses on survivorship. She had prepared a letter of wishes, which asked for a post-death severance, but the letter was not legally enforceable on this point. The executors argued that the solicitors had been negligent in their advice to the testator, in drafting the will, and in preparing the letter of wishes. However, the claim was dismissed. This was because, on the facts, the testator had expressed to the solicitors that she did not wish to sever the joint tenancy, at least not at the time when the will was prepared. During the meeting, she indicated that she would discuss this further at a later date, but she never did so. She had also been advised that the letter of wishes would not be enforceable. She executed her final will knowing that the properties had not been severed. The solicitors had therefore prepared a will which did reflect the testator's intentions, which distinguishes the case from *Frearsons* (above).

In the case of *Martin v Triggs Turner Bartons (A Firm)* [2009] EWHC 1920 (Ch), [2010] PNLR 3, the client had asked for a will to be drafted. It established a sizeable discretionary charitable trust, which included a power for the trustees to advance capital to the client's widow. The instructions were that the trustees could advance the whole trust fund except the last £100,000. The will was drafted a bit differently, saying that the trustees could only advance a maximum of £100,000. The claim was successful in terms of a breach of duty to draft the will according to the client's instructions. The quantification of loss was more challenging, since the power of advancement was discretionary. The court agreed on a settlement which partitioned the trust fund, with one part going to the widow and the other part being held for the charities. The widow was also entitled to compensation for the money she had spent on a claim for rectifying the will.

In *Wales v Dixon* [2020] EWHC 1979 (Ch), which was considered in **Chapter 5** (as to whether a gift to nieces and nephews could be construed as including not only blood relations but also nieces and nephews by marriage), the judge expressed concern that instructions had been taken from an elderly testator solely over the phone (and, indeed, the draft will was posted the very same day, suggesting that it had been quickly written up) and that no family tree had been drawn up by the solicitor (which could have avoided the construction claim). As the court was able to construe the gift as including nieces and nephews by marriage, no claim against the law firm was considered. However, if the nieces and nephews by marriage had been excluded in the construction claim, they certainly could have explored the possibility of bringing a negligence claim against the law firm in question, with reference to the judge's observation that the clause in question was 'badly drafted'.

That said, the duty placed on solicitors and will-drafters is limited to ensuring that the will reflects and carries out the testator's intentions. There is no duty to ensure that the beneficiaries actually receive the property. As discussed in **Chapter 14**, there are many reasons why a beneficiary might not obtain the property. The property might have been used to pay debts or a gift might have adeemed.

16.1.3   Duty to give advice on execution

The solicitor is also under a duty to explain to a client how to properly execute the will and to check, at least on the face of the will, that it has been properly executed (*Gray v Richards Butler* [2000] WTLR 143). In the case of *Humblestone v Martin Tolhurst Partnership* [2004] EWHC 151 (Ch), [2004] PNLR 26, the client had asked for a will to be prepared, leaving his estate to his partner. The will was correctly prepared and sent to the client to be executed. The client's parents signed as witnesses, but the client was not present. At a later point, the client dated the will, but did not actually sign it himself. It was returned to the solicitors for safekeeping. On receipt, the firm stated that the will seemed to be in order, when clearly it was not. The client later died, and due to the improper execution, the parents took his estate through intestacy. The partner was successful in a negligence claim against the solicitors, for failing to check that the will had been properly executed.

16.1.4   Duty to provide information

The solicitor or will-drafter may be under a duty to provide relevant information about the creation and execution of the will. Parties who seek to challenge the will may issue a *Larke v Nagus* request (from the case of *Larke v Nagus* (1979) 123 SJ 337) to the solicitor or will-drafter, requesting disclosure of the will file (which may include attendance notes, letters to the testator, and drafts of the will). The solicitor is not legally compelled to comply with such a request, but it is considered 'best practice', as confirmed in *Gardiner v Tabet* [2020] EWHC 1471 (Ch).

However, the court has power under s 122 of the Senior Courts Act 1981 to order any person whom the court reasonably believes 'has knowledge of any document which is or purports to be a testamentary document' to give evidence as to that matter before the court. Further, in s 123 of the Senior Courts Act 1981, the court can issue a subpoena and compel any person who has in their 'possession, custody or power any document which is or purports to be a testamentary document' to deliver that document to the court. The powers in ss 122 and 123 are not restricted to solicitors or will-drafters but extend to 'any person'. For a solicitor or will-drafter, complying with a *Larke v Nagus* request may be more sensible than to risk being compelled to by the court.

The reason why the law allows for such disclosure (which, to some extent, may undermine the concept of client–solicitor confidentiality) is that the parties challenging a will may not have first-hand knowledge of the circumstances in which the will was made. Only the solicitor or will-drafter may have that information. The will file, containing for example a solicitor's comments in an attendance note, may be useful evidence in a claim, such as helping to determine if the testator had testamentary capacity, knew and approved of the contents of the will, or if the will was properly executed. A request for disclosure is therefore a precursor to a substantive probate claim.

16.2 Non-contentious probate

When a testator dies, their will is put into probate, as explained in **Chapter 11**. Probate proceedings may be needed to resolve various problems or disagreements. These can take the form of either non-contentious or contentious probate proceedings. Non-contentious probate is defined in s 128 of the Senior Courts Act 1981 as being probate proceedings where there is no 'contention' as to the right to issue a grant of probate, but it does include various legal actions where disagreements may arise, including issuing caveats. Non-contentious probate includes all ordinary day-to-day probate business of proving wills and issuing grants, which would include questions (and disagreements) as to who is entitled to the grant (as disused in **Chapter 9**).

The statutory definition does leave a bit to be desired in terms of clearly delineating between contentious and non-contentious probate. All non-contentious probate matters are dealt with in the Family Division. Contentious probate is transferred to the Chancery Division. MacDonald J noted in *Ali v Taj* [2020] EWHC 213 (Fam) that 'non-contentious probate business does not become contentious simply by reason of a dispute between the parties involved'; rather, it is the statutory definition that decides whether a dispute is contentious or not. That case concerned an application for the executors to give an account of their conduct, which was deemed to be non-contentious probate, even though there was clearly disagreement between the parties as to whether the executors had properly carried out their duties.

Disputes over who should be appointed PR over the estate can also be deemed non-contentious (*Re Clore (No 1)* [1982] Fam 113). That case concerned an application to 'pass over' the named executor, under what is now s 116 of the Senior Courts Act 1981. Ewbank J noted that this was a very contentious dispute, but it was nonetheless non-contentious probate. Passing over was discussed in **Chapter 9**.

16.3 Contentious probate – challenges to a will

Contentious probate concerns any claims against the will or the PRs for wrongful administration. Anyone who has an 'interest' in the estate can issue contentious probate proceedings (Civil Procedure Rules 1998, r 57.7(1)). This includes any beneficiary (under any will or on intestacy), anyone entitled to a grant of probate or administration, anyone entitled to bring an Inheritance Act claim, and, as shown in *Randall v Randall* [2016] EWCA Civ 494, [2017] Ch 77, any creditor of the above. A creditor of the deceased is not entitled to bring a contentious probate claim, since they have no interest in the validity of any will or who is appointed as PR for the estate. As seen in **Chapter 13**, a creditor will have a claim regardless of the above issues.

A common contentious probate claim is challenging the validity of the will. This chapter will not repeat in detail the grounds on which a will can be challenged, as the requirements for a valid will were set out in **Chapters 2** and **3**. In summary, the will can be challenged on the basis that the testator did not have testamentary intention or testamentary capacity, or because any of the formality requirements have not been met.

Whether it is the claimant or the PR who has the burden of proof varies between the different claims, as explained in those chapters. The court can find against the will and refuse to admit it into probate. Alternatively, the court can find in favour of the will, which is then proven in solemn form. The various forms of grant that can be issued were discussed in **Chapter 11**.

16.4 Contentious probate – administration claims

Once a PR is appointed, they have legal obligations to properly administer the estate. These duties were considered in the administration chapters (see **Chapters 11 to 14**). Administration proceedings may be issued if there is any dispute as to how the PR should or has carried out these administration duties.

Administration proceedings can concern many different issues:

- A PR can seek guidance from the court on how to carry out their duties.
- The PR or a beneficiary can make an application to remove and replace a PR, under s 50 of the Administration of Justice Act 1985;.
- A claim for devastavit can be made, alleging that the PR has not properly carried out their duties.

16.4.1 PR or trustee?

The law on breach of administration duties and breach of trust is essentially the same. Claims against PRs for wrongful administration often use the terminology of 'breach of trust', even though this is strictly incorrect. A PR remains a PR during the administration process. Administration includes collecting in estate assets, paying off debts and distributing specific gifts. Thereafter, the will or intestacy rules generally provide that the residue is to be held on trust for the residuary beneficiaries. At this point, the PR becomes a trustee (*Green v Gaul* [2006] EWCA Civ 1124, [2007] 1 WLR 591). A claim against a PR is called a devastavit, whilst a claim against a trustee is for breach of trust. However, the content of the claims, the remedies and the defences are in essence the same. The main difference, referred to in the 'Defences' section (see **16.5** below), is that the limitation period for certain claims only begins to run once administration is completed and the PR has become a trustee of the residue.

16.4.2 Right to seek guidance from the court

A PR or trustee can, at any time, ask the court for guidance on what to do. If there is a question of how the will or a trust is to be interpreted, the PR can also ask a lawyer with 10 years' High Court qualification to give advice (Administration of Justice Act 1985, s 48). For any other issue, the PR can ask the court. The court has an inherent jurisdiction to manage all trusts (*Schmidt v Rosewood Trust Ltd* [2003] UKPC 26, [2003] 2 AC 709). The inherent jurisdiction applies equally to the administration of estates. Therefore, to avoid potential liability, the PR should seek the court's guidance if there are any doubts as to what the PR should do.

16.4.3 Removing and replacing a PR under the AJA 1985, s 50 or the inherent jurisdiction

Section 50(1) of the Administration of Justice Act 1985 allows the court to replace a PR or, where there are two or more PRs, remove some but not all of them. An application to remove or replace a PR can be brought by a PR or by any beneficiary of the estate. A beneficiary is someone who takes under a will or who would be entitled on an intestacy (s 50(4)).

Section 50 does not depend on a PR having done something wrong, such as breaching their duties. Instead, many cases turn on a breakdown in the relationship between PRs, to the point where the administration process is affected. The key principles governing s 50 were set out in the case of *Harris v Earwicker* [2015] EWHC 1915 (Ch). The court said that the 'guiding principle is whether the administration of the estate is being carried out properly' and whether it would be in the beneficiaries' 'best interest' to remove or replace a PR. Certainly, if there has been a breach of duty, the court is more likely to exercise its authority under s 50. If there has not been a breach of duty, but merely a breakdown in the relationship, either between the PRs themselves, or between the PRs and the beneficiaries, the court has to consider whether the administration can continue. If any breakdown in the relationship 'makes the task of the personal representatives difficult or impossible', the court may exercise its authority under s 50.

In the case of *Heath v Heath* [2018] EWHC 779 (Ch), three brothers were executors of their mother's will. In it, they received equal shares of the estate. However, one brother had provided care for their mother in her later years. He claimed that she had written a new will, which favoured him, but he refused to actually show the will to the court (which raised serious doubt as to whether it really existed). He also claimed to be entitled to more than a one-third interest in the property because of his work in taking care of their mother. The other two brothers claimed that the third was obstructing the administration process and, given his claim to a larger interest, had a conflict of interest between his position as an executor and his position as a potential claimant against the estate. On their application, the Court removed the third brother. To protect his interest, he was replaced by an independent solicitor.

A PR can also be removed by the court using its inherent jurisdiction, following the same principles it would use when exercising its inherent jurisdiction to remove a trustee (*Thomas & Agnes Carvel Foundation v Carvel* [2007] EWHC 1314 (Ch), [2008] Ch 395). The key consideration is the 'welfare of the beneficiaries'. The court has to ask itself whether the PR has done something, or not done something, that has harmed the welfare of the beneficiaries. If so, the PR can be removed. The test is not radically different from the one used in s 50, as explained above.

16.4.4 Devastavit

Where a PR commits a breach of duty, it is referred to as a devastavit. This is an old Latin term meaning 'he has wasted'. It means, in short, that if the PR has caused a loss to the estate, the PR must provide compensation to restore the estate to where it should have been. A devastavit can be committed in many different circumstances. This corresponds to the duties set out in the administration chapters.

As seen in **Chapter 13**, there is no liability for a delay in seeking probate (*Chappell v Somers & Blake* [2003] EWHC 1644 (Ch), [2004] Ch 19). The law cannot force someone to seek probate. Under the principle in *White v Jones* (set out above), a solicitor may be liable to the estate and the beneficiaries if they cause delay. For example, the solicitor might delay seeking probate once instructed to do so by an executor or potential administrator.

Once appointed, however, the PR must start acting. As seen in the administration chapters, the PR has three main duties. They have to call in the estate, pay off all lawful debts, and then distribute the estate to the correct beneficiaries. Below are some examples of devastavits.

16.4.4.1 Failing to call in debts

The PR has to call in the estate. This includes ensuring that all debts owed to the estate are repaid. This was discussed in **Chapter 12**. Most debts are founded on a simple contract, meaning there is a six-year limitation period to call in the debt (Limitation Act 1980, s 5). If no repayment date is set, the period of six years runs from the time the loan was called in (Limitation Act 1980, s 6). If a PR fails to call in a debt within this time, or fails to ensure the money is received after the debt is called in, they will be liable to the estate for the money lost.

16.4.4.2 Failing to look after estate assets

Once the estate has been called in, the PR must look after the assets with reasonable care. As discussed in **Chapter 12**, the PR has the power to insure the estate assets (Trustee Act 1925, s 19). There is no liability for assets which are stolen, though the PR may still be liable for the value of the asset if it had not been properly insured.

The PRs may not spend more money on handling the estate than is necessary, and the PRs may be asked to account to the court for their expenditure. In the case of *Kibby v Skillings*, 25 October 2016 (unreported), the executors had spent some £600,000 on things such as securing and storing estate assets as well as evicting squatters from a property. The court agreed with the beneficiaries that £100,000 was a more reasonable cost for the work done, and the executors were ordered to compensate the estate for the difference.

16.4.4.3 Selling estate assets at an undervalue

The PR is free to sell estate assets in order to raise funds to pay off estate debts. If an asset is sold at a gross undervalue, a creditor or beneficiary can apply to have the transaction set aside or for the PR to pay compensation to the estate (*Rice v Gordon* (1848) 11 Beav 265, 50 ER 818). It is important that the PR takes reasonable steps to obtain a fair market value for the asset. The PR should already have obtained the market value of the asset when valuing the estate for IHT purposes.

Again, in *Kibby v Skillings* (above), the executors sold a painting for £50,000. The beneficiaries claimed that this was at an undervalue, as the buyer soon thereafter resold the painting for £700,000. Speculative property, such as artwork, can be difficult to value, but the court agreed that £50,000 was clearly too low. The executors had to pay £325,000 in compensation to the estate (less the money they had spent on carrying out the sale).

16.4.4.4 Paying excessive funeral costs

As seen in **Chapter 13**, the PR may be responsible for arranging the deceased's funeral and can then obtain compensation from the estate. However, the funeral costs have to be reasonable (*Edwards v Edwards* (1834) 2 Cr & M 612, 149 ER 905). The PR will not be entitled to compensation out of the estate for unreasonable funeral costs, and if the PR takes the money, the PR may be liable to compensate the estate.

16.4.4.5 Failing to pay off debts

The PR is under an obligation to pay off all the deceased's debts with 'due diligence' (*Re Tankard* [1942] Ch 69). If the PR fails to do so, the PR may be liable to compensate the estate for any additional interest payments or costs incurred. The PR cannot distribute estate assets whilst debts are still owed, unless these are specific gifts not needed to pay off the debts.

16.4.4.6 The PR distributes property to the wrong recipient

The PR has to ensure that the estate assets are distributed to the correct beneficiaries. A devastavit is committed if the PR hands over property to someone who is not entitled to it (*Re Diplock* [1948] Ch 465). The PR is liable to compensate the correct beneficiary for the loss and this is the beneficiary's primary remedy.

However, a creditor (if distributed assets are needed to pay off debts) or a beneficiary retains the right to follow or trace the property into the hands of the recipient, unless it would be inequitable to do so or if the asset has been sold in a good faith transaction (*Re Diplock*).

key terminology

Following: a beneficiary can follow a specific asset into the hands of a third party and claim it back.

Tracing: a beneficiary can claim the value of a lost asset in substitute property, such as the proceeds of sale. This is particularly relevant if an estate asset is sold in good faith. Here the beneficiary can claim the proceeds of sale instead.

(*Foskett v McKeown* [2001] 1 AC 102, [2000] 2 WLR 1299)

The specific rules on tracing are covered in more detail in an Equity & Trusts textbook. The key point is that a wrongful recipient can be asked by the court to return the asset. The right to follow a specific asset stops if the asset was purchased in good faith. Here, the disappointed beneficiary can only claim the proceeds of sale. Following and tracing also do not apply where it would be inequitable to do so. In *Re Diplock*, money was mistakenly paid to a charity, which spent it on improving its facilities. Strictly speaking, the disappointed beneficiaries could have claimed a constructive trust over those facilities, which would have entitled them to order a sale of the land. However, the court refused, saying it would be wrong to impose a constructive trust on the charity, given that it had already spent the money. This must be considered if property has been given to the wrong beneficiary; if they have already spent money they received, or sold an asset they received, it might be improper to claim it back from them. Instead, the remedy is limited to claiming compensation from the PR.

16.4.4.7   Delay in distribution

Once the debts have been paid off, the PR must distribute the balance of the estate to the appropriate beneficiaries. The PR can be liable if there are unreasonable delays in the distribution. If so, the PR can be compelled to pay interest on the estate asset as compensation to the beneficiary (*Blogg v Johnson* (1866-67) LR 2 Ch App 255). The PR does not have to distribute the estate within the first year after the deceased's death, as set out in s 44 of the Administration of Estates Act 1925 (the so-called executor's year).

16.5   Defences available to the PR

There are various defences available to a PR in administration proceedings.

16.5.1 Section 27 notice

The s 27 notice was discussed in **Chapter 13**. When the PR starts the administration process, they should issue a notice to this effect in local newspapers, as prescribed by s 27 of the Trustee Act 1925. The notice should advertise for potential beneficiaries and creditors. The PR must give the parties at least two months to respond with details of their debt. Thereafter, the PR is entitled to begin paying off known debts and thereafter distributing the estate. Any creditor or beneficiary who turns up at a later date cannot bring a claim against the PR. That party might be able to recover already distributed assets, using tracing, as discussed above. However, as shown, there is no guarantee that the creditor or beneficiary will be able to recover assets which have already been distributed.

16.5.2 *Benjamin* orders

Benjamin orders are named after the judgment in *Re Benjamin* [1902] 1 Ch 723. In that case, a father left the residue of his estate to his 13 children in equal shares. One of his sons, Philip, had disappeared several years before. Despite an extensive search, worldwide, Philip was simply gone. The court allowed the executor to distribute the estate to the remaining 12 children, operating on the presumption that Philip had predeceased the testator. However, the court did not formally pronounce Philip dead, meaning that if he did reappear, he would be entitled to claim back a 1/13 portion from his 12 siblings. Similarly, in the case of *Re Green's Will Trusts* [1985] 3 All ER 455, the court held that the testator's son was presumed to have died in the Second World War, and that the executors could proceed on that basis.

Benjamin orders have also been issued in respect of missing creditors. In the case of *Re Gess* [1942] Ch 37, the court authorised the executors to proceed without identifying all estate creditors, since potential creditors would be in Nazi-occupied Poland.

A *Benjamin* order is important to the PR or trustee, since they become protected from potential future claims. It also protects the missing beneficiary, since they are entitled to try to claim their money back from other recipients, subject to the rules on tracing (*Re MF Global UK Ltd (In Special Administration)* [2013] EWHC 1655 (Ch), [2013] 1 WLR 3874).

16.5.3 Missing beneficiary insurance

PRs can also take out what is known as missing beneficiary insurance, to provide financial protection in case a missing beneficiary were to reappear at a later date. In *Evans v Westcombe* [1999] 2 All ER 777, the court recommended the use of missing beneficiary insurance, especially in smaller estates, as a more cost-effective means of protection compared to going to court to seek a *Benjamin* order. Normally, the cost of obtaining the insurance is treated as an administration expense and can be claimed by the PR out of the estate (indeed, the same is true for the legal costs of obtaining the *Benjamin* order, which can make the insurance even more cost-effective for the estate, as there will be more money left for the beneficiaries).

16.5.4 Trustee Act 1925, s 61

Section 61 provides an important protection to trustees and PRs. It allows the court to excuse a trustee from any wrongdoing, in situations where the trustee has acted 'honestly and reasonably' and 'ought fairly' to be excused from liability. Whilst it is always open for trustees to plead s 61, it will be rare that the court goes along with it. Each case is fact specific, but the trustee has to show that they acted honestly and reasonably. This is inherently difficult if there has been a breach of trust or a devastavit. It is more challenging when the PR or trustee was acting as a professional (*Re Rosenthal* [1972] 1 WLR 1273). The PR or trustee must show that they followed all the correct processes in carrying out their duties (*Santander UK v RA Legal Solicitors* [2014] EWCA Civ 183).

16.5.5 Trustee Act 1925, s 62

Section 62 allows for an indemnity to the trustee in specific circumstances. If a beneficiary has instigated, requested or consented in writing to a breach of trust, the trustee is entitled to an indemnity out of that beneficiary's trust assets. The trustee has this right even if they have subsequently been removed due to the breach (*Re Pauling's Settlement Trusts (No 2)* [1963] Ch 576).

16.5.6 Limitation Act 1980, s 22

Section 22(1) of the Limitation Act 1980 stops a beneficiary from bringing a claim to obtain their interest in an estate after a period of 12 years. Section 22(2) prevents a beneficiary from claiming interest on a legacy after a period of six years.

The time period only begins once the administration is completed. In the case of *Green v Gaul* [2006] EWCA Civ 1124, [2007] 1 WLR 591, the court said that the time period in s 22 'will not begin to run until the administrator has paid the costs, funeral and testamentary and administration expenses, debts and other liabilities properly payable out of the assets in his hands, and provided for the payment of any pecuniary legacies'. This is ordinarily the time when a will executor becomes a will trustee.

16.5.7 Limitation Act 1980, s 21(3)

This section states that a beneficiary cannot bring a claim for breach of trust, such as a wrongful payment, after a period of six years. Again, the time period will not begin to run until the testamentary trust has arisen at the end of the administration process (*Davies v Sharples* [2006] EWHC 362 (Ch)).

16.5.8 Administration complete

A PR has two key defences against creditors in situations where the estate is insolvent and runs out of assets. The two defences are administration complete (formerly known as *plene administravit*) and administration complete except (formerly known as *plene administravit praetor*).

The defence of administration complete says that a PR is not personally liable to creditors for estate debts in situations where the estate runs out of assets (*Inland Revenue Commissioners v Stannard* [1984] 1 WLR 1039). This is provided, of course, that the PR has paid off debts in the correct way (see **Chapter 13**). Creditors can only claim against future estate assets (for example, if debts owed to the estate are yet to be paid). Administration complete except applies where the PR states that the estate has run out of assets, except specific property. The creditors can then only claim against that specific property. The PR might be personally liable for the debts if they have not followed the correct process.

16.6 Executor *de son tort*

A person may be liable if they are not a properly appointed PR but act as if they were. The third party is called an executor *de son tort*. This includes people who would be entitled to be administrators but who begin dealing with the estate assets before obtaining a grant of administration. Their liability only extends to the property they actually deal with. This is different from executors, who obtain authority from the will, and therefore can begin dealing with the estate assets even before obtaining a grant of probate.

To be liable, the executor *de son tort* must take control of the property and deal with it as if they were the owner. The threshold appears to be rather high. In the case of *Pollard v Jackson* (1994) 67 P&CR 327, a tenant remained in possession of a downstairs flat after the landlord, living in the upstairs flat, died. The tenant also took possession of the upstairs flat and disposed of some of the deceased's property. Twelve years on, the tenant tried to become the registered owner through adverse possession. The deceased's daughter was found in Canada, and she brought a claim against the tenant for his dealing with the deceased's property. The Court of Appeal dismissed the claim, saying that the tenant was not an executor *de son tort*, even though he had taken physical possession of the upstairs flat and also destroyed the deceased's personal possessions. Instead, the tenant obtained the freehold to the whole property through adverse possession.

The defendant must do 'something to intervene in the administration so as to assume the obligations of a trustee or executor' (*Haastrup v Okorie* [2016] EWHC 12 (Ch)). In that case the court suggested that a burglar would not become an executor *de son tort*, since a burglar only takes the property but does not assume the obligations of a PR. This helps explain the outcome in *Pollard v Jackson*; the squatter took unlawful possession of the property but did not assume the responsibilities of a PR.

Even if the executor *de son tort* does not assume the authority of an executor, but receives property from the actual PR in a scheme to defraud creditors, they are liable as if they were executors (Administration of Estates Act 1925, s 28).

16.7 Criminal liability for fraud

The PR can also face criminal liability for fraud if they misuse the estate assets for personal gain. Section 1 of the Fraud Act 2006 identifies three specific types of fraud: first, in s 2, fraud by false representation, which is to say, the defendant knowingly makes a misleading or untrue statement about fact or law, with the intention of making a benefit for themselves or causing another to suffer a loss; secondly, in s 3, fraud by failing to disclose information that the defendant is under a duty to disclose, again with the aim of making a benefit for themselves or causing a loss to another; and, thirdly, in s 4, fraud by abuse of position, which arises where the defendant is in a position of authority where they are expected to protect the financial interests of another person, and instead dishonestly abuse that position to make a gain for themselves or to cause a loss to another.

In the case of *R v Tuckwell* [2019] EWCA Crim 1659, the defendant was one of several named executors in his wife's will. When his wife died, the defendant took sole control of the estate and lied to the other executors and the beneficiaries (who were various family members, including the defendant's own daughter), claiming that he was the sole executor. He also misled the beneficiaries about the terms of the will. In the course of doing this, the defendant transferred the estate assets into his personal name and used them for his own personal benefit. When this was discovered, the defendant pleaded guilty to one count of fraud, contrary to s 1 of the Fraud Act 2006. It was not specified if this was fraud by false representation or by abuse of position. Either could apply, but the defendant certainly made false representations about the terms of the will with the aim of making a gain for himself. The Court of Appeal handed down a sentence of four-and-a-half years imprisonment (accounting, in the usual way, for both aggravating and mitigating factors on the facts of the case).

Such events are hopefully rare, but of course it behoves families to be more open about their testamentary wishes before death (to avoid someone being able to mislead the family as to the terms of the will) and, as the family did in this case, to be willing to question a PR's actions if those actions appear unusual or not in accordance with what the complainant knew about the deceased's testamentary wishes.

16.8 Further reading

Allen, Sebastian, 'White v Jones: What if the Claimant was not the Client?' (2012) 18 Trusts & Trustees 390–401.

Weale, James, 'Probate Litigation: The Incidence of Costs' (2015) 21 Trusts & Trustees 449–56.

summary

This chapter has brought together many issues discussed earlier in the textbook. Contentious probate concerns challenges against the validity of a will or the appointment of a particular PR. Solicitors and professional will-drafters may be liable in negligence for delays or poor drafting, where the will does not reflect the intentions of the testator. Such wills can be rectified by the courts, but the solicitor may still be liable for any loss, including the cost of the rectification proceedings. A PR commits a devastavit if they do not properly administer the estate, and a third party can be liable too if they intermeddle with estate assets. PRs have a wide range of defences available to them.

INDEX